Policy and management in the British Civil Service

Policy and management in the British Civil Service

Geoffrey K. Fry

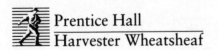

Prentice Hall
Harvester Wheatsheaf

London New York Toronto Sydney Tokyo Singapore
Madrid Mexico City Munich

First published 1995 by
Prentice Hall/Harvester Wheatsheaf
Campus 400, Maylands Avenue
Hemel Hempstead
Hertfordshire, HP2 7EZ
A division of
Simon & Schuster International Group

Typeset in 10/12 pt Sabon
by Dorwyn Ltd, Rowlands Castle, Hants

Printed and bound in Great Britain by
T.J. Press (Padstow) Ltd

Library of Congress Cataloging-in-Publication Data

Fry, Geoffrey Kingdom.
   Policy and management in the British Civil Service/Geoffrey K.
Fry.
    p. cm.
   Includes bibliographical references (p.   ) and index.
   ISBN 0-13-353830-3 (alk. paper)
   1. Civil service reform—Great Britain. 2. Civil service—Great
Britain. 3. Great Britain—Politics and government—1979—
I. Title.
JN428.F78 1995
354.41004—dc20
                                           95-8786
                                              CIP

British Library Cataloguing in Publication Data

A catalogue record for this book is available from
the British Library

ISBN 0-13-353830-3

---

1 2 3 4 5 99 98 97 96 95

To Harry and Joan Hanson

Contents

Preface

This book is about the British Civil Service since 1979 and about the origins of the changes which have taken place. It is not a textbook, but an interpretative essay of assessment.

To judge from past experience, and as would be expected, not all readers will agree with the assessment made. This has certainly been so before. A book of mine called *The Administrative 'Revolution' in Whitehall*, published in 1981, was dismissive about the importance of the changes made in the machinery of government in the 1960s and 1970s, hence the inverted commas. This upset those who had earnestly chronicled changes which should have been recognised at the time, and not merely later, to have been mainly cosmetic and usually worthless. Then again, while the historical material in my book, *Statesmen in Disguise* (1969) was accepted, the criticisms made about the work of the Fulton Committee offended against the conformity of the day. Yet who now thinks that the Fulton Report was radical? The changes since 1979 were viewed with caution in another of my books, *The Changing Civil Service* (1985), and in academic articles. What has taken place in the British Civil Service since 1979 does not seem to me to fit either of the two famous explanations of patterns of administrative change, the Lindblom incrementalist model and the Elton 'revolutionary' model, both discussed in Chapter 6 of this book. Yet, especially since the Next Steps Report of 1988, and certainly by the standards of the past, the order of change since 1979 seems remarkable, and only that which took place in and around the two world wars, particularly the Second World War, seems at all comparable in importance. In those periods, though, the Civil Service was being built up. Now, it may be being broken up. Some might call this a counter-revolution, as would befit a Conservative revolution. Some would hope for a restoration, a reaction, a 'return to normalcy', to the days before 1979, or at least before the true date, 1988. Whether or not the changes have been revolutionary (and one of their major architects thinks not), they have been of a scale and importance which invites analysis.

The writer is well aware of the changes that have been taking place in the Civil Services of other countries, and the text, bibliography and references bear testimony to this. Nevertheless, each country is different, which is what makes them interesting, and recent British experience owes surprisingly little to outside examples. Indeed, Britain's closest outside relationship, that with the European Union, involves bureaucratic expansionism.

The Treasury and the Office of Public Service and Science, and that department's predecessors, have been generous to the author with their time and help with material for this book. I am grateful to Sir Robin Butler, the Head of the Home Civil Service, for permission to have access to the papers of the Fulton Committee within the period of the Thirty Year Rule, and to produce related material in this book. The work was funded by ESRC Award Number R000231033. I am grateful to Dr Ann Gold for permission to have access to, and to quote from, the papers of Lord Boyle, and I am grateful also to the Chairman of the Conservative Party for access to archive material, as I am to the Keeper of Public Records and the Controller of HM Stationery Office for permission to quote from material that is subject to Crown copyright. I am grateful to K.A.G. Murray, formerly of the Civil Service Commission, for making available to me material that was privately published. I am grateful as well to the editors of *Political Studies*, *Public Administration* and *Public Policy and Administration* for permission to use material published in another form in those journals.

As in earlier books, I am indebted to those who debate Civil Service issues, although I rarely, if ever, share their views. This is true of *The Economist* newspaper. I record with thanks the help given in particular by the Civil and Public Services Association, the National Union of Civil and Public Servants, the Institution of Professionals, Managers and Specialists, the Association of First Division Civil Servants and the Council of Civil Service Unions. When the *Whitley Bulletin* was first issued in 1921, it was intended to be a journal of record about the Civil Service. It fulfilled this role admirably, as did *The Bulletin of the Civil Service Unions*, which was its successor. *The Bulletin* ceased publication at the end of 1994 because there was insufficient central Civil Service material for it to record. This illustrates the radical nature of the recent changes in the Civil Service.

It is the case that I could not have completed this book, or the others before it, without the facilities of, and the help of the staff employed in, the Brotherton Library of the University of Leeds, and I acknowledge the professionalism shown.

As with earlier books too, I have had considerable help and encouragement from colleagues at the University of Leeds. Gordon Forster, Christopher Challis, Kevin Theakston and Duncan McCargo helped me this time, and, as before, the polymath, Owen Hartley provided invaluable support. I take full responsibility for what is written in this book.

Harry Hanson began the tradition of academic study of public administration at the University of Leeds, and it is to Professor Hanson and Joan Hanson, a marvellous friend to my wife and family and myself, that I dedicate this book.

Geoffrey K. Fry
December 1994

1 A revolution in the British Civil Service?

The 'sea change' taking place within the British Civil Service amounted to 'nothing less than a revolution in progress', declared John Major, the Chief Secretary to the Treasury in the then Thatcher Conservative Government, in 1989. The Ibbs Report of the year before and the Next Steps agencies devolved from government departments in consequence were 'a logical development' of the application of the Financial Management Initiative within the civil service. The departure from traditional, centralised, monolithic organisational structures to arrangements increasingly characterised by the 'devolution of budgets and financial control to units of management and, wherever possible, to individuals' represented 'radical change'. The future Prime Minister insisted: 'This is a revolution' (Major, 1989, pp. 1, 10, 13, 23).

This was not a lone view. Whitehall was undergoing a 'silent revolution', Richard Luce, the then Minister for the Civil Service, had stated in 1986:

> When we came to office [in 1979] we believed we owed it to the taxpayer to introduce in the public service procedures which will produce some of the same kinds of disciplines that exist in the private sector. A highly efficient Civil Service to back up the wealth creators was a key part of our overall strategy. The pace and extent of change in the Civil Service since then have been dramatic.

What had taken place had been 'a revolution in management methods and fundamental attitudes in the Civil Service' (Cabinet Office, 1986, p. 1). This was with the Ibbs Report still to come. The Next Steps programme resulting from that, according to William Waldegrave, the Minister for Public Service and Science, speaking in 1993, could be fairly described as representing 'the most fundamental and far reaching reform of the Civil Service for 140 years' (Waldegrave, 1993a, p. 8). While emphasising the importance of the creation of the Next Steps agencies, 'the process of agentification' as he called it (ibid., p. 18), Waldegrave considered, though, that even the 'Thatcherite revolution' had left large parts of the public sector 'essentially unreformed' (ibid., p. 7). Thus there was plenty of scope for the application of the Citizen's Charter of 1991, with its 'revolutionary' reassertion of the primacy of outputs (ibid., p. 11), and for market testing and competitive tendering for central government functions. All told, Waldegrave believed, 'Britain had the most comprehensive public service reform programme' in the world (ibid., p. 12).

Within the Higher Civil Service too, there have been public expressions of the view that radical change has been in progress since 1979. 'Today, the Civil Service is going through the most profound changes it has seen for over a century', Anne Mueller, the then Second Permanent Secretary in the Cabinet Office, declared in a public lecture in 1985:

> The new Civil Service is still constructed on the merit principle but aims at a new professionalism which will secure better value for money for the taxpayer and the citizen. To this end it is focusing on performance and outputs and individual responsibility for securing desired results. (Mueller, 1985a, p. 3)

The same official believed that 'a management revolution is already underway in the Civil Service which will greatly increase its effectiveness', observing:

> This is not just concerned with cost cutting and increased efficiency, essential though that is. It involves targeting investment more closely to identified needs and ensuring that these needs are met in the most effective way. It also means making the best use of people, and so improving personnel management as well as financial management. The key initiatives in train are the Financial Management Intitiative launched by the Government in 1982 and the Personnel Work Action Programme arising from major reviews of personnel management carried out in 1982–83. Long before 2000 these complementary initiatives will have transformed management in the Civil Service. (Mueller, 1985b, pp. 5–6)

The shape of the Civil Service of the future suggested by the related document, *Working Patterns*, circulated by the Treasury towards the end of 1987, certainly looked radically different from that of the past in important respects. In 1993, the Head of the Home Civil Service, Sir Robin Butler, wrote in terms of a 'management revolution' taking place in the Civil Service: 'the gentle process of evolution which started in the 1960s has turned into a revolution of the 1980s and '90s' (Butler, 1993, p. 398). Things had moved on from the Ibbs Report stage. The Next Steps programme had seemed to be 'one hook on which we could hang the future development of the Civil Service', John Ellis, the Secretary of the Council of Civil Service Unions, told the House of Commons Treasury and Civil Service Committee in 1993, but 'along comes, within three or four years of getting it started . . . this idea that you must start subjecting what you are doing to the market place test' (HC 390-II, 1992–3, evidence, q. 497). The scale on which market testing and contracting out was being contemplated and pursued, Ellis informed the Committee, had led people within its ranks to question 'whether the Civil Service has any future at all' (*ibid.*, q. 425).

It was a 'self-evident truth', according to one unsympathetic contemporary historian, that 'Mrs Margaret Thatcher has had more impact on the Civil Service than any peacetime Prime Minister since Mr Gladstone' (Hennessy, 1989a, p. 114). The commentator concerned was confident that 'the cumulative effect of her managerial reforms between 1979 and 1987 would leave Mrs Thatcher [an] historic figure in Civil Service terms', a reputation which the full implementation of the Ibbs Report would serve to enhance (*ibid.*, p. 118). Next Steps plus market testing and competitive tendering meant that the Conservative Government which succeeded that of Mrs Thatcher had 'a very clear and pretty radical reform programme' for the Civil Service, according to William Waldegrave, the Minister most directly concerned, giving evidence to the House of Commons Treasury and Civil Service Committee in 1993 (HC 390-II, 1992–3, evidence, q. 1145). The Major Government was 'doing things far more radical than anybody has ever done before', Waldegrave maintained (*ibid.*, q. 1144), and this was what worried John Garrett, one of the Labour MPs on the Committee, who informed Waldegrave:

> You will go down in history as the Minister who did a great deal to abolish the Civil Service. . . . What is your strategy for a Civil Service consisting of a hundred agencies, say, with a very large degree of autonomy and 100,000 contracts for everything from legal services to cleaning, to maybe even ministerial support? That does not seem to me to be a Civil Service any more. (*ibid.*, q. 1143)

The policies that the Conservatives were pursuing were thus defined as being of a different order from the supposedly radical reforming proposals of the Fulton Committee on the Home Civil Service of 1966–8, for John Garrett had been professionally associated with that Committee's work as a member of its Management Consultancy Group, and only Norman Hunt, who had been the Committee's most prominent member, had been as ardent a Fultonite. The machinery of government and the convention of ministerial responsibility had not been within its remit, but the mustering by the Fulton Committee of no fewer than 158 recommendations for change had given its report the appearance of comprehensiveness. This impression was reinforced by the work of the Management Consultancy Group, which had innovatively married contemporary mangement thinking with the more conventional Fabian ideas for reforming the Civil Service, which concentrated on such matters as structure, recruitment and training. What, above all and increasingly, differentiated the position of the Fultonites from that of their Conservative rival reformers was their belief in the desirability and continuance of a large-scale career Civil Service. This position was entirely unsurprising, given that the Fulton Committee was located firmly within the Fabian reforming tradition, and, hence, was wedded to public administration solutions to problems of public policy, as indeed was the Labour Government of the 1960s which appointed it. The Heath Conservative Government of 1970–4 eventually proved to be similarly fond of such solutions. Either side of the Heath Goverment, and for a time within its life, economic liberalism made the intellectual running within the Conservative Party, and preparations for office in the 1960s and again from 1975 onwards were imbued with its outlook, which was antipathetic to extensive career bureaucracies like the Civil Service, preferring market solutions to problems of public policy. As will be demonstrated, the Conservative Party had little need of the Fulton Committee's work, and, indeed, such common ground as there was had been left well behind by the time of, say, the White Paper of 1991, *Competing For Quality*.

'You are . . . destroying an institution of literally world wide renown', John Garrett said accusingly to the Tory Minister, William Waldegrave, in 1993 (*ibid*., q. 1145), in defence of the career Civil Service. This *cri de cœur* could be taken as signalling the handing over of the radical crown. There is no necessary merit in either radicalism or conservatism. It depends on the circumstances and the outcomes. The drive against domestic bureaucracy since 1979 could also be said to cohere uneasily with the practice of Conservative Governments, including those of Mrs Thatcher, increasingly subjecting so much of British public policy to the influence of, and sometimes control by, an external bureaucracy, the European Commission. Even so, in relation to that domestic bureaucracy, we have already noted that politicians involved and higher civil servants and the representatives of the broad mass of civil servants were of the belief that radical, even revolutionary, change was under way in the British Civil Service. Whether this is really so or not invites analysis, and, with political will having been crucial to the order of change attained, as well as to the continuance of the policies concerned, the point to begin would seem to be with an examination of the Conservative Party and its attitudes towards the Civil Service.

2 The Conservatives and the career Civil Service before 1979

Conservative Governments from 1979 onwards, and especially those of which Margaret Thatcher was the Prime Minister, have been commonly believed to have departed from traditional Tory attitudes towards the career Civil Service, which were supposed to have previously treated that Service as being akin to an estate of the realm. The argument that will be advanced here will be that Conservative attitudes towards the Civil Service conventionally have been more complicated than this, and that really since 1965 when in Opposition and then again from 1975 Conservative policy planning anticipated the antagonism towards the Civil Service as an interest the Thatcher Governments were to display.

Conservatism always has been more than what Conservative Governments do, but the reality that there have been so many such Governments over the last hundred years and more has meant that Conservative principles are difficult to identify among the facts of practice. 'No man can be a collectivist alone or an individualist alone. He must be both', Winston Churchill declared in 1909 (Greenleaf, 1983, p. 9). The Conservative Party has borne this out in embracing a 'High Tory' or Statist tradition, which is more than Paternalism in the sphere of social provision, and a libertarian tradition, which is mainly economic liberalism. Taste, which in some cases may amount to conviction, and/or circumstances may well decide which combination of views the Conservative leadership or the Conservative Party or an individual Conservative adopts, inevitably with varying degrees of consistency. The 'contradictions' of Conservatism have tended to encouragé an overtly 'pragmatic' form of leadership of the kind that Stanley Baldwin perfected and John Major appeared to follow, though Margaret Thatcher was to be closely associated with the economic liberal tradition within the Conservative Party, at least once she became its Leader and then the Prime Minister.

1 THE CONSERVATIVE TRADITION AND THE CIVIL SERVICE: SALISBURY TO HOME

The classic 'High Tory' interpretation of the constitutional role of the career Civil Service remains that expressed by Lord Balfour, the former Conservative Prime Minister, who, writing in 1928, described the Crown and the Civil

Service as being the two elements within the British Constitution 'able to mitigate the stresses and strains inseparable from party warfare', while recognising that 'great indeed are the differences between them'. The Civil Service was 'no more than a wheel in the "efficient" part of our Constitution'. The Crown was 'typical of the "dignified" part'. The Civil Service was 'below Party' and the Crown 'above it', and 'yet both of them are, in a very real sense, independent of it, and both are indispensable'. Of the role of civil servants, Balfour observed:

> They do not control policy; they are not responsible for it. Belonging to no Party, they are for that very reason an invaluable element in Party Government. It is through them, especially through their higher branches, that the transference of responsibility from one Party or one Minister to another involves no destructive shock to the administrative machine. There may be change of direction, but the curve is smooth. If administrative continuity has (so far) been quite unbroken even by the most abrupt vicissitudes of Party warfare, it is largely to the silent work of the Civil Service that this happy result is due. (Balfour, 1928, pp. xxiv–xxv)

The best-known exponent of the Tory interpretation of history, Sir Lewis Namier, once famously described British constitutional arrangements in terms of a 'framework for the free play of Parliamentary politics and Governments' being supplied by 'the two permanent elements, the Crown and the Civil Service', the latter being 'an unpolitical Civil Service whose primary connection was with the Crown, and which, while subordinated to Party Governments, is unaffected by their changes'. Namier thought that it was 'not by chance' that the Crown and the Civil Service 'together left the political arena' (Namier, 1955, pp. 13–14). Those who dissent may well feel that there is no obvious link between, say, the circumstances surrounding the formation of Sir Robert Peel's Conservative Government in 1841, after which the Crown's political role was diminished, and the slow and uncertain development from the mid-1850s onwards of a career Civil Service recruited by competitive examinations. Another Tory, a poet this time, C.H. Sisson, when still a senior official, wrote that the 'legitimate concern with the continuance of the Realm, which characterizes the work of the administrator in the Civil Service and gives him his genuine indifference to party is more than accidentally connected with the fact that he is what is called a servant of the Crown' (Sisson, 1966, p. 154).

A political party so often in office as the Conservatives, on the face of it, would seem bound to have or have had a special relationship with such established institutions as the Crown and the Civil Service. In the case of the Crown, it was not until after the introduction of a system of elections for the Tory leadership in 1965 that the Monarch was formally excluded from the process by which, when in office, successors to Conservative Prime Ministers were selected. As for the career Civil Service, writers from Harold Laski onwards maintained that the Service was socially and politically prejudiced against the Labour Party, and thus, presumably, biased in favour of the Conservatives. Across Whitehall, the weight of departmental opinion was said to be antagonistic to the Labour Party, and the Treasury and the Foreign Office in particular were portrayed as being citadels of opposition to socialism. A more socially democratic Civil Service, and a more open one with an administrative style of greater professionalism, became the Fabian ideal, and Harold Wilson's Labour Government appointed the Fulton Committee of 1966–8 to help to bring this about.

If Laski and those who later thought like him were right, then working relationships between Conservative Governments and their leading Civil Service advisers would be especially harmonious, particularly in the case of Ministers of 'High Tory' persuasion, even making allowance for differing political contexts and the inevitably wide range of individuals involved over time. Lord Salisbury and Lord Curzon would seem to be exemplars of the 'High Tory' persuasion. Lord Salisbury, who had been opposed to the introduction of competitive entry to the Civil Service (Smith, 1972, p. 97), proved to be critical of such established institutions as the Colonial Office (Cecil, 1932, p. 303), the Admiralty (*ibid.*, p. 188) and, indeed, of the British system of government as a whole when it came to waging war. Salisbury spoke and wrote of the Treasury at times in a manner later to become familiar among that department's more radical critics. He wrote of 'the peculiar position given by our system to the Treasury . . . which is very galling to other departments', and observed:

> That the Treasury should say that any expenditure is excessive or thriftless, in regard to the objects for which it is intended, is obviously within its functions. But in practice the Treasury goes much further. It acts as a sort of Court of Appeal on other departments. Because any policy at every step requires money, the Treasury can veto everything and can do so on proposals which have nothing financial in their nature and pass judgement upon which it has no special qualifications. The line I admit is hard to draw – but it is natural for the head of a department to feel annoyed if, by applying the financial brake, the Treasury hampers a policy in which it does not concur . . . It is much more keenly felt if the interference of the Treasury wins, not at arresting a policy which it disapproves, but at securing sufficient delay to enable it to disapprove if it wishes.

Lord Salisbury publicly stated that 'the exaggerated control of the Treasury has done harm', and his distrust of the Treasury seems to have been one reason why he took what was then the unusual step of combining the Foreign Secretaryship with being Prime Minister, the latter role giving him the constitutional authority to select the Cabinet and to overrule the Treasury and so be able to shape the environment in which foreign policy was decided (Blake and Cecil, 1987, pp. 160–1). Broadly similar social origins did not make for a good working relationship between Lord Curzon and his officials when he became Foreign Secretary. As one biographer observed:

> Curzon acquired a reputation among his officials as an inconsiderate chief. It was not only, as his private secretary Vansittart wrote, that 'he annexed their work as the Germans annexed Shakespeare'. He would treat even his Permanent Under Secretary, Sir Eyre Crowe, with near contempt, constantly sending for him to

return to the Foreign Office at night in spite of his victim's tragic guttural complaint: 'I have to travel in the Unterground.' (Rose, 1969, p. 300)

It was small wonder then that the Foreign Office took to James Ramsay MacDonald when he combined the roles of Prime Minister and Foreign Secretary in the first Labour Government of 1924. 'The Foreign Office is far too pleased' with MacDonald, complained the former diplomat, George Young; 'they say they have got rid of a cad in Curzon and found a gentleman in MacDonald'. As MacDonald actually had working-class origins, Beatrice Webb's explanation was that 'J.R.M. is a born aristocrat and he will tend to surround himself with "well bred men", in spite of their reactionary attitude towards affairs – another Balfour!' (Cole, 1956, p. 9).

To judge from references in his reminiscences, Sir Austen Chamberlain appreciated the role of higher civil servants and even their wit and wisdom (Chamberlain, 1935, pp. 307–13). As Foreign Secretary between 1924 and 1929, Chamberlain's working relationship with his Permanent Under Secretaries, Sir Eyre Crowe and then Sir William Tyrrell, seems to have been cordial (Dutton, 1985, p. 237). Chamberlain was credited by one biographer with the 'ability to make the best use of experts without . . . becoming a mere instrument in their hands' (Petrie, 1940, p. 246), though a fellow Cabinet Minister believed Chamberlain 'to have become a mere phonograph of Crowe' (Gilbert, 1979, p. 348; q.v. Dutton, 1985, p. 255). This may have been because Austen Chamberlain did not take internationalist sentiment to similar levels, while still associating himself with the League of Nations and, on one occasion, applauding what he saw as the League's first Secretary, Sir Eric Drummond, taking with him 'the traditions of [the] British Civil Service' (Chamberlain, 1930, pp. 3–9). When Lord Halifax became Foreign Secretary in 1938, the Malburian R.A. Butler, Halifax's Under Secretary of State, was to complain of and to resolve to change 'the old F.O. team where PPSs, Ministers and officials had all got OE [Old Etonian] ties and called each other by their Christian names and had exactly the same brains' (Roberts, 1991, pp. 86–7). Though a product of Eton himself, Lord Halifax, as a supporter of Prime Minister Neville Chamberlain's foreign policy of appeasement, achieved no particular rapport with the Foreign Office, where he encountered some strongly expressed opposition to that policy (Birkenhead, 1965, pp. 418–19). The appeasement policy was not a straightforward matter, of course, with few of its critics failing to make optimistic assumptions at various times about American intentions or French military capabilities or Britain's capacity to wage war, if needs be independently, against a range of prospective foes. Later much was made of the removal of Sir Robert Vansittart from the Permanent Under Secretaryship of the Foreign Office in 1938, and his translation to the honorific post of Chief Diplomatic Adviser to the Government. This was because the change was said to have been made solely as the result of Vansittart's anti-German sentiments being unwelcome to Chamberlain. The then Prime Minister and Halifax certainly did tire of Vansittart's elaborate manner of presenting his views as well as their vehemence (*ibid.*, p. 422), but the originator of the idea to remove Vansittart was actually Sir Anthony Eden (Carlton, 1981, p. 105), whose relations with him had long been antipathetic, a reality not obscured by letters beginning 'My dear Anthony' and 'My dear Van' (James, 1986, p. 116). Neville Chamberlain had experienced a good working relationship with higher civil servants when Minister of Health in the 1920s (Dilks, 1984, pp. 336–7), and as Chancellor of the Exchequer in the 1930s he was on excellent terms with Sir Warren Fisher at the Treasury (O'Halpin, 1989, p. 191) and seems to have had confidence in that department (Peden, 1979, p. 17). When Prime Minister, though, Chamberlain proved distrustful of what he called 'the Foreign Office mind' (Carlton, 1981, p. 111). Eden seems to have enjoyed considerable support in the Foreign Office at the time of his resignation from the Chamberlain Government in 1938, whereas in 1956 over the Suez crisis, according to Eden's official biographer, it was the reverse, although the number who did support the Suez policy was rather greater than was generally believed, particularly during the early stages (James, 1986, p. 555). The same observer recorded working relationships in the Foreign Office as having been affected adversely by Eden's volatile temperament (*ibid.*, p. 623). Sir Evelyn Shuckburgh, who was to question Eden's sanity at the time of Suez (Shuckburgh, 1986, p. 365), went so far as to describe Eden as having been 'a great Foreign Secretary between 1951 and 1955' despite being 'frequently . . . difficult to work with' (*ibid.*, p. 15; cf. Young, 1988, pp. 1–28). It is reasonable to doubt whether, even before the Suez crisis, the socially privileged and Conservative Eden experienced as good, let alone better, working relations with the Foreign Office than, say, Labour's proletarian Ernest Bevin had done.

The Foreign Office was not seen as really being part of the Civil Service at all by Winston Churchill, according to Sir Desmond Morton, who had 'some sympathy with that view' and who recorded Churchill's 'loathing' of those people he did regard as civil servants 'really because the senior ones had always acted as some sort of brake upon his more excitable proposals within their purview' (Thompson, 1976, p. 71). If civil servants were 'that most unjustly and ignorantly abused class', as Churchill once observed (James, 1974, p. 2606), he was not slow himself in later career to wish to share the blame for 'the biggest blunder of his life . . . the return to the Gold Standard' in 1925 (Moran, 1966, p. 303) with, among others, his Treasury advisers and to show distrust of the Treasury thereafter. Like all prominent politicians, of course, Churchill too paid public tributes to the Civil Service. In 1922, for instance, he 2spoke of 'the great Civil Service' in the following terms:

> Powerful, incorruptible, anonymous, the Civil Service discharges a function in this country which is invaluable, and without which immediate disaster would overtake any Administration which attempts to carry on the business of the State . . . what a vital thing it is to have some instrument which is thinking not in days or months or in Parliaments, but is thinking of the affairs of the British Empire in terms of a whole lifetime. (James, 1974, p. 3217)

In much the same spirit, Stanley Baldwin endorsed what he perceived as Balfour's interpretation of the role of the Higher Civil Service as 'the shock absorber of the chariot of the State' (Baldwin, 1935, p. 63), celebrated the Civil Service's 'independence, its anonymity and its aloofness from political controversy' (*ibid.*, p. 52) and attributed to the British Civil Service 'an incomparable prestige throughout the world for capacity, intelligence and integrity' (*ibid.*, p. 62). Yet, in 1926, when, as Prime Minister, Baldwin played a major part in establishing the Central Electricity Board, he went out of his way to emphasise that 'when I speak of a Board . . . I do not mean a government department. What we have in mind is a Board managed by practical men closely in touch with the industry' (*The Times*, 16 January 1926). So, despite the virtues that he had ascribed to the Civil Service, Baldwin did not choose to assign it to the task of running what was, except in form, a nationalised system of electricity generation, or at least he did not believe that the Conservative Party of 1926 would tolerate this.

Though, in that year, Lord Balfour chose to describe the Civil Service in terms of 'a single corporate unity' to be ranked with the Army, the Royal Navy and the Royal Air Force as 'great institutions' of the state (Balfour, 1927, pp. 142–5), less admiring Conservatives in the House of Commons were supporting a motion that the 'continued efficiency' of the Civil Service depended upon 'the strict maintenance of its constitutional position as a subordinate branch of administration' (194 HC Deb. 5s. c. 290–334). The 'new fangled and fantastic machinery of a Cabinet Secretariat', as Sir Henry Craik put it (*ibid.*, c. 293), was one source of unease. In 1922, Craik, together with Lord Eustace Percy and other Tory critics, had pressed for the abolition of the Cabinet Secretariat, believing it to be unconstitutional for officials to be present at Cabinet meetings. The authority of Ministers was said to be challenged by this presence and the form of discussions affected, and the recording and circulation of minutes was deplored, because they were bound to be rendered in a manner which did not fully reflect the real nature of those discussions (155 HC Deb. 5s. c. 213–78). Bonar Law, when Conservative Prime Minister, did not mind restricting the remit of the Cabinet Secretariat and, indeed, made a manifesto pledge to do this (Craig, 1975, p. 36), but he ruled out abolishing the Secretariat, being determined to retain the services of Sir Maurice Hankey (Blake, 1955, p. 501). Another target for Conservative critics and a longer-lasting one was the role of Head of the Civil Service especially as practised by Sir Warren Fisher when he was Permanent Secretary to the Treasury between the wars. Leopold Amery, no admirer of the Treasury of that time, dismissing it as 'a surly watchdog' (Amery, 1953, II, p. 358), was to write in his *Thoughts on the Constitution* that 'the general control of the Civil Service [should be] taken out of the hands of the Treasury' (Amery, 1947, p. 96). The title of a book published as late as 1950 by Harry Legge-Bourke, *Master of the Offices*, encapsulated the distrust of some Conservatives about arrangements for senior promotions within the Civil Service that seemed in practice to diminish ministerial opinion. As

Chancellor of the Exchequer in 1926, Winston Churchill, while recognising Sir Warren Fisher's responsibility to the Prime Minister for 'advising him in general matters affecting the Civil Service', reminded Fisher that 'you are so far as the administration of the Treasury is concerned responsible to me', and Churchill rebuked Fisher for acting as though 'you exercised some independent authority which you conceive to be resident in your office. This is obviously unconstitutional' (Gilbert, 1979, pp. 689–90). Several Conservatives in Parliament at that time, not least the persistent Sir Henry Craik, thought that Fisher's position as Head of the Civil Service was unconstitutional in principle, but Stanley Baldwin as Prime Minister upheld the arrangements (191 HC Deb. 5s. c. 2093–5; 192 HC Deb. 5s. c. 518–20). Of Fisher, Baldwin was later to remark upon the 'determined effort . . . made by the present Head of the Service not only to deepen the sense of corporate unity but to promote movement within the Service so as to fit diversity of gifts to diversity of duties' (Baldwin, 1935, p. 65). Equating the Civil Service with the Armed Forces as Fisher tried to do and, as we have seen, Balfour did, ignored the different relationships that higher civil servants had with Ministers compared with the leading military people, as well as differences of function. Further, treating the Higher Civil Service as one for promotion purposes as Fisher did with such relish would seem conflictual with the increased 'diversity of duties' by then accorded to government departments (Fry, 1969, pp. 52–8). The establishment of the Conservative Research Department in 1929, and its later development by Neville Chamberlain, was indicative of Tory unwillingness to be dependent on the resources of government departments (Ramsden, 1980, pp. 12–94). Against that, fears expressed from within its ranks that a Higher Civil Service composed of examination entrants would find it socially difficult to establish satisfactory working relationships with Conservative Ministers in particular (Dale, 1941, pp. 153–5) proved exaggerated. Until Harold Macmillan's aberrant appointment of John Wyndham in 1957 as an unpaid Private Secretary (Egremont, 1968, pp. 160–95), Conservative Prime Ministers increasingly came to rely upon higher civil servants to staff their Private Offices (Jones, 1976, pp. 13–38). This did not necessarily mean that the official hierarchy was always respected, as Neville Chamberlain showed when preferring the advice on foreign policy advanced by Sir Horace Wilson, the Government's Chief Industrial Adviser, to that of the Foreign Office (Feiling, 1946, p. 327; cf. Petrie, 1958, pp. 156–82).

There never was any neat divide between the statist tradition within the Conservative Party and that of economic liberalism, as a consideration of, say, Neville Chamberlain's record as Minister of Health and as Chancellor of the Exchequer would illustrate. The statist tradition would seem by its nature to have to be less hostile to the Civil Service, since its preferred solutions to problems of government would be less dependent on the market. As adherence on the part of some Tories to economic liberalism would suggest, the divide between the Conservatives and the Liberals was also not always a clear one, even if few crossed the formal boundaries with Winston Churchill's panache. Churchill's difficulties over the Gold Standard in 1925 owed less to malign Treasury advice than his own residual Liberalism. Present in the thinking of one of the architects of 'Tory democracy', Lord Randolph Churchill, was antipathy towards public expenditure. As his son recorded: 'He submitted the Civil Service estimates to an unremitting scrutiny' (Churchill, 1906, p. 232). In much the same spirit, Winston Churchill as Chancellor in 1925 rebuked Sir Warren Fisher for submitting a minute 'showing the impossibility of any reduction in the emoluments or numbers of the Civil Service' (Gilbert, 1979, p. 600). Gladstonian sentiments proved durable despite the expansion of the state brought about by the Liberal reforms of 1906 and then the Great War. Conservative adherents to economic liberalism shared this outlook with Liberals in, say, wielding the Geddes Axe on public spending in 1922, and the May Report of 1931 was commissioned by the Labour Chancellor of the Exchequer, Philip Snowden. There were Conservative attitudes inimical to the growth of bureaucracy that could be identified (Greenaway, 1992, pp. 129–60), but they were not exclusive. The size of the Civil Service and the increased powers accorded to government departments were as much a concern to a Liberal such as Lord Hewart deploring *The New Despotism* as they were to the likes of a Conservative like Lord Eustace Percy (Percy, 1933, pp. 3–14).

The combined effects of the Keynesian revolution in economics and on expectations about public expenditure and hence, the role of the state, and also of the electoral revolution of 1945 (Fry, 1991, pp. 45–55), necessarily depressed economic liberalism in relation to statism within the Conservative Party as it accommodated to the changes. For the foreseeable future, the appeal had to be that of the ability to run the Keynesian Welfare State better than the Labour Party. Though the central bureaucracy was thus bound to remain extensive even on the Conservatives' return to office, this did not preclude the exploitation of its present supposed evils, with Winston Churchill complaining in 1947, for instance, that the extent of the controls over the economy exercised by government departments risked making Britain into a prison, 'one vast Wormwood Scrubbery' (Gilbert, 1988, pp. 302–3). Walter Elliot demanded to know 'where will Civil Service expansion end?' (Elliot, 1948, pp. 250–2) and Churchill professed to detect a 'scandal' in the 'excessive top-hamper' of officials (Gilbert, 1988, p. 402), while also stressing his 'highest regard for our civil servants. It is no fault of theirs if they are now made too numerous, it is the fault of this Government' (*ibid.*, p. 324). Civil servants themselves, of course, remained part of the middle classes whom at the time the Conservatives, not least for electoral considerations, were portraying as being needlessly disadvantaged (Lewis and Maude, 1949, pp. 111–29). The Conservatives' election manifesto in 1950 made the ritual references to 'enormous waste' in government departments and to 'plenty of scope for retrenchment' (Craig, 1975, pp. 141–2), and that of 1951 talked of the need to 'simplify the administrative machine and prune waste and extravagance in every department' (*ibid.*, p. 170), complaining of 'all powerful and remote officials in Whitehall' (*ibid.*, p. 169) and asserting that 'the United Kingdom cannot be kept in a Whitehall straitjacket' (*ibid.*, p. 173). This supposedly stern set of attitudes did not preclude a promise in 1950, subject to the financial position, 'to proceed at an early date with the application in the Government Service of the principle of equal pay for men and women for services of equal value' (*ibid.*, p. 143). That, in office, Conservative behaviour towards the Civil Service would be reformist at most was evident from the work of a group of Conservatives reporting in 1946 (Headlam *et al.*, 1946) and from R.A. Butler's pronouncements on the subject (Butler, 1948, pp. 169–72). Both sources envisaged the Headship of the Civil Service, and with it that Service's central management, being removed from the Treasury, but the Conservative Governments soon to follow took no action.

When Churchill returned to the Prime Ministership in 1951 he tended whenever possible to bring in or to retain those familiar to him from the wartime Coalition arrangements, and this applied to civil servants as well as to Ministers and personal advisers. Churchill's insistence on Sir Norman Brook remaining as Secretary of the Cabinet meant that Sir Edward Bridges stayed at the Treasury as Head of the Civil Service well beyond the conventional retirement age (Seldon, 1981, p. 112). When Churchill insisted on John Colville, a wartime associate from the Foreign Office, becoming his Principal Private Secretary ten years too early in career terms and despite David Pitblado having been recently appointed to the post, Bridges devised a joint appointment (Colville, 1985, pp. 631–2). Of Brook's role, Colville later wrote:

> The mantle of Elijah Bridges fell amply on to the shoulders of Elisha Brook. Churchill trusted him implicitly, relied on his judgment and listened to his advice with attention. From October 1951 to April 1955 Brook never put a foot wrong and, as Churchill's energies began to flag, Brook filled in the gaps and ensured the competent conduct of Government business with unerring skill.

Colville maintained that Churchill retained to the last his capacity for independence of decision (Wheeler-Bennett, 1968, pp. 108–9), and the Prime Minister also displayed disrespect for bureaucracy when, for example, overruling the Ministry of Food and abolishing sugar rationing in 1953 in time for the Coronation (*ibid.*, p. 59).

Distrust of the Treasury on the part of Churchill was not diminished by the politically convenient appointment of R.A. Butler, as Chancellor of the Exchequer, which was made in the same spirit of electoral appeasement as that of Sir Walter Monckton as Minister of Labour. Even the emollient Monckton was said to have felt 'well concealed irritation' at 'the lectures of the Permanent Secretary, Sir Godfrey Ince' (Birkenhead, 1969, p. 297). Butler, though sceptical about the wisdom of 'the gentlemen in Whitehall' when in Opposition (Butler, 1949, p. 321), seemed to find higher civil servants agreeable enough as a breed when in office. As his official biographer observed:

Rab never believed in building a Chinese wall between a Minister and his official subordinates. Even his scribbles on official minutes – 'No. 10 seems to be going mad' or 'Tell him to go to hell' (this about the Chairman of one of the five clearing banks) – were modified neither by caution nor by inhibition; and sometimes his sense of fun would simply get the better of him, as when on a memorandum he approved of, instead of formally expressing thanks, he would simply draw a little Valentine – a heart with an arrow going through it pointing directly towards the initials of the writer. (Howard, 1987, pp. 368–9)

When he became Chancellor in 1951, Butler was told by the Treasury officials, Sir Edward Bridges and William Armstrong, that Britain faced the prospect of an economic crisis of 1931 proportions (Butler, 1971, pp. 156–7). The distrustful Churchill ensured that for a time at least Butler had the unwanted assistance of a Ministerial Advisory Committee and also of a Ministerial aide, Sir Arthur Salter, a former civil servant. The unadmiring Lord Woolton on the Committee blamed the Treasury officials for the crisis (Woolton, 1959, pp. 371–2). This crisis did not in fact occur, but another one might have done if Butler had been allowed to go on and implement the Robot scheme, devised by Treasury and Bank of England officials to float the pound sterling in 1952. Though accounts differ, Churchill's eccentric arrangements, which also included placing his personal adviser, Lord Cherwell, within the Cabinet (Birkenhead, 1961, pp. 284–94), played a part in denying the Treasury and Bank of England influence of the order exercised in 1925. Freed of such restraints by 1955, Butler followed official advice in composing his April Budget, having to introduce more restrictive measures in the months that followed.

It may be that Butler's family links with Civil Service traditions led him to be more trusting of bureaucracy than, say, Lord Woolton, whose unrewarding experiences in the splendidly named role of Civilian Boot Controller in the War Office during the First World War, issuing directives such as the High Legged Boot Order, had induced the opposite attitude, for all the acknowledged intelligence and probity of the higher officials (Woolton, 1959, pp. 43–51). Lord Cherwell's determined and eventually successful campaign to transfer responsibility for the development of atomic energy from the Ministry of Supply to what became the United Kingdom Atomic Energy Authority in 1954 was partly based on dislike of Civil Service organisation and practices (Birkenhead, 1961, pp. 295–316). Lord Chandos, another member of Churchill's Government when plain Oliver Lyttelton, described the Civil Service as 'this wonderful machine [which] responds to clear cut decisions if they follow frank discussions and a willingness to face the essential argument and to take a dialectical toss without chagrin'. Lord Chandos, though, was also clear that 'the Civil Service is not organised for the day-to-day management of affairs', and added:

The Civil Service is also too much withdrawn from some parts of the national life. For example, civil servants regard with suspicion and distaste illiterate and vulgar men who have made a lot of money. 'If Heaven had looked upon riches to be a valuable thing, it would not have given them to such a scoundrel' is their attitude, and this again is apt to make them over suspicious of the motives and over anxious of the methods of business. Strangely, the commercial morality of government departments sometimes does not reach the minimum standards which the instinct of survival imposes on the business world. I can remember senior officials without a smile on their faces saying 'Well, Minister, we have studied the contract with great care and we see no way in which we can get out of it.' They do not grasp that in business a reputation for keeping absolutely to the letter and spirit of the agreement, even when it is unfavourable, is the most precious of assets, although it is not entered in the balance sheet. (Chandos, 1962, pp. 349–50)

The ambivalence of Conservative attitudes towards the Civil Service and its methods was evident in the Churchill Government's pursuit of its target of building 300,000 houses a year. The Prime Minister assured the Minister of Housing and Local Government, Harold Macmillan, that 'the boys', meaning Sir Edward Bridges and Sir Norman Brook, would know how to set about this (Macmillan, 1969, p. 363). Macmillan was less sure, and behind the familiar talk about the need to 'cut red tape and simplify procedure' (*ibid.*, p. 399), he had a clear model which he wished to follow, drawn from his wartime experience at the Ministry of Supply, one characterised by 'improvisation and a certain ruthlessness' (*ibid.*, p. 374) allied to the form of 'business methods' that Macmillan called 'Beaverbrookism' (*ibid.*, p. 400). Macmillan wrote of the Permanent Secretary at the Ministry of Housing, Sir Thomas Sheepshanks, that 'he knew nothing of the problems of industry or of production', and while 'Dame Evelyn Sharp would not object to the unconventional methods we must adopt clearly there must be somebody to play the role of Director General as in the wartime production Ministries.' Sir Percy Mills was recruited on a temporary basis from private business (*ibid.*, p. 395), though only after the objections from what Macmillan called the 'trade union' of officialdom restored since the war had been overruled (*ibid.*, p. 397). Macmillan noted that Sheepshanks objected to the role assigned to Mills and to the Minister's methods as being 'unconstitutional' (*ibid.*, p. 401). Macmillan also recorded dislike of 'grandmotherly control by the Treasury' (*ibid.*, p. 409), whereas in reality the political necessity for the Government of attaining the 300,000 houses target gave Macmillan a wartime scale of freedom from Treasury constraints on spending which gave point to the wartime style of organisation, and which may also have been sufficiently dislocative of econmic strategy to contribute to the difficulties that eventually emerged in 1955.

Though Enoch Powell had felt able to write in 1953 that 'hatred of bureaucracy' was a common and continuing feature of Conservatism (Powell, 1953, pp. 163–4), and cuts in Civil Service numbers were a part of the economy measures which the Eden Government thought it necessary to introduce in early 1956 (Eden, 1960, p. 324), this did not translate into political antagonism, at least on the part of the Conservatives, in the years down to 1964.

Further in 1956, for instance, the Eden Government agreed to the Priestley Royal Commission's recommendations that, in principle, granted civil servants comparable pay with that received by outside counterparts. In practice, inevitably, incomes policies came to interfere with Civil Service pay settlements, leading to threatened confrontation with such as the Civil Service Clerical Association which led to threats of a 'go slow' and to Harold Macmillan as Prime Minister making a diary entry in 1962, recording joking remarks of the 'how *could* the Civil Service go any slower?' variety (Macmillan, 1973, p. 51). This may well have been no more significant than Lord Home's later tribute to civil servants that 'in the huge majority of cases I have found them competent, skilful, inventive, resilient and careful of the public good' (Home, 1976, p. 195). As the author of *The Middle Way*, a Government headed by Macmillan, not least for reasons of electoral calculation, was always likely to reject an economic liberal agenda and to sustain the Keynesian Welfare State. That was bound to mean at that time maintaining a large-scale Civil Service much in the manner that a Labour Government would have done. There were subsequent suggestions that over thirteen years of office there had grown up a special relationship between the Conservatives and the Higher Civil Service, partly on grounds of social coherence (Williams, 1972, pp. 344–59). Certainly, Macmillan was at ease with higher civil servants, feeling able to write of Sir Norman Brook, for example, as 'a man who was not only one of the greatest of public servants but a loyal friend and delightful companion' (Macmillan, 1972, p. 121). As Brook was originally a product of Wolverhampton Grammar School, Macmillan's admiration for him was plainly not based on common social origins. Macmillan seemed to think that social distinctions were eroding, so that 'you often couldn't tell at meetings today which was the civil servant and which the business executive' (Evans, 1981, p. 163). The Civil Service remained an obvious career outlet for scholarship products like Brook, but it was the Conservative Party that was to change.

II 'A NEW STYLE OF GOVERNMENT'? THE HEATH EXPERIMENT AND THE CIVIL SERVICE

When, in 1963, a group of Conservatives published a pamphlet called *Change or Decay*, proposing reform of the Civil Service and the organisation of central government (Robson Brown *et al.*, 1963), it was evident how little their thinking differed from the Fabian reforming agenda. By 1970, though, when David Howell published a further pamphlet on the same subject, called *A New Style of Government*, it was clear that some Conservatives at least had freed themselves of this intellectual debt and that they had established an independent position.

The expulsion of the Conservatives from office in 1964 not only called into question the instrumental case for continued adherence to statism on the existing scale, it also led to the adoption in the Conservative Party of an elective leadership, a development prospectively undermining of High Toryism. An elected leadership was bound to mean a more programmatic approach, and it came into being at a time when economic liberalism was at least partly restored to a prominence that was to be promotive of a more radical attitude towards the machinery of central government and, with it, the Civil Service.

Reforming the machinery of government was certainly treated as being of importance in Conservative policy preparations when in Opposition in the 1960s, especially once Edward Heath became the Party's Leader. The attention given to policy planning between 1965 and 1970 could be taken as evidence of an unwillingness to be dependent in future upon the resources of the Civil Service. Of the work done, one Tory was later to write that 'there was a marked absence of the intellectual quality and depth of the comparable documents published between 1945 and 1951' (James, 1972, pp. 290–1). On the other hand, Douglas Hurd felt able to observe:

> The work was greater in quantity and higher in quality than any which a political party had previously attempted in Opposition. There had been a sustained attempt to go beyond the coining of phrases and the striking of attitudes, and to probe the real causes of Britain's poor performance. (Hurd, 1979, pp. 12–13)

Butler's *Industrial Charter* and similar pronouncements immediately after the war scarcely amounted to policy plans. They had been little more than elegant public relations exercises aimed at convincing sufficient of the electorate of the unremarkable fact that the current Conservative leadership accepted the Keynesian Welfare State which the wartime Coalition Government led by Churchill had very largely planned itself. By the 1960s, it was widely recognised in British politics that the Keynesian Welfare State was malfunctioning. Given that it was a contemporary electoral imperative to continue to pursue full employment and the other goals conventional wisdom deemed attainable under this particular economic and social order, the Wilson Labour Government, like its immediate Conservative predecessors, sought remedies by recasting the means of attainment, most notable the machinery of government. If Heath had an identifiable policital position it was that of being a Macmillanite paternalist, an outlook that was disguised for some because it was a role for which he was socially miscast and, hence, in which he seemed unconvincing. Heath wrote of the Conservative Party that 'our basic principles are well known and easily distinguished from the statist emphasis even of moderate socialism' (Ramsden, 1980, p. 241). This was not so, and as a result, and contrary to Hurd's analysis, Heath frequently resorted to rhetoric in often ineffective attempts to draw distinctions between his own form of Conservatism and Fabian reformism in terms of public policy, at times being driven into forms of economic liberal rhetoric. Party management in Opposition required the economic liberal position to be acknowledged, of course, but, whereas the economic liberals were free to question both means and ends in analysing the policies associated with the Keynesian Welfare State, Heath had no such freedom, given, not least, the commitment to full employment.

The Conservative Party's policy preparations in Opposition in the years down to 1970 may well have been more extensive than the minimal efforts of earlier Oppositions, but this did not prevent them from being inadequate as a guide to practice in several crucial areas. The justification for policy planning in Opposition was spelt out by Robert Carr, who became Secretary of State for Employment in 1970, and who observed that 'if you come in as a Minister and you don't know your subject then you really are at the mercy not only of your civil servants, but of other particular lobby groups' (Campbell *et al.*, 1990a, p. 37). The Industrial Relations legislation prepared in Opposition, however, did not anticipate the non-registration tactic that the trade unions employed. Brendon Sewill, the then Director of the Conservative Research Department, recalled:

> The economic policy group, partly as a result of Arthur Cockfield's great excellence in the tax field, was led off into wonderful schemes for tax reform. . . . But the central question, which was very apparent right through the 1960s, of what you did about incomes policies, none of which worked, was not tackled. The question of monetary policy was never mentioned.

Sewill added:

> There was a curious blank spot because everybody thought that inflation was the great problem but no one was actually prepared to say that the Keynesian principle that full employment was of paramount aim should be abandoned. Everybody said the trade unions were too powerful but nobody was prepared to say the only way to reduce their power was to increase unemployment. Nobody was prepared to take that mental leap away from the total Keynesian tradition in which everyone had grown up during the 1940s, 1950s and 1960s. (Campbell *et al.*, 1990a, p. 38)

Few radical departures from the Keynesian dispensation were likely from a policy-planning process in which besides Heath as Chairman, the main overall responsibility fell, in turn, to Sir Edward Boyle and then Reginald Maudling. At one stage in 1965, there were thirty-six policy groups in formal existence (Ramsden, 1980, p. 238), but from 1966 onwards the policy groups tended to be replaced by task forces, steering groups or panels of experts working directly to Shadow Ministers and to the Research Department, though the policy group on trade unions was a notable exception (*ibid.*, pp. 266–7). The policy groups served a wide variety of functions, and that on the European Economic Community, for instance, seemed to have no role beyond enabling Heath to cover the extent of his commitment to obtaining British membership. Sewill recalled that 'the policy group didn't actually discuss what the terms should be or what the price should be' (Campbell *et al.*, 1990b, p. 35). Angus Maude's contemporary observation about the Conservatives' policy preparations 'that a technocratic approach is not sufficient and that we must have some philosophy' (Ramsden, 1980, p. 251) ignored the reality that tax reform was one of the few areas of policy in which anything resembling technocracy was being practised, and that the only distinctive philosophy available, which was economic liberalism, did not appeal to the Party leadership except, at times, as a source of slogans.

The machinery of central government was an area of prospective action about which Heath had decided views at the outset, several of which he set out in a talk at Swinton College as early as November 1964. Heath believed that 'the whole system of Parliamentary and Cabinet Government [has] exhibited very great weaknesses in coping with the problems of the modern world' and even saw it as being at a disadvantage in competing with the more authoritarian powers'. Greatest of all were:

> the manifest difficulties of getting the economic priorities right. . . . What we seem to have done in this context is to have overthrown the market mechanism without putting anything effective in its place. Instead of getting clear decisions on priorities we get compromise decisions which are so far failing to produce the necessary results.

Heath thought that the 'fair shares for all' basis of Cabinet decisions was 'the worst possible way of trying to get priorities right', and considered that 'the plain fact is that the modern Cabinet spends too much time on detailed points and far too little on the discussion of policy.' He believed that the institutional support for the Prime Minister needed strengthening, but made no definite proposals, though he was clear about the need for a smaller Cabinet. He ruled out an overlords arrangement, on the grounds that all Ministers needed the resources of departments to sustain them and that Ministers deemed subordinate would not tolerate supervision over policy. So, while recognising that it also raised difficulties about Ministerial accountability to Parliament, Heath envisaged changing 'the structure of the department so that you have a federal organization under a Minister, and thus have a smaller number of Ministers in the Cabinet itself', and observed:

> This is one direction in which we were beginning to move. We have done this in the defence field, we had got to the stage of amalgamating the staffs of [the] Commonwealth Relations Office and Foreign Office and announced that we would amalgamate the Colonial Office with it in a year's time. In the same way we had worked out a solution for the Board of Trade which would have become a three pronged federal department, having Trade as one prong, Industry as another, with Regional Development and the Technology of Industry as a third. This, I believe, made complete sense: you would have had one Federal Minister, as Secretary of State responsible, and a Minister of State running each of the three prongs.

Heath recorded the view that the industrial side of the former Department of Scientific and Industrial Research should have been put in with the Board of Trade and not with Education, and observed that 'a really big issue at the moment is the Social Services. Should not Health and Pensions and National

Assistance be brought together in one federal department?' (Boyle Papers: MS 660/23778/2–5).

'Is it not a strange situation, in which a large part of the job of a Cabinet Minister is bound to be about matters of general policy, that he has nobody whatever to advise him?' Heath asked, believing this to be both unsatisfactory and unable to be remedied with the existing staffs. Heath considered the introduction of Ministerial *cabinets* into departments, without committing himself, and added:

> Far from the Civil Service running the Government, as the public sometimes believes, on too many occasions the Civil Service does not say plainly what it thinks policy ought to be. Within the departments, the fundamental problem is a different one. The Civil Service has been unparalleled in the job of administration, but is not equipped to take the initiative in so many of the technical fields today. In the case of the Minister, under our democratic system, there is no reason why he should be any better equipped.

Heath believed that:

> The real specialists must be brought in on secondment for periods of three to five years. The established Civil Service doesn't really take to this sort of thing and they could perhaps be helped by the establishment of a much greater interchange within the departments themselves. The Treasury in particular ought to move around more into the spending departments. A review will have to be made, too, of the method of work within the Civil Service; we may indeed have got to a stage where the whole system of minutes and letters has reached such a stage of perfection that it is in fact a block in the way of speedy and efficient work.

Heath added:

> We must also be sensible about the size of the Civil Service. One of the things which worried me most about our period in Opposition is that we may become silly, as I believe we did between 1945 and 1951, about the size of the Civil Service. If we are going to be properly serviced in the modern world we have got to have the people to do it and pay them properly. (Boyle Papers: MS 660/23/3–4)

That the Civil Service was insufficiently efficient and yet there was no sense in contemplating cuts in the numbers of civil servants was scarcely a radical message from Edward Heath; and discussion of the Civil Service at the Swinton College meeting in November 1964 tended to be unadventurous. Lord Normanbrook chaired the relevant group and later recorded that:

> We discussed criticisms, beginning with recruitment. In the Administrative Class there is still a predominance of Oxford and Cambridge, but as the best students from all types of secondary education now tend to go there, this does not mean a preponderance of Public School. . . . The criticism of amateurishness in the Administrative grade was on the whole rejected by the group. The Administrative Class are not amateurs at administration, which is all they purport to do. The large number of technical people . . . provide the up-to-date advice. What is expected of the administrator is not that kind of knowledge, but the ability to talk

to experts in their own language. There are now enough administrators with a background of economics, if not of science.

The group recognised that 'Governments necessarily live from hand to mouth and only a special effort gets the study of long term problems', and 'some of the group thought of a central organization which would provide impetus and continuity for this kind of work.' The group observed:

> We thought that on the whole there was a reasonable flow of ideas within Government, but that there was a danger in the temptation to call in the technical expert. By and large he is not likely to produce an answer which is practicable without processing, and we felt nervous about government by technocrats.

The group recommended that there should be a margin on the establishment of the Civil Service to enable exchanges of 'youngish' staff with industry and with local authorities. The group thought that 'the other half of the exchange, bringing people in from outside, is quite possible at trainee level and is done, but at higher levels it is much more difficult.' The group concluded:

> We all felt that the main weakness of the Civil Service was in the lower echelons rather than the higher which were more or less alright in number and quality. Our conclusion was that there was the greater scope for improvement, both in mechanization and in getting rid of sogginess in attitudes and procedures, and that it was in relation to the Executive and Clerical grades that comparisons with business and commerce is least favourable to the Civil Service. (Boyle Papers MS 660/23776/9–10)

Alone of the main political parties, the Conservatives did not choose to submit formal evidence to the Fulton Committee on the Home Civil Service of 1966–8, although Sir Edward Boyle was a member of that body, and Edward Heath met Lord Fulton and some other members of the Committee for informal discussions, and three former Ministers presented oral evidence. Reginald Maudling said at the outset of his evidence that 'senior civil servants were outstandingly good at their job and men of the highest ability by any standards,' and he tended to be uncritical (PRO: BA 1/6). Aubrey Jones, while admiring the first-class quality of the Administrative Class, was uneasy about the use and, indeed, the availability of specialist advice within departments. Jones wanted specialist advisers to be brought in from outside, not least 'to provide a counter balance to permanent officials'. Jones thought that 'the collectivity of senior officials was stronger than the collectivity of Ministers, first, because in general they were more able, and, secondly, because they commanded a larger, more elaborate, and cohesive machine.' Jones was critical of the management arrangements in government departments, and he viewed favourably the idea of hiving off blocks of Civil Service work away from departments without feeling able to specify candidates (PRO: BA 1/3). In his evidence, Enoch Powell extolled the virtues of the lay administrator in the Civil Service; the work 'needed no great depth of expertise'. Powell also expressed economic liberal sentiments about the need to cut expenditure not least as a means of identifying priorities ('the sound of squeaking pips speedily revealed where people were least unwilling to economize'), while also denying the relevance of 'the business analogy' in the organisation of departmental work (PRO: BA 1/4).

When Edward Heath met some members of the Fulton Committee at an informal meeting on 19 June 1967, what he had to say resembled to some extent the views that he had advanced at the earlier Swinton College discussions. Heath also observed:

> On the Civil Service side, one defect was a lack of straight thinking. The approach was too pragmatic and in particular inclined to bend itself too much in advance to the Minister's expected line of thought. It should be a primary task of the Civil Service to show the Minister the result that straight thinking produced; it was then up to the Minister to bend it if he had to. It was also remarkable how civil servants improved when they were taken away from their departments and put into a team with its own ministerial directive, for example the team which had been set up for the Brussels negotiations. This enabled decisions to get away from the lowest common denominator of agreement that the Cabinet system imposed. The team worked out what was the right answer and then sought to persuade their respective departments – a constructive reversal of the normal pattern.

Heath thought that:

> The main problem was how to produce innovation. It was no good expecting Ministers to innovate; the road which led to appointment as a Minister did not encourage new constructive thinking. Innovation must therefore come from the Service. To get it into the Service, it would be necessary to take in outsiders for short periods; if they stayed too long they lost their innovating drive. It would also be desirable to set up a small central team of economic and scientific experts independent of departments to advise Ministers on the competing technological claims on resources which continually come forward from departments, for example, Concord . . .. There was also a need for more high level, centrally run O. and M. This, and the independent team of experts referred to above, would be yet further additions to the central complex of Civil Service management and the Cabinet Office.

Heath told the Committee that:

> The Conservative Party had come to the conclusion that hiving off could work where the organization was commercial in character, but was doubtful elsewhere . . .. He was not sure whether an adequate career structure could be erected on the purely executive side, and thought that it would always be necessary to allocate the brightest and most effective to the policy making and negotiating side.

Heath was inclined towards 'selecting administrators on the basis of their general ability rather than on the subject of their education. What was wanted was a trained mind.' However, he would like to see 'more who had training in science and logic (of a statistical and numerate kind). This was more valuable than economics.' Finally, Heath expressed the view that 'the whole government machine was too secretive.' He had recently had highly expert and informed discussions in the United States about ABM systems with academics at Harvard, which would have been inconceivable in Britain (PRO: BA 1/38).

The machinery of central government seemed to be a subject that the Conservatives or at least Edward Heath could not seem to leave alone for long. The Boyle group came up with proposals in 1965, which were to have similarities with the pattern eventually adopted in 1970 (Pollitt, 1984, p. 83) and unsurprisingly so, given that not least political considerations ensured that there were only so many ways in which the functions could be allocated. Yet, in 1968, a group of former senior civil servants, chaired by Lady (formerly Dame Evelyn) Sharp and comprising Sir Eric Roll, Sir Harold Hardman and F.A. Bishop, reviewed the machinery of central government, producing three reports, the last of them submitted in July 1969, passing judgement on the Boyle group's proposals, and devising a structure consisting of 'seventeen major (Ministerial) departments' including an Office of the Prime Minister and the Cabinet into which the Civil Service Department would be merged. The Sharp group considered that 'individual Ministers should be responsible for areas of policy which would be neither so large nor so heterogeneous that Ministerial control would be – as it is often today – a mere fiction'; and added:

> Reducing the number of departmental Ministers is valuable; but we believe that it is more important to reduce both the range and also the number of tasks directly performed by each and thus liable to call for direct intervention by the Cabinet. For this reason we have suggested that in many areas the political decisions should be separated from the routine management ones, by giving the day-to-day tasks concerned to non-Ministerial agencies with clearly defined terms of reference. This should relieve Ministers of both a managerial and a related Parliamentary burden, and should allow them to concentrate on the areas where their continuous intervention is really necessary. (Conservative Party Archive: CRD 3/14/5)

From the summer of 1969 onwards, Heath used the services of a 'Businessmen's Team', several of whose projects related to the machinery of government, including proposals which anticipated the future practice of Programme Analysis and Review (PAR) and institutional developments, notably the Property Services Agency and the Manpower Services Commission (Pollitt, 1984, pp. 85–6).

It may be that 'Heath had a more personal monopoly of authority in the Party than any leader since Neville Chamberlain', and Sir Michael Fraser as Deputy Chairman of the Party had a special co-ordinating role in relation to policy planning (Ramsden, 1980, p. 237), but policy research after 1966 became a disparate activity. Eventually, besides the Research Department, there was a Conservative Systems Research Centre, as well as Public Sector Research Unit. At the beginning of 1969, Sir Michael Fraser even wrote to Brendon

Sewill in terms of there being 'private armies' at work in the field of policy preparation (Conservative Party Archive: CRD 3/14/9). This was besides the various policy groups regularly coming up with expensive commitments, as Sir Edward Boyle remarked (Ramsden, 1980, p. 269). For example, the majority of the Policy Group on Public Sector Pensions, reporting in March 1969, was generous in its proposals for index linking, and only a minority felt the need to record that 'we see no reason why public servants should become a privileged class in so far as at agreed intervals their pensions shall be increased as of right on account of inflation', and the view that 'the civil servant is already the rich man of the pensions community' (Conservative Party Archive: PG 16/65/94).

The Public Sector Research Unit's activities proved difficult to integrate with the rest of the Conservatives' preparations for office, but, in retrospect, its work, though at times it went down blind alleys, proved to be the most imaginative that the Party undertook and an important source of later practice. David Howell recalled:

> We had been interested for a long time in the work that Robert McNamara was doing at the Pentagon, and it was in 1965 that Ernest Marples, Mark Schreiber and I went to the U.S.A. and came back enthused about Planning Programming and Budgeting Systems (PPBS), having established contacts with Charles Schultze, who was pressing ahead with this as head of the Bureau of the Budget. In March 1967, the Conservative Party established a Public Sector Research Unit, headed by Ernest Marples, and involving Mark Schreiber and myself, which reported directly to the Leader of the Party. (interview, 1989)

At the time, although there was much talk about the need for a more technocratic approach in British politics, only Marples was widely perceived as being suitably qualified, and one reason why Edward Heath set up the Public Sector Research Unit seemed to be to keep Marples involved and politically prominent. Heath's remit for the Unit ran as follows:

> First – to make recommendations as to how to improve the speed and effectiveness of decision making in government. Secondly – to make recommendations as to how better value for money can be obtained in the public sector. Thirdly – to make recommendations as to what changes are necessary in systems, controls and techniques in the public sector, especially in respect of Treasury control, so that the improvement of efficiency is continually a process of management. Fourthly – to make recommendations upon the application of 'best practice' in modern management throughout the world to government in Britain. Fifthly – to make recommendations on the changes necessary in the recruitment, training and deployment of staff in the public sector to achieve these aims, including the creation of suitable opportunities for the innovator.

Marples interpreted his and the Unit's first task as being 'to work out methods for a substantial and permanent reduction in the size of the public sector by reshaping it in terms of both ownership and management' (Conservative Party

Archive: CRD 314/7). Widespread privatisation was beyond Heath's agenda, but David Howell was already thinking in terms of structurally divorcing policy work from management in government departments, and, where possible, devolving the latter to the private sector (*The Times*, 14 March 1967; Fry, 1993, p. 264). Marples himself went on to achieve little and a member of the Research Department informed Reginald Maudling in early 1969 that 'Marples has now more or less retired to his vineyard', and observed of Howell and the remaining Unit's staff:

> Many of the ideas that they are exploring sound excellent, but so far we have been at a loss to get anything very specific out of them, for example for manifestos or policy documents. My own worry is that much of the good work that they were doing is in fact only marching in parallel with the work that is now being carried out by the new Civil Service Department. (Conservative Party Archive: CRD 3/14/9)

The overriding advantage of a political party conducting its own research, though, was the obvious one of minimising its future reliance on the resources of the Civil Service, and this would seem to be even more essential when the intention was to reorganise the work of government departments and to render the Civil Service more efficient. The work of the Public Sector Research Unit seemed to be seen by some as being couched in highly technical administrative language that defied interpretation by the uninitiated (Ramsden, 1980, p. 257). In fact, almost all of its output was straightforward and easily understood, and, to take just two examples from the range of investigations undertaken, it was a sensible preparation for office to promote a study of government decision making by RTZ Consultants and of public procurement by Arthur D. Little (Conservative Party Archive: CRD 3/14/8). David Howell later recalled:

> The Selsdon Man thing is a bit of a legend. The Selsdon Park meeting took place over a weekend in late January 1970. It was made highly visible by a pronouncement by Sir Peter Rawlinson about law and order. The Sunridge Park meeting in September 1969 lasted a week and in terms of preparation for office it was much more important. It was organized by the Public Sector Research Unit. As well as people from the Party, it was attended by eighteen businessmen, including Sir Derek Rayner in his first manifestation, and specialists from other countries. Charles Schultze attended and he made an electrifying contribution to the discussions. (interview, 1989)

The range of work done at the Sunridge Park meeting was certainly impressive (Conservative Party Archive: ACP 70/70). The Public Sector Research Unit became associated with the developments which eventually led to the establishment of the Central Policy Review Staff. The idea originated independently in a paper by Mark Schreiber in 1965 in which he proposed the setting up of a Public Sector Efficiency Unit (Conservative Party Archive: PG/ST/65/31). The Party's Policy Group on Science and Technology became involved in developing the idea of what had come to be called a Crown Consultancy Unit, suggesting in 1968 it 'should be directed by a senior Treasury official' and that 'this general approach is not questioned' (Conservative Party Archive: PG/ST/66/40). It was in fact questioned by Mark Schreiber himself, who wrote to James Douglas of the Research Department to say that he disagreed strongly, arguing that three things were needed to make a Crown Consultancy Unit effective. The first was political authority and this could only come from the Prime Minister himself. The second was 'the innovative thrust of a creative minded entrepreneurial type who is motivated by results' and drawn from 'outside the government machine' not being 'steeped in the traditional way of doing things and who is unaware of and even unsympathetic to the difficulties of making changes'. The third was 'the support and co-operation of the Civil Service establishment who will have to implement the many radical changes involved'. What worried Schreiber was that:

> Sir William Armstrong is reported as expressing the hope that the Fulton Report will determine the pattern for the Civil Service for a considerable period – he reluctantly says 'I hardly like to suggest 100 years' but that is clearly the way the man's mind does work – hardly that of an innovator.

Edward Heath minuted 'I agree' (Conservative Party Archive: CRD 3/14/4), and the next report from the Policy Group on Science and Technology proposed arrangements along the lines that Schreiber had indicated, while noting a suggestion that the Crown Consultancy Unit 'should be called the Office of Government Reorganization and Efficiency – OGRE' (Conservative Party Archive: LCC (69) 250).

This suggestion was not taken up by David Howell in his pamphlet, *A New Style of Government* in May 1970, which set out the Conservative programme for recasting central government, and it also found no place in the White Paper, which the Heath Government published in October 1970, entitled *The Reorganization of Central Government* (Cmnd 4506), the opening paragraph of which stated:

> This Administration has pledged itself to introduce a new style of government. More is involved than bringing forward new policies and programmes: it means resolving the issue of the proper sphere of government in a free society; and improving the efficiency of the machinery intended to achieve the aims it sets itself within that sphere.

It was emphasised in the White Paper that:

> The product of this review will be less government, and better government, carried out by fewer people. Less government, because its activities will be related to a long term strategy aimed at liberating private initiative and placing more responsibility on the individual and less on the State. It will be better government, because the tasks to be done will be better defined and fewer in number, requiring fewer Ministers and fewer civil servants to carry them out. (Cmnd 4506, 1970, p. 4)

An important feature of the White Paper was the establishment of 'a small multi-disciplinary Central Policy Review Staff in the Cabinet Office' (*ibid.*,

p. 13), which Heath later said that he created 'first and foremost so that the government strategy could be continuously reviewed and regularly reported upon' (Heath and Barker, 1978, p. 382). The rationalisation of nine government departments into four, including the mergers which created the Department of Trade and Industry and the Department of the Environment, was also announced in the White Paper, and the future Defence Procurement Executive was anticipated too (Cmnd 4506, 1970, pp. 7–13). New initiatives were also announced, in one instance relating to the dispersal of more Civil Service work away from London, partly for reasons of economy and efficiency, and the Hardman Report (Cmnd 5332, 1973) eventually followed this up. More broadly, and initially involving a team of business people based in the Civil Service Department, a review of public expenditure programmes and of departmental tasks was introduced under which 'every activity, from the most traditional to the most recent innovation, will be subjected to the same rigorous tests: is it relevant? and does it have to be done by central government?' Whether functions were 'rightly articulated in the department's organizational framework' or whether they should be 'hived off' to accountable units was also to be examined, as were 'the possibilities of stopping activites altogether, of reducing them and of transferring them to the private sector' (Cmnd 4506, 1970, pp. 14–16).

'I drafted the White Paper, *The Reorganization of Central Government*', David Howell later recalled, 'subject to the intervention of Sir Burke Trend, who must take responsibility for the definition of the role of the Central Policy Review Staff presented there.' Howell observed:

> Looking back at *The Reorganization of Central Government* perhaps the mistake was not to think small. In the late 1960s we looked to the methods of big corporate business to put a bomb under the Civil Service. We might have done better to look at successful small businesses. As it was, the big merged departments – the Department of the Environment, the Department of Trade and Industry – were like unfinished pyramids. The intention was to separate out the policy work from the rest.

Howell added:

> We brought a team of businessmen into government in 1970 headed by Richard Meyjes from Shell, and including Derek Rayner from Marks and Spencer, Robin Hutton from Hambros, Ronald East from G.K.N., David Cruikshank from Bovis, and Kenneth Lane from R.T.Z. The results were mixed. Richard Meyjes was effectively told to go away when he tried to review the National Health Service, and the Government eventually reorganized that Service in the way that the doctors wanted it done. Elsewhere, the results were mixed. The Defence Procurement Executive, the Property Services Agency, and the Manpower Services Commission were established. In the case of the M.S.C., the Department of Employment had declared such an arrangement to be unworkable and the most that they were prepared to offer was a separate Division, but in the end the Commission was established. In 1972, the team of businessmen was broken

up . . . the Treasury wanted accountable management and delegated authority like a hole in the head. Things fell back to Programme Analysis and Review. This was a second best. What we had wanted was to put the whole expenditure on a programme basis with the departments reduced to policy rumps, whereas PAR just dealt with selective areas. Departments just threw their rubbish at PAR, leading to huge reports which no Minister had time to read, which was the idea. (interview, 1989)

As originally conceived within the Conservative Party, what became the Central Policy Review Staff (CPRS) would have been at the heart of PAR activity, but the policy strategy role that the CPRS was assigned meant that it gave PAR a low priority. Former members of that body were later to write that 'the CPRS put quite a lot of time and effort into PAR', the failure of which they partly attributed to the reality that 'departments had too much influence over the choice of programmes to be reviewed and naturally often put forward candidates of only minor importance' (Blackstone and Plowden, 1988, p. 48). The only report by the CPRS to be published when Heath was Prime Minister did anticipate some of the attitudes to be adopted by later Conservative Governments. The report on *The Organization and Management of Government R. and D.* was written by the Head of the CPRS, Lord Rothschild, himself. Though the original version was toned down to make it less acerbic (Blackstone and Plowden, 1988, p. 42), the Rothschild Report's observation that basic research was often 'a form of scientific roulette' and its recommendation that research and development should operate in future on a 'customer-contractor basis' (Cmnd 4814, 1971, p. 3) provoked controversy.

The establishment of a body like the CPRS to monitor the Government's long-term strategy raised many issues, including constitutional ones, but in one sense it was an impossible task because when Edward Heath said of his Government that 'our strategy is clear' (Campbell, 1993, p. 31), it was evident from the outset that this was not so. For the supposed 'strategy' embraced both sides of Conservatism at one and the same time, meaning statism on the one hand, to which Heath subscribed by political preference, and economic liberalism on the other hand, to which Heath had made public commitments. To domestic political problems, which were the ones that electorally mattered most, there could be public administration solutions and there could be market solutions, and the factors of the situation might well decide which ought to apply. What could not work was to apply these differing solutions together. 'We have created what we promised, a new style of government', Edward Heath told the Conservative Party Conference in 1970, taking up David Howell's phrase, who, in turn, echoed Heath when writing of 'the quiet revolution – a change in the role of government, the way it works, the way it believed public aims and goals should be achieved' (Howell, 1971, pp. 4–5). Heath's radicalism was evident in the manner in which he secured British membership of the European Economic Community, but as far as the Keynesian Welfare State was concerned even a sympathetic biographer observed that Heath's purpose was 'reforming it at the edges, to make it function better' (Campbell, 1993, p. 313).

Edward Heath was later to emphasise that he recognised that 'the machinery of government does not exist for itself' and the attention that he gave the subject was 'not because I like playing with machinery as such' (Heath and Barker, 1978, p. 365), but the sheer scale of the reforms of the structure of the National Health Service and of local government as well as of central government did suggest disproportionate interest. That the White Paper, *The Reorganization of Central Government*, could be warmly praised by a veteran Fabian administrative reformer (Robson, 1971, p. 90) indicated that no radical breakthrough had been made. The Wilsonian creation of the Department of Health and Social Security in 1968 took much the same form as Heath had anticipated in 1964, Peter Walker, an incoming Conservative Minister in 1970, later wrote in terms of Heath and his Government inheriting Labour plans to establish 'giant departments' in the form of the Department of the Environment (DOE) and the Department of Trade and Industry (DTI) (Walker, 1991, p. 76), which, while ignoring earlier Conservative preparations, did underline the continuity of approach. Harold Wilson was to describe the CPRS as 'a project that was being worked up before Labour left office in 1970' (Wilson, 1976, p. 95), but, as we have noted, the Conservatives had done their own thinking. Heath's ideas about the machinery of government, and most importantly his reservations about the functioning of the Cabinet, seem to have been largely formed by 1964. To some extent, Heath then seemed to be casting around for confirmation that these ideas could be translated into practice, which is not to say that the further preparations for office in this area were cosmetic or solely to keep an Opposition busy, not least because of the nature of the activities of the Party's Public Sector Research Unit.

That 'Mr Heath had a high regard for the Civil Service' was later remarked upon by his Political Secretary, Douglas Hurd, who added that 'because of his justified respect for his senior advisers Mr Heath tended to exaggerate what could be achieved by new official machinery.' It may be that, as Hurd added, 'a little more scepticism about machinery would have been wise' (Hurd, 1979, pp. 92–3), but adherence to the statist tradition within Conservatism would naturally tend to be less encouraging of such an outlook than economic liberalism. To judge from the White Paper of 1970, Heath did seem to have adjusted his attitude about the size of the Civil Service compared with his views of 1964, but the manner of his reference to federal departments in terms of 'for those who want to reduce the number in the Civil Service this was one way of dealing with it' (Heath and Barker, 1978, p. 373) was suggestive of detachment. The number of civil servants seemed to stay much the same at about 700,000 during the years between 1970 and 1974 (*Civil Service Statistics 1970*, 1971, p. 20; *Civil Service Statistics 1974*, 1975, p. 4) in some contrast with the expansion in public sector employment at the time of over 400,000 (Semple, 1979, p. 98). In discussing 'hived off' agencies, Heath drew attention to the need to have 'a reasonable career structure' for the civil servants concerned (Heath and Barker, 1978, p. 371), and of the imported businessmen only Sir Derek Rayner went on and ran an agency, the Defence Procurement Executive (*ibid.*, p. 370), the other heads being civil servants. It was the Heath Government which established the Review Body on Top Salaries, which was to persistently make recommendations for the upgrading of Higher Civil Service salaries. It was the Heath Government which was the only Government after 1964 that implemented in full the findings of the Priestley formula for Civil Service pay. It was the Heath Government which introduced index-linked pensions for civil servants (Fry, 1985, pp. 96–121). The Heath Government's 'U turn' away from the economic policies of 1970 into the Barber boom and the erection of the paraphernalia of a statutory incomes policy and of the Industry Act of 1972 were matters of political responsibility, but of Heath as Prime Minister even the admiring James Prior was later to write:

> As time went on, he relied more and more on a trio of senior civil servants, led by William Armstrong, Head of the Civil Service, with Douglas Allen, Permanent Secretary at the Treasury, and Conrad Heron, Permanent Secretary at Employment in support. They were able and loyal advisers, but they were not politicians. This . . . fuelled the charge of corporatism which was increasingly being levelled at this Government. (Prior, 1986, p. 77)

The working relationship between Heath and Sir William Armstrong, like that of Chamberlain and Sir Horace Wilson before them, seemed too close for constitutional comfort. 'At the top of the Civil Service there is order, reason and reassurance – until the roof caves in', Douglas Hurd was later to observe (Hurd, 1979, p. 92), and, under pressure from the insufficiently appeased National Union of Mineworkers, the Heath Government collapsed into electoral defeat.

III THE THATCHER OPPOSITION AND 'THE RIGHT APPROACH' TO THE CIVIL SERVICE

The problem-solving approach that had characterised Edward Heath's approach to policy making in Opposition in the 1970s was not one that Margaret Thatcher adopted after displacing him as Conservative Leader in 1975. Mrs Thatcher, Sir Keith Joseph and Angus Maude, who was made Chairman of the Research Department, had been of the view in the years down to 1970 that principles and ideas should be settled in advance of detail. So, as the historian of the Research Department observed, between 1975 and 1979 'there was no imposing array of policy groups as before 1970' and few resulting policy pledges by the standards of modern Oppositions, and yet the Conservative Party 'succeeded . . . in building for itself a clear identity' (Ramsden, 1980, pp. 308–9). As the only distinctive principles and ideas available were those provided by market philosophy, the Conservative leadership's identity at least was bound to be an economic liberal one, and this time, in contrast with the 1960s, it was not just within the Party that the intellectual tide was running in that direction. Margaret Thatcher swam with this tide, and eventually struck out to reach what for many in the Party must have seemed to be the wilder shores. Heath, of course, had swum in differing directions, for a while at the same time, and, not surprisingly, he had sunk.

Such had been the humiliating manner of the circumstances in which the Heath Government had left office that one of the Conservative policy groups subsequently formed was concerned with authority of Government, examining how the 'crisis of authority' could be combated (Conservative Party Archive: PG 40/75/18). That 'overload' at the centre combined with the exercise of trade union power had rendered Britain 'ungovernable' was a fashionable belief in the wake of the events of 1974 (e.g. King, 1976), but the situation was never beyond remedy by a different form of political leadership. The IMF crisis of 1976 and its imposed settlement marked the end of the Keynesian era, but well before that the economic liberal revival had gathered pace. What was perceived to be the doctrine of monetarism added little to what Adam Smith had written 200 years before. Nevertheless, in discussion of economic policy, the writings of Friedrich Hayek and of Milton Friedman won increasing attention, and the implications of what became in character an Anglo-American debate about the role of government were encapsulated in the title of a contemporary book, *Democracy in Deficit: The political legacy of Lord Keynes* (Buchanan and Wagner, 1977). Though a body like the Institute of Economic Affairs would promote a discussion in the form of *Bureaucracy: Servant or master?* (Niskanen *et al.*, 1973), it tended to have as little direct interest in the machinery of central government as such or in the organisation of the Civil Service as had the Bow Group in the past or the Centre for Policy Studies from 1975 onwards, and the Adam Smith Institute was formed too late to be influential at this time. However, the opposition to bureaucratic expansion and self-seeking and budget maximisation was as clear as it was in the growing 'public choice' literature (e.g. Buchanan, 1960; 1975; Buchanan and Tullock, 1962; Tullock, 1965; 1976; Niskanen, 1971; Breton, 1974; Buchanan *et al.*, 1978). Whatever the sophistication of such theorising, its impact seems almost certainly to have been dwarfed by that of Leslie Chapman's book, *Your Disobedient Servant*, published in 1978. For this was an 'insider' account which revealed gross operational inefficiency and waste of public expenditure in the Ministry of Public Building and Works and its succcessor, the Property Services Agency, on a scale that was encouraging of ideas that there was considerable scope for cuts in Civil Service numbers and activities.

'The incoming government might well, immediately it takes office, set up a Committee on Government Expenditure, like the Geddes Committee of 1922, to recommend cuts and to report within a matter of months', Nigel Lawson wrote to John Nott in November 1975, advocating 'the adoption of some variant of the old "balanced budget" doctrine' involving cash limits and staff controls. Lawson added:

> The Civil Service has become an interest group just like any other. It is as keen to reduce the number of civil servants as M.P.s are to reduce the number of Members of Parliament. Yet the number of civil servants has got to be reduced. Thus it is necessary to increase the power of Ministers *vis-à-vis* officials. This will not be easy, but may be facilitated in two ways: first, by requiring that inter-departmental meetings of officials may not take place without the prior agreement of the Ministers involved, who may ask for an account of the meeting afterwards; and, second, by having more meetings of Ministers without officials present. (Conservative Party Archive: CRD 4/13/9)

Peter Walker had used the latter practice when Secretary of State for the Environment in the Heath Government overriding initial Civil Service opposition. Though Walker came to have good working relationships with the likes of Sir Matthew Stevenson and Sir David Serpell, he felt that high fliers within the Service would benefit from 'experience in the front line', and Walker was unimpressed by 'Ministry of Transport civil servants' (Walker, 1991, pp. 75–7), and at the Department of Energy he found that 'the Civil Service team was not the strongest' (*ibid.*, p. 114). The 'extreme conservatism' of the Civil Service was noted by Nicholas Ridley in an Aims of Industry pamphlet published in 1973. 'From my own experience they made it hard for us to carry out some aspects of our Conservative policy', Ridley recorded, and added:

> I suspect that the Civil Service is a political party of monolithic view, which believes in a whole series of policies because it thinks they are in the 'national interest'. It has its own incubus, its own political dynamism, its own colossal research department. It thinks it has the solutions that are most nearly perfect. (Ridley, 1973, pp. 4–5)

To strengthen the position of Ministers, Ridley wanted them to have the support of French-style *cabinets* including 'several senior people' drawn from the Civil Service and also 'one or two outside advisers'. Recognising that the Civil Service could not be relied on 'to reorganize and slim down public administration', Ridley observed:

> The first essential for tackling this problem is to separate the functions of policy making from administration. Granted that it is not always easy to draw the line between these two, there are in fact a whole mass of functions which can easily be classified as administrative; and hived off to be run by a public agency. Employment exchanges, the administration of the social services, regional and industrial grants, road building, Companies House, insurance control, prison management, are but a few of the many examples that could be given. Each of these functions should be separated from direct control by Whitehall, and set up as a separate agency with its own Chief Executive. The Chief Executive should operate with precise terms of reference, and be personally responsible for his agency's standard of efficiency, including any mistakes made by his subordinates. He should make periodic reports to Parliament. (*ibid.*, pp. 11–12)

While it was unsurprising that an economic liberal like Ridley embraced 'public choice' theorising and wrote, it seemed with relish, of 'sacrilegious' ideas such as performance pay for civil servants (Niskanen, 1973, pp. 86–93), that a Tory like William Waldegrave could write dismissively of government departments that 'they are without a theory of discipline, of accountability, or of organization' (Waldegrave, 1978, p. 27), and of 'an over mighty Civil Service' which had to be brought under control (*ibid.*, p. 81) was suggestive of a wider Conservative discontent about the Service and its efficiency.

That *The Right Approach* and *The Right Approach to the Economy* were the most prominent policy documents produced by the Conservatives in Opposition under Mrs Thatcher, and that the best-remembered policy pronouncement of the Heath years in Opposition was *A New Style of Government* could be seen as encapsulating their differing approaches and priorities. The scale of the work done in relation to the machinery of central government in the years down to 1970 tended anyway, though, to diminish the need for further extensive activity, especially as it had been wildly ranging and an economic liberal agenda could be selected from its varied proposals. As early as 1975, David Howell spelt out such an agenda to the Party's Public Sector Policy Group. It involved the 'questioning and subjecting to systematic analysis the purposes and objectives of a wide range of government activities in almost all government departments', and 'a campaign to replace traditional departmental hierarchies with proper management structures in all appropriate areas throughout Whitehall', and 'hiving off activities' and 'creating an overall framework for better management control, better information flows, and a more effective political input into and control of Whitehall'. This is what Howell saw as having been the Conservative Government's approach between 1970 and 1972, 'after which major political interest was lost in cutting government and the businessmen were allowed to go without being replaced.' Howell also listed that candidates for 'hiving off' submitted in the Public Sector Research Unit's Black Book of 1970 (Conservative Party Archive: CRD 3/13/8). In other words, the basic groundwork had been done already.

'Britain needs a system of government that is both more simple and more effective', the Interim Report of the Party's Machinery of Government Policy Group declared in the belief that:

> The Public Service State has broken down. It is seen to be remote and ineffectual, and there is an increasing realization that power has passed into the hands of the bureaucracy and a few large pressure groups. The central machine takes too many decisions that ought not to be and need not be its business. Its function should be simply to take decisions that can only be taken [at] that level and in no other way. There must be reforms designed to divest government of its overwhelming role. . . . There will be functions that need not be carried out by government at all, others that are best left to the operation of the market.

The Group did not attach importance to changing the existing pattern of central government departments, which meant that proposals advanced by

Kenneth Baker and an academic John Barnes, for splitting the Treasury and establishing what the Group called 'a North American Bureau of the Budget' were not adopted. The Group did believe that the Civil Service Department should be brought within the Treasury eventually, not least because it had 'a vested interest in maintaining the power-strength of the bureaucracy', but the Group treated the 'political row' that would result and the opposition of the Civil Service unions as ruling out an immediate change. That the Group seemed to see the Civil Service as an interest that needed to be appeased in the short run did not exclude expressions of criticism of that Service more marked than in the Heath years. Thus John Barnes, who was involved in the machinery of government preparations in both the 1960s and the 1970s, wrote:

> The Conservative Party has noted the ratchet effect of socialism, but their con-demnation of the politics and policies of consensus as practised since the War has to some very considerable extent ignored the mechanisms which gave direction to the consensus, the most obvious of which is the part played by the Civil Service in policy making.

On this view, the Civil Service was exercising excessive power. It was 'a closed corporation' that needed to be opened up and brought under closer political control (Conservative Party Archive: CRD 3/13/5).

Such criticism of the Civil Service, like plans for recasting Whitehall depart-ments and their practices, meant little, of course, without political will. It does seem, as David Howell observed, that:

> The seeds of the Thatcher Revolution were planted in the mid-1960s, with the people in the Conservative Research Department and the Public Sector Research Unit being the original gardeners. . . . Ted Heath's Government was sidetracked into other directions. What we needed was the Thatcher Factor. (interview, 1989)

3 The uneasy relationship: the Thatcher Government and the Higher Civil Service

'The civil servant's power over policy preparation, interdepartmental liaison, crisis management and the control of the public sector has grown beyond the reach of a ministerial tradition still rooted in the nineteenth century', *The Economist* (17 May 1980, p. 9) stated a year after the Conservatives had returned to office led by Margaret Thatcher, observing:

> A series of studies . . . have all portrayed civil servants as accustomed to running the country in spite of Ministers rather than on their behalf. The constitutional model has collapsed. The Minister no longer proposes, while the official disposes; the official more often opposes, and the Minister then runs away. . . . So adept is the Civil Service at eliding the difference between Labour and Conservative administrations that it leads to a presupposition of U turns whenever radical Governments enter office.

Before 1979, and it seems for a short time afterwards, it was a form of conventional wisdom to believe that the Higher Civil Service really ruled Britain. Whether or not this had been the case, those who held such views had to abandon or at least modify them as the Thatcher era progressed. One committed economic liberal recalled with relish:

> From the inception of the first Thatcher Administration in 1979, the Civil Service was 'taken on'; a body of men and women which had grown ever larger since the War was cut back to the point where it became the smallest Civil Service since the War. The number of peerages and knighthoods given to senior civil servants markedly declined; relations between Ministers and their officials were – to quote one senior official off the record – 'absolutely awful' (Letwin, 1992, p. 40)

'Advisers advise and Ministers decide', Mrs Thatcher as Prime Minister declared with characteristic clarity in October 1989 (158 HC Deb. 5s. c. 1044), and Norman Fowler, one of her former Ministers, later wrote of the phrase that 'it is not a bad commentary on the Thatcher years. It was Ministers, not advisers, who drove through the distinctive policies like privatization and industrial relations reform' (Fowler, 1991, p. xi). If Norman Fowler was able to write in retrospect as if higher civil servants knew their place was this because they had been put back into it? Why else would relationships have been 'absolutely awful' or, as Sir Ian Bancroft, as a former Head of the Home Civil Service, put it, 'cooler' and 'more formal' than before (Young and Sloman, 1986, p. 49)? Indeed, the relationships between the Thatcher

Government and the Higher Civil Service and the wider civil Service too were sufficiently conflictual to mean that, for the first time since the immediate aftermath of the Northcote-Trevelyan reforms in the 1850s, it came to be a matter of serious public debate whether it was desirable or not for there to be a career Civil Service and, more particularly, a Higher Civil Service so composed, and, as will be seen, a change of Prime Minister did not bring this debate to an end.

I 'CAPTURE THEORY,' THE HIGHER CIVIL SERVICE, AND THE THATCHER FACTOR

'The Conservative victory in May 1979 was more than just another change of Government; in terms of political and economic philosophy, it was a revolution', according to Sir Leo Pliatzky, a former Permanent Secretary (Pliatzky, 1982, p. 176). What was actually envisaged was a counter-revolution. The nub of the case which Margaret Thatcher and the other economic liberals in and associated with the Conservative Government advanced against the previous Keynesian dispensation was that it was not an economic and social order which had proved capable of arresting, let alone reversing, Britain's long relative economic decline. By 1979, this was difficult to dispute. To the extent that ideas determine the party political contest, the restoration of the neo-classical creed, in its modern guise of monetarism, to the position of economic orthodoxy enabled its adherents in and connected with the Thatcher Government for several years to dictate the domestic political debate to their adversaries, who possessed only tried and failed ammunition with which to reply. Whether this Conservative ascendancy would remain reflected in terms of electoral predominance necessarily depended on what voters defined as results, and positive results at least required the emergence of an entrepreneurial class in Britain capable of more than holding its own in international competition. To put the matter mildly, this was a tall order, and it would have been a remarkable achievement if there had been hard evidence of progress towards its attainment within the two Parliaments that the scale of the 1979 electoral victory initially indicated was available for the 'Thatcher experiment'. Inevitably, the Thatcher Government found that it was one thing to preach the neo-classical orthodoxy of a Budget balanced at lower levels of taxation and expenditure as being the climate in which business would flourish, but quite another to practise it in the face of the maze of intractable economic problems which the Conservative Government had inherited together with often electorally popular and always massively expensive commitments to state social provision. The economic liberals in and connected with the Government saw themselves as contending with what Mrs Thatcher herself called 'the Welfare State mentality' embedded in the Keynesian dispensation, represented in Britain by what she termed 'special interest groups' that made the country into 'an entitlement society' (*The Spectator*, 2 March 1985, p. 10). Indeed, so formidable were the opposing interests that what Sir Leo Pliatzky called 'a Monetarist half revolution' (Pliatzky, 1982, p. 187) was all that was possible, certainly in the short run. As such neo-classical remedies as were deemed politically feasible were applied to the economy, the Thatcher Government, as part of its ambition to put private enterprise back on the throne, treated the public sector as a usurper. Of the various 'special interest groups' to be overcome, the career Civil Service, heavily unionised from top to bottom, was a prime target for attack, and one relatively close to hand.

'The sheer professionalism of the British Civil Service, which allows Governments to come and go with a minimum of dislocation and a maximum of efficiency, is something other countries with different systems have every cause to envy', Margaret Thatcher wrote in her memoirs (Thatcher, 1993, p. 18). Similar sentiments had been expressed by Lord Hewart many years before, when, before accusing civil servants of wishing to impose through 'bureaucratic encroachments' what he called 'the new despotism' (Hewart, 1929, p. 21), he had written of Britain having 'the best Civil Service in the world' (*ibid.*, p. 13). It was not surprising then that, although Mrs Thatcher recognised the virtues of the Civil Service, and especially of those of its members who worked closely with her in Downing Street, her administration did not preclude behaviour characterised by distrust and dislike. At times, Mrs Thatcher seemed to be 'almost Maoist in her suspicion of established institutions' (Anderson, 1986, p. 6). The former Permanent Secretary, Sir William Pile, who had worked with Mrs Thatcher when she was Secretary of State for Education and Science between 1970 and 1974, thought that she distrusted all large organisations: 'she was wary of size in itself . . . and obviously the Civil Service was a big body and had a life of its own' (Young and Sloman, 1986, pp. 25–6). Sir Frank Cooper, formerly Permanent Secretary at the Ministry of Defence, did not detect in Mrs Thatcher any dislike of 'civil servants in their own right' but of 'anybody who [was] not helping in the wealth creation process' (*ibid.*, p. 49). Unlike her three immediate predecessors as Prime Minister, Mrs Thatcher had never been a civil servant, a fact which the Civil Service unions were as swift to appreciate (*Whitley Bulletin*, June 1979, p. 85) as they were slow to recognise the likely consequence of lack of empathy towards the Civil Service as an interest. Mrs Thatcher seemed to have drawn lessons about Civil Service obstructionism from her unhappy time at the Department of Education and Science. At one stage, she tried to have her Permanent Secretary, Sir William Pile, dismissed on the grounds that he was dangerously left wing, but, on official advice, Edward Heath as Prime Minister had turned down her request. After this, 'iron entered my soul', Mrs Thatcher was recorded as having said (Young, 1993, pp. 71–4). 'You have an awful department', Mrs Thatcher was reported as having told Sir Keith Joseph in 1983, when he was Secretary of State for Education and Science (Baker, 1993, p. 161). To judge from her own account, Mrs Thatcher closely associated 'the gentleman in Whitehall' with the 'prolonged experiment' in 'democratic socialism' conducted in Britain between 1945 and 1979, which had been 'a miserable failure in every respect', because 'far from reversing the slow relative decline of Britain *vis-à-vis* its main industrial competitors, it accelerated it' (Thatcher, 1993, pp. 6–7).

The Higher Civil Service, like the career Civil Service of which it was a part, was a natural adversary for the Thatcher Government because of its guilt by association with the former economic and social order. The waging of the total war of 1939–45 had primarily explained the growth of the Civil Service on its modern scale, and readiness for a further conflict partly accounted for the continuance of a large Service; but what oiled the machinery of government and what persistently led to the state being called upon to do more was the assumption of the Keynesian dispensation that the money was always there. Moreover, the notion that the state was the universal provider carried with it the implication that those who ran the machinery supposed to provide universally would themselves be provided for, in principle, relatively favourably in terms of pay according to the Priestley Commission of 1953–5. So the interests of the career Civil Service became bound up with the Keynesian order. While it is not suggested that the tradition of public service has ever been unimportant in the British Civil Service, a career bureaucracy inevitably has materialistic concerns; and a dispensation such as the Keynesian, in which the money was more often than not deemed to be available, provided a climate in which pay and promotion arrangements could function more easily than under more restrictive conditions. Moreover, the Keynesian politics of Butskellism meant that, although who won the elections mattered to the politicians and the politically committed, the differences between social democratic Labour Governments and paternalistic Conservative Governments tended to be marginal, and when, if only at first sight, they appeared to be more than this, as in 1970, things soon reverted to the Keynesian norm.

Whatever the position of the career Civil Service was supposed to be in British constitutional theory, it was predictable that the Thatcher Government would encounter opposition from that Service when, as it perceived the matter, it reasserted the position of the elected Government in relation to the permanent bureaucracy. The 'organizational imperatives' of bureaucratic self-defence against outsiders, as Philip Selznick demonstrated in his classic study of the Tennessee Valley Authority (Selznick, 1966, pp. 10–11, 256), were writ large in the British career Civil Service, which the Thatcher Government seemed to perceive as having 'captured' a role for itself in the machinery of government that was inappropriate for it to aspire to, let alone play. Further than this, whereas 'capture theory' in the United States had been used by economists and political scientists to analyse the effective take-over of bodies such as independent regulatory commissions by the economic interests that they were supposed to regulate (Stigler, 1971, pp. 3–21; 1972, pp. 207–35; Posner, 1974, pp. 335–8; Katzman, 1980, pp. 182–3), the Thatcher Government treated the Civil Service as itself acting as an economic interest and as one which merited tighter control of its activities. Such sentiments, of course, were familiar enough among economic liberals, whether in the relatively recent theorising about government bureaucracy or in the findings of the Geddes Committee in the 1920s. Labour as well as Conservative Governments had felt cause for dissatisfaction in their dealings with the career Civil Service, prominent though the search for a scapegoat for the political parties' own inadequate preparations for and deficiencies in office seem to have been as a motive for the criticisms later made by politicians and political sympathisers. What was distinctive about the Thatcher Government, in comparison with its immediate predecessors, was that it displayed a combative attitude towards the career Civil Service from the outset. Further than this, it was soon evident that the Thatcher Government's forceful reassertion of the primacy of elected politicians, particularly, but by no means exclusively, in relation to its attempt to practise economic liberalism, was to be met by a measure of opposition from the career Civil Service.

The Civil Service was literally confronted by the most radically inclined Government since that of Clement Attlee, who had declared in March 1948 that 'we always demand from our civil servants a loyalty to the state, and that they should serve the Government of the day, whatever its political colour. That undertaking is carried out with exemplary loyalty' (448 HC Deb. 5s. c. 3418). This seemed to be more of a tribute to the integrity of the Civil Service than applause for its impartiality (*The Times*, 23 November 1953). For, the contemporary Head of that Service, Sir Edward Bridges, had been clear that leading civil servants interpreted the convention of ministerial responsibility as meaning that they had the right to advance the 'practical philosophy' of departmental traditions when presented with the policy proposals of Ministers (Bridges, 1950, p. 19). Plainly, the Ministers did not always prevail. The impartiality of the career Civil Service was never really tested in the manner in which Harold Laski had anticipated in the 1930s. The experience and effects of the Second World War redefined what was 'politically possible', and the establishment and early working experience of the Keynesian managed economy and of the Welfare State provided Sir Edward Bridges with a favourable context in the first half of the 1950s in which to celebrate the Northcote–Trevelyan inheritance of a career Service recruited independently of Ministers. When an Oxford Professor, K.C. Wheare, mildly observed in 1954 that the 'most serious occupational disease' of the British higher civil servant was 'to degenerate into professors in disguise' (Wheare, 1954, p. 34), Bridges welcomed the analogy:

> As I see it, both in academic life and in the Civil Service you need this combination of intellectual integrity . . . with the ardour of the chase. Moreover this combination of qualities has been of value to the Civil Service in another way. It is the pride of the Civil Service that it is non-political, and that it can serve Governments of all parties with equal loyalty and obtain their confidence. And this

confidence is, perhaps, the more easily obtained by a Civil Service whose general attitude is slightly detached and withdrawn. (Bridges, 1954, p. 321)

Richard Wilding, the higher civil servant who had been the secretary to the Fulton Committee, elaborated these themes, in 1979:

> Insufferable Talleyrand was, as so often, insufferably right with his *'surtout, pas de zèle'*. There is, at the end of the day, a contradiction between a strong moral commitment to any given policy and the requirement to be the wholly loyal and effective servant of the Minister of the next Administration who reverses it. In this respect, the Civil Service necessarily breeds Laodiceans. We must, I think, distinguish energy from commitment. It is absolutely necessary to pursue today's policy with energy; it is almost equally necessary, in order to survive, to withhold from it the last ounce of commitment. At the same time, however, I believe that it *is* possible to care, and care passionately, to throw in, as it were, the last ounce of commitment, for the idea of service itself; and to invest that commitment in one particular institution, the Civil Service, with all its manifest imperfections. (Wilding, 1979, p. 8)

However, neither Civil Service as an institution nor the administrative style that Wilding celebrated attracted the level of admiration that they had enjoyed at the time of Bridges's declaration of faith in the Warren Fisher inheritance of generalist administrators. The twenty-five years since then had witnessed sustained criticism of the ethos of the Higher Civil Service, certainly of its Administrative Class, and partly in response, in the post-Plowden, post-Fulton period there took place what C.H. Sisson dismissively called 'a growth of the mythology of management' (Sisson, 1971, p. 282). For all the fashionable emphasis that there had been on the professional manager as the ideal administrator, the Thatcher Government inherited a Service in which, as Sir Robert Armstrong, soon to be its Head, was later to make clear, its leading officials saw themselves primarily as policy advisers (HC 236-II, 1981–2, p. 1226). In 1979, these advisers found themselves advising a Government which, in important areas of policy, did not feel the need for their advice.

The Thatcher Government's treatment of the career Civil Service was in such stark contrast with the attitudes of extreme dependence which seemed to characterise the Governments of the Wilson–Heath–Callaghan era that the radical nature of its behaviour was in danger of being exaggerated. This would not be to say that the status of the Civil Service was unaffected by the Thatcher Government. That Government declined to treat the Service as an interest in its own right. The poltically aggressive Civil Service unions – which from the late 1960s onwards had developed from the staff associations of the old Whitleyism – were beaten in the Civil Service strike of 1981, caused when the Conservative Government unilaterally dispensed with the Priestley pay system. The Civil Service Department was then disbanded, and, in an unprecedented blow at the Civil Service's self-esteem, its Head, Sir Ian Bancroft, was asked to take early retirement. He later described the Thatcher Government's attitude towards the Civil Service as 'Poujadist, populist and silly' (*World in Action*, ITV, 21 January 1985), as opposed, presumably, to social democratic, elitist and 'reasonable'. The Thatcher Government struck at the hierarchy of the career Civil Service in other ways too, initiating a programme of cuts in numbers which amounted to 15 per cent overall between 1979 and 1984, and 16.2 per cent at Senior Open Structure levels near the top of the Service over the same period (*Civil Service Statistics 1984*, p. 5 and correction). The Wardale inquiry was asked to make recommendations about whether or not the Under Secretary grade should be abolished. Though the grade was to survive, one effect, perhaps intentionally, of such inquiries, and, indeed, of the various confrontations and 'de-privileging' activity, was to force the Service on to the defensive. Not content with that, the Rayner efficiency studies and the introduction of MINIS and then of the Financial Management Initiative of 1982 were aimed at changing the Service's culture, and this was the objective too in Prime Ministerial interventions in high-level promotions.

'I took a close interest in senior appointments in the Civil Service from the first, because they could affect the morale and efficiency of whole departments', Mrs Thatcher was later to write (Thatcher, 1993, p. 46). There were those who felt that the scale of the then Prime Minister's involvement in such appointments was unhealthy in two senses. One was that she was instrumental in promoting personal favourites, and in blocking the advancement of others who had crossed her. The other objection was that she was alleged to give preferrence to officials who shared her political outlook. What was being engaged in, Clive Ponting was not alone in believing, was supposed to be 'politicization of the Civil Service by the back door' (Ponting, 1985, pp. 7–8). Early on in her premiership, Mrs Thatcher actually took to visiting government departments by the front door. These tours were later seen by some as sinister in intent, with assessments of senior civil servants being made on the basis of first impressions. James Prior was one Minister who welcomed the visits in principle, but found that made to the Department of Employment disagreeable in practice, for it showed Mrs Thatcher 'at her worst':

> She got into an argument with one of the best and most dedicated civil servants I have ever met, Donald Derx. She insisted on picking an argument without knowing the facts or the legal position on secondary industrial action. . . . It ended by Donald Derx saying, 'Prime Minister, do you really want to know the facts?' I suspect that, as a result of this, Donald had a black mark against his name and appeared to be passed over for promotion. It was a pity that she was not able to accept that by standing up to her, he was displaying qualities which a civil servant must have if he is to serve his Minister properly, and which she of all people used generally to accept. (Prior, 1986, pp. 135–6)

If Mrs Thatcher used 'generally to accept' opposition to her views being expressed by higher civil servants, the Derx case would seem to have been the exception rather than the rule, and if one wanted an offsetting example of a senior civil servant's career benefiting from conflicts over policy with Mrs Thatcher, an instance would be that of Sir Anthony Parsons, who went on to become her Foreign Policy Adviser in Downing Street (Young and Sloman,

1986, p. 51). Some higher civil servants' careers may well have benefited from working proximity to Mrs Thatcher, constituting what one observer called 'the Cabinet Office effect' (Richards, 1993, pp. 24–5). Mrs Thatcher herself wrote:

> I was enormously impressed by the ability and energy of the members of my Private Office at No. 10. I usually held personal interviews with the candidates for Private Secretary for my own office. Those who came were some of the very brightest young men and women in the Civil Service, ambitious and excited to be at the heart of decision making in government. I wanted to see people of the same calibre, with lively minds and a commitment to good administration, promoted to hold the senior posts in the departments. Indeed, during my time in government, many of my former Private Secretaries went on to head departments. In all these decisions, however, ability, drive and enthusiasm were what mattered; political allegiance was not something I took into account. (Thatcher, 1993, p. 46)

Of course, the Cabinet Office and the Prime Minister's Office were not the same thing, and of one of the controversial appointments made, the translation of Sir Clive Whitmore, the Prime Minister's Principal Private Secretary, to become the Permanent Secretary to the Ministry of Defence in 1982, it could be observed that Whitmore had spent almost the whole of his previous career in that Ministry (RIPA Working Group, 1987, p. 44). As for the promotion of Sir Peter Middleton from Deputy Secretary to become Permanent Secretary to the Treasury in 1983, reportedly against official recommendations favouring Sir Anthony Rawlinson, some thought that Middleton's adherence to monetarism explained his early advancement. One notes that the former Labour Chancellor of the Exchequer, Denis Healey, later wrote of Middleton that 'he fully deserved his later promotion to Permanent Secretary over the heads of older men. One of the few things Mrs Thatcher and I have in common is a taste for a little lively insubordination in those who work for us' (Healey, 1989, p. 442).

What Clive Ponting and the others who saw Mrs Thatcher's critical use of Prime Ministerial powers relating to Higher Civil Service appointments (which, after all, dated from 1920) as back-door politicisation needed to demonstrate was that the promotions made were illegitimate in the sense that those given advancement were unqualified for the posts concerned and that they were elevated above their level of ability. Competence may well have been given preference rather than ideologues of a shared political outlook. After all, at a lower level Ponting himself, who seems to have made no secret of his social democratic beliefs, initially gained in career terms from the Prime Minister's recognition of his energetic part in the Rayner exercises (Ponting, 1985, p. 11). The First Division Association, representing higher civil servants, observed about senior Civil Service appointments in the Thatcher era:

> Anecdotal evidence suggests it is style rather than belief which tends to be considered important. The style which appears to appeal to the Prime Minister is the 'can do' approach, best characterized by decisiveness and an ability to get things done, rather than the more traditional approach which lays greater emphasis on analysis of options with recommendations for action based on that analysis.

The RIPA Working Group (1987, pp. 43–4), which was informed of this, concluded that there was no evidence of politicisation and this was also the assessment made in another scholarly study (Richards, 1993, p. 23). Even if Mrs Thatcher had wanted to advance the prospects of economic liberals within the Higher Civil Service she might well have found them in short supply in the Keynesian generation that formed the promotion pool. Mrs Thatcher chose to work with the system, but in a manner which provoked opposition, and there were those among her allies who thought she was insufficiently radical.

II THE HOSKYNS VERSUS WASS DEBATE ABOUT THE HIGHER CIVIL SERVICE

The Thatcher Government was conservative in relation to the Higher Civil Service in the sense that it expected that body to revert to what that Government deemed to be that Service's constitutional role. The Higher Civil Service was nothing less than 'an instrument which will enable [a Government] to carry out all it wants', Richard Crossman (1972, p. 77) once wrote, while observing darkly that this co-operation was subject to the status, the hierarchy and the procedures of the Civil Service being left alone (*ibid.*, pp. 22–3). As the Thatcher Government did not choose to exempt Higher Civil Service from its economic liberal attentions, disharmony resulted. Norman Strauss, one of Mrs Thatcher's political advisers recruited for a time from Unilever, detected contempt for Ministers in the Higher Civil Service, the culture of which, he believed, was antipathetic to change. Strauss and Sir John Hoskyns, the head of the Prime Minister's Policy Unit, had wanted a Prime Minister's Department established to emphasise political control over the Civil Service. Mrs Thatcher turned this down, though, as we have seen, she did make more use than her predecessors had done of long-existing Prime Ministerial powers relating to senior appointments to try to promote cultural change that way (*World in Action*, ITV, 21 January 1985). Once he had left to become Director General of the Institute of Directors, Sir John Hoskyns went on to argue for an explicitly politicised Higher Civil Service. Sir Douglas Wass, once he had left the Treasury, came to the defence of the career Civil Service. There then ensued the first debate about this matter for generations, involving, inevitably, consideration of existing Minister–civil servant relationships; and, if the controversy ever showed much sign of slackening, events like the GCHQ affair, the Ponting case, the Westland affair and the *Spycatcher* case soon came along to keep things on the boil.

Britain was 'fighting for its life', Sir John Hoskyns declared in 1982, and yet its Government had to rely on a Higher Civil Service which was pessimistic about the chances of success in this struggle. Sir John had spent twenty years in a computer business before selling it, after which he joined the Centre for Policy Studies in 1975, where he wrote policy papers for Mrs Thatcher as

Leader of the Opposition and for the Shadow Cabinet. He served in Downing Street with his own terms of reference as the Prime Minister's Senior Policy Adviser. As his belief in electoral reform suggested, Sir John was hardly the conventional Conservative businessman, admitting to voting Labour in 1970 and then Liberal in the first 1974 Election before becoming Tory in the second. He then displayed some signs of the zeal of the convert, while seeming less of a Conservative than an admirer of Mrs Thatcher, seeing her approvingly as having 'a mission oriented approach' and as 'wanting to do things rather than just to be the Prime Minister' (*David Dimbleby in Conversation with Sir John Hoskyns*, BBC1, 7 December 1982). 'Radical aims, better organization, proper methods, new politics and fresh thinking must go together', Sir John believed, 'It's all or nothing. Turning a country around is a big job' (Hoskyns, 1984, p. 10). Sir John plainly did not think that Britain's political establishment as at present constituted was up to that job. It was organised only for day-to-day performance, not anything resembling 'strategic leadership' (Hoskyns, 1983, p. 140). This 'leadership vacuum' followed from a structure in which 'a deeply pessimistic Civil Service looks for political leadership . . . to a tiny handful of exhausted Ministers. These same Ministers look in vain to their officials to provide policy options which, to be any use, would have to be too "politically controversial" for the officials to think of' (*ibid.*, p. 143). This was 'why most post-war Governments have, like hamsters in a treadmill, gone round and round in a strategic box too small to contain any solutions' (Hoskyns, 1984, p. 8). Sir John did not believe that the 'antique conventions, culture and machinery, which failed us between 1950 and 1980, will somehow succeed between 1980 and 2000'. As at present organised:

> For the purposes of government, a country of 55 million people is forced to depend on a talent pool which could not sustain a single multinational company. Indeed, it is extraordinary that such a system seems, nevertheless, regularly to produce quite remarkable individuals. But there are rarely enough of them to build a remarkable Government. And, these days, we need remarkable government.

So, Sir John proposed, 'the Prime Minister should no longer be restricted to the small pool of career politicians in Westminster in forming a Government.' The workload on Ministers had to be reduced, although Sir John did not say in what ways. Whitehall had to be 'organized for strategy and innovation, as well as for day-to-day political survival'. It had to be possible 'to bring adequate numbers of high quality outsiders into the Civil Service' (*ibid.*, pp. 14–15).

As in wartime, 'motivated outsiders' had to be deployed both at the centre and in the individual departments, Sir John believed, observing:

> We need to replace a large number of senior civil servants with politically appointed officials on contracts, at proper market rates, so that experienced top quality people would be available. They might number between ten and twenty per department. Some of them would fill senior positions in the department. Others might work as policy advisers to the Cabinet Minister concerned. There is

no reason why, in some cases, the Permanent Secretary should not be an outsider, with a career official as Second Permanent Secretary responsible for the day-to-day running of the department.

The political appointees would come from private business, and Sir John wanted taxpayer support for political parties to maintain shadow teams of officials in Opposition which would then accompany their party into office. In addition to this 'injection of fresh blood in the departments', Sir John said that there was 'a need for a small new department, responsible for the development and overseeing of the Government's total strategy across all departments, integrating policy and politics into a single whole'. He had in mind 'a reconstructed Cabinet Office' which would be 'headed and partly staffed from outside, though it would also include a substantial number of high flying career officials' (Hoskyns, 1983, pp. 146–7). While disapproving of the effects of the Official Secrets Act (Hoskyns, 1984, p. 12), Sir John did not allow his 'radicalism' to be deflected by suggested reforms. For his ambition was to parallel the changes brought about by the Rayner scrutinies in the sphere of operations management with 'a management revolution in policy work', the very area in which higher civil servants believed themselves to be 'already expert'. Nothing less would be appropriate for the 'new politics' inaugurated in 1979 (*ibid.*, p. 9).

Towards the end of his career, when in the position of Permanent Secretary of the Treasury and joint Head of the Home Civil Service, and then in early retirement when delivering the Reith Lectures for 1983, Sir Douglas Wass established himself as the main defender of the career Civil Service against contemporary critics such as Sir John Hoskyns. Sir Douglas observed:

> Looking back on nearly forty years' experience of government, I am struck not by its deficiencies . . . but by its strengths. I am struck too by the adaptability it has shown to changing circumstances, always preserving what was best, but being ready to discard what had become obsolete and irrelevant. This evolutionary quality of our system of government reflects our pragmatic and cautious approach as a nation to change and reform.

While he instinctively warmed to this approach, Sir Douglas recognised that it could breed 'complacency and suspicion of change'. He saw himself as favouring change. The yardsticks which he applied in gauging the need for change were efficiency and responsiveness:

> Efficiency because of the incessant need for any institution to achieve its objectives at lowest cost to those who have to bear it, and responsiveness because the test of government in any democracy is ultimately its acceptability to those it governs. (Wass, 1984, p. 119)

Sir Douglas was certainly not lacking in suggestions for institutional change. While he believed the Cabinet to be 'in real terms . . . the ultimate embodiment of the executive government in this country' (*ibid.*, p. 10), it was a body that he thought needed 'to strenghten' its 'directing capability'. His mechanism for achieving this resembled the Central Policy Review Staff abolished by the Thatcher Government in 1983, though he was critical of the Think Tank's record (*ibid.*, pp. 36–40). A believer at least in a form of 'open government', to try to raise the level of public debate and the quality of the information to which the public had access, Sir Douglas proposed the establishment of:

> a single, large, permanent Royal Commission from which panels would be drawn to carry out specific studies. It would be the Commission itself, not the Government, which decided what issues to investigate, what terms of reference to give its panels, and who should sit on them.

Two hundred or so persons would be involved. Appointments would be made by the Crown on the advice of the Prime Minister (*ibid.*, pp. 115–16). Sir Douglas ruled out the further institutional experiment of establishing a Department of the Opposition, despite being critical of the performance of Opposition parties since the war. Instead, he favoured 'a limited experiment' under which 'a small number of civil servants' would be seconded 'to the Opposition on the basis of a fixed period of not more than five years and on the firm understanding that they would then be returned to the Civil Service and given a purely managerial post away from the political stage' (*ibid.*, pp. 75–80).

Sir Douglas ruled out any major changes affecting the Civil Service. He observed:

> The line which separates the politically committed and publicly responsible Minister from the political neutral permanent official is drawn at a particularly high level in Britain. In practically no other country is there so little change in the administrative apparatus when a new Government takes office. Officials who advise in favour of particular policy, and devise means of implementing it, cheerfully accept the same responsibilities in regard to the diametrically opposite policy when the Government of the day changes. The presumption on which the system operates is that the Civil Service is unswervingly dedicated to the democratic Parliamentary process and to the paramountcy of Ministers in decision taking. The professional ethic it has embraced required it to give unqualified loyalty to its departmental Ministers and to seek to the best of its ability to put the Government's policies into execution. In advising Ministers it should take their policital objectives as given and regard it as its duty to secure those objectives in the most efficient and publicly acceptable way.

The line between policy and administration was not so easy to draw in practice, Sir Douglas recognised, and this meant that 'in the real world Ministers and civil servants are inextricably mixed up with each other. And they can only function on the basis of a close and harmonious partnership in which each has the trust of the other.' Sir Douglas was aware that 'in recent years this trust has not always been taken for granted.' He denied that the Civil Service had any right to an 'independent' role or that it generally sought one. The existing system was responsive to ministerial initiatives, and he saw no need to go beyond the recently introduced practice of bringing in a small number of politically committed special advisers into government departments. There would be several disadvantages in going further than this and adopting American style arrangements whereby political appointees automatically took over the leading administrative posts in departments on a change in government. Sir Douglas added:

> Businessmen or academics cannot be expected to know how to run a government department any more than a civil servant can be expected to manage an industrial concern without a lot of training and experience. The mechanics, the procedures and methods of government, the constraints of the administrative process, all these things are new to outsiders; and because they are not familiar with them they make mistakes which experienced hands would not. One of the virtues of the British system is that we change Governments smoothly, without the violent dislocation which is a feature of the Washington scene.

Further, Sir Douglas said, the politicisation of the Higher Civil Service would lead to a situation where 'the time horizon over which policy is formulated would become markedly biased towards the short term. One of the advantages of a permanent cadre of heads of departments is that their very performance inclines them to take the long view of the problems they are dealing with.' If 'senior posts were no longer filled by career officials', Sir Douglas observed, 'then Ministers would lose much of the benefit of a department's collective and historical knowledge.' More than this,

> from the point of view of the Service as a career, young men and women of ability would not be attracted if they knew that the most senior posts were likely to be denied to them. There would be a major problem too of ethics over business appointments when political advisers and managers left the Service on a change of Administration.

Sir Douglas compared the British Civil Service with 'the ancient Netherlands Order of the Golden Fleece, a company whose duty it was to give advice to the Dutch ruler and to be bound by solemn oath to speak freely, honestly and under privilege'. He believed that a career civil servant was a practitioner in administration who possessed 'a skill of professional calibre' which required 'a mastery of the arts of politics as well as a command of intellectual analysis and of management', and that the senior official could aspire to 'an objectivity that sometimes escapes the political enthusiast' (*ibid.*, pp. 43–59).

By the mid-1980s, it had become 'fashionable in academic and journalistic circles to argue that the process of politicising the Senior Civil Service is irreversible', as Stephen Linstead, an Assistant Secretary in the Department of Industry and Trade, pointed out, when joining the debate:

> The present Administration has certainly exercised vigorously its undoubted right to vet new senior appointments to satisfy itself that candidates will not reopen its firmly established policies. These developments are a long way from wholesale politicization in the sense of an Administration seeking to replace top officials with people of its own political hue. Neither the present Government nor any of

the other major political parties claims an intention of doing so. . . . There are respectable public policy grounds for opposing politicization of the Civil Service. . . . The present system was introduced as a specific reform, after considerable debate, to stamp out patronage and corruption: those who seek to alter the system must bear the onus of showing that the ills will not recur. . . . Nor (contrary to the impression conveyed by some British commentators) is the U.K. the only democracy to carry the non-political tradition to the top grades. There are plenty of examples in the older Commonwealth and in Western Europe. (*FDA News*, May 1985, p. 4)

Large-scale politicisation of the Civil Service runs into difficulties at the first hurdle: from where in a society like the British one would it be possible to attract the able people needed to do the jobs concerned? Industry and commerce was Sir John Hoskyns's answer, believing as he did that 'the way businessmen think and act is more relevant than that of most of the politicians, civil servants, academics and commentators who have concerned themselves with the nation's problems thus far' (Hoskyns, 1984, p. 16). If nothing else would change the defeatist culture of Whitehall, Sir John at one stage was prepared to envisage the mass pensioning-off of much of the Higher Civil Service (*David Dimbleby in Conversation with Sir John Hoskyns*, BBC1, 7 December 1982). Scepticism seems justified about British private companies, a breed not noted for their success in international competition, having talent to spare on the Hoskyns scale. Further than this, Sir John was solely concerned with the working arrangements of a Conservative Government 'responsibly trying to make capitalism work' (Hoskyns, 1984, p. 3). In the event of an alternative government, Labour and/or, in those days, Alliance, and later Liberal Democrat, where would the political appointees come from then? The most likely source would seem to be economists and social scientists in higher education. Without assurances that jobs could be returned to in institutions then, and in the foreseeable future, looking for staff economies, the numbers of able people likely to be attracted across seemed destined to be insufficient. Such considerations could not be trivial for those excluded from perhaps the only independent profession, that of private means.

Although the Presidential system complicates comparisons, the American Federal Executive provides some idea of what a more politicised British Civil Service might look like. For all the powers of appointment that an American President has, one reason why the notion of Presidential government has been well described as an illusion is that the Federal bureaucracy is insufficiently politically responsive (Heclo and Salamon, 1981, pp. 113–46). Naturally, there are those who want 'better Presidential appointments' (Mackenzie, 1981, p. 277). That the history of the American national bureaucracy suggests that efforts to enhance popular control of government seem to have largely worked to the benefit of bureaucrats (Nelson, 1982, pp. 747–78) seems to have had no effect at all upon the respect for the principle of merit appointments which characterises most studies of American Civil Service arrangements. It is the exceptional American observer who speaks up for the spoils system at all (Peters and Nelson, 1979, pp. 263–7). The ablest study of the American national bureaucracy, conducted by Hugh Heclo in the mid-1970s, found that there was no consistent pattern of division between career and non-career posts in different agencies (Heclo, 1977, pp. 36–41). The picture of 'in and outers' did not square with the reality of most political executives only coming into government work once, and then almost always in the one agency (*ibid.*, pp. 87–112). Such were the consequences of combining political executives and career bureaucrats in an agency-bound manner that Heclo advocated the creation of a mobile class of merit appointees, called Federal Executive Officers, to make the national bureaucracy more efficient (*ibid.*, pp. 249–61). The Senior Executive Service established by the Civil Service Reform Act of 1978 did not seem to match Heclo's aspirations, the realisation of which would have led to the establishment of a body of officials resembling Warren Fisher's British Administrative Class.

Ironically, domestic admiration for Fisher's creation, even when obscured within the Open Structure and the Administration Group of the Home Civil Service, has become more and more qualified as the years have passed since the centenary of the Northcote–Trevelyan Report was celebrated. The malfunctioning of the Keynesian order led, first, to wide questioning of the role and abilities of the Higher Civil Service, then the Fulton Committee and then the raising of the issue of politicisation. When Sir Douglas Wass, defending the Civil Service, criticised the former Central Policy Review Staff for being too small to really question areas of departmental expertise and initiative (Wass, 1984, pp. 37–8), he proved to be a comfortable target for the scorn of Lord Rothschild, the former Director of the CPRS, who talked of Wass's 'departmental dream world' (Hennessy *et al.*, 1985, p. 107). The Higher Civil Service, having scorned expertise in the past, could not easily lay claim to it now. Sir Warren Fisher had led the Service down the wrong road. This is not to say that the CPRS did not merit its abolition by the Thatcher Government. Only one member of the CPRS was believed to have voted Conservative in 1983 of all Elections, and the insider view of the members' allegiances was that 'they had S.D.P. tendencies and were certainly out of sympathy with Norman Tebbit's view of the world' (Blackstone and Plowden, 1988, pp. 30–1). The Prime Minister's Policy Unit, which actually comprised Conservatives, was better suited to the task of attempting to fill 'the hole at the centre' of the system. If the Thatcher Government wanted centrist advice, this was always unlikely to be in short supply from the Higher Civil Service. Yet, the Thatcher Government showed no sign of wishing to emulate the Reagan Administration in the United States, which to a limited extent had a similar political outlook, and which made a determined effort to impose its will on the permanent bureaucracy through the vigorous use of provisions for political appointments (Salamon and Lund, 1981, pp. 337–413). The Thatcher Government did not take up the modest *Re-skilling Government* proposals for experiments in

French-style ministerial *cabinets* which Sir John Hoskyns with others carefully constructed and costed and then published in 1986 after wide-ranging consultations (Hoskyns *et al.*, 1986; Institute of Directors, 1986a; 1986b). The Thatcher Government preferred to soldier on, working with the Higher Civil Service, with the Prime Minister at least not being averse to acts of antagonistic behaviour which were at times reciprocated and at others undertaken without provocation, with the consequence of an uneasy relationship between the elected Government and the career Service that proved promotive of constitutional analysis.

III THE ARMSTRONG MEMORANDUM AND THE CONSTITUTIONAL RECKONING

The 'capture theory' view of the role that the Higher Civil Service had come to play, which the Thatcher Government implicitly subscribed to, rested on a conservative, some would say outdated, view of the role of the high official. Nowadays, as the constitutional lawyer Geoffrey Marshall observed, 'a clear and succinct account of the principle or convention of ministerial responsibility is not easy to give. One reason may be that the convention is, like most British conventions, somewhat vague and slippery – resembling the procreation of eels.' Nevertheless, Marshall added, politicians carry on as if the convention does exist (Marshall, 1984, pp. 54–5). This was not entirely unreasonable, since, despite the changes wrought by the growth of government as affecting the span of control, and by the consequences of the Crichel Down case and the appointment of the Ombudsman as regards perceptions of the constitutional position, Ministers still remain responsible in the sense that they are liable to report upon the activities of the government department of which they are a political head to the Crown, to the Prime Minister and Cabinet, and to Parliament. Civil servants remain non-political in the sense that they normally receive their appointments independently of Ministers, that they are not allowed an avert political allegiance and that they are not required to perform politically on the floor of either House of Parliament. Civil servants are required to appear before Parliamentary committees, but they are still publicly responsible neither for the advice that they have given to Ministers, nor for the efficiency with which they carry out their work.

Allegations of the Ponting kind that the Thatcher Government was 'politicising' the Higher Civil Service in one sense ignored the reality that politics has never been absent from the career Civil Service, which operates in the midst of it. As Sir Gwilym Gibbon once observed, nobody ever said that the higher civil servant should be a 'political eunuch'. What the career civil servant must abstain from being was a 'political gospeller' (Gibbon, 1943, p. 86). To take an example, the valedictory despatch sent in 1979 by Sir Nicholas Henderson to the then contemporary Foreign and Commonwealth Secretary,

David Owen (*The Economist*, 2 June 1979, pp. 29–40) may have been little more than the conventional wisdom of a generation, or the expression of routine social democratic sentiments, as Tony Benn believed (Benn, 1981, p. 51), but the despatch did take up a political position. When George Brown, as Labour Foreign Secretary in the 1960s, complained that the Foreign Office was resistant to policy change, he was told by Sir Cecil Parrott that:

> whatever politicians may say when they're in Opposition, they soon find out when they get into office and read the confidential papers that they can't possibly do what they said they would do. They must instead follow the line of their predecessors in office, because there's just no other line any Government can follow. (Wallace, 1977, p. 52; q.v. Jenkins and Sloman, 1985, p. 100)

The Foreign and Commonwealth Office itself recognised the NATO Alliance and membership of the European Community as the 'twin pillars' of its position (Jenkins and Sloman, 1985, pp. 71–97). If David Owen, who, essentially, did not challenge this position, found himself dealing with 'some officials' who 'would fight the implementation of a decision taken by the Secretary of State' (*ibid.*, p. 103), it would not be surprising if another Foreign Secretary committed to, say, pulling down one of the pillars, experienced a greater degree of obstruction. External affairs may have some of the characteristics of a special case, because the room for manoeuvre normally seems to be even more limited than in most areas of domestic policy. Nevertheless, the existence of established departmental policy positions – some at least defended, it seems, with vigour – must constitute a modification of the notion of the career Civil Service providing a politically neutral framework for Ministers.

That any party-political activity remains debarred for the leading civil servants who constitute the top 3 per cent or so the Service's ranks, from Principal level upwards, and that a further 70 per cent or so below that are banned from national party political activity (Armitage Report, 1978, para. 157; *CCSU Bulletin*, July 1984, pp. 91–4; *CCSU Bulletin*, February 1985, pp. 28–30) gives the career Civil Service a superficially non-political appearance which is belied by the fact of the scale of unionisation of the Service. By the time that the Thatcher Government had reached office, the Civil Service unions had made themselves much more consciously part of the wider trade union movement, and thus much more politically prominent, than, generally, the old staff associations had tended to do; and especially once they had established the centralised Council of Civil Service Unions, these bodies represented a challenge to the elected government of a kind that the Thatcher Government was disinclined to sidestep. The Civil Service strike of 1981 could hardly be said to be without political intent, because a defeat for the Government would have weakened its economic strategy. As it was, the Government won, and in 1984, wisely or not, one of the ways it followed up its victory was to ban union membership for civil servants working at the Government Communications Headquarters at Cheltenham and its outstations. The furore which this action aroused tended to distract from the wider issue. Whether a career Civil Service could be heavily unionised when it was supposed to be a politically neutral body was a question that was easier to pose than to answer in a way compatible with an open society (Fry, 1985, pp. 122–45).

The disharmony that characterised relations between the Thatcher Government and the career Civil Service was of the kind hinted at in Crossman's speculations. As long as the Civil Service's privileges were largely left alone, then, in principle, the career Civil Service was a co-operative instrument for policy execution. Given departmental policy positions, in practice this was scarcely an arrangement that was politically neutral, but it was one conducive to a form of loyalty. When the Thatcher Government engaged in 'deprivileging' the Civil Service in some cases disloyalty resulted. Of the 'leakers' of confidential information in the Civil Service who were uncovered, Clive Ponting expressed disgruntlement at the Thatcher Government's behaviour towards the Service's material interests (Ponting, 1985, p. 7), and related resentments were expressed by Sarah Tisdall and Ian Willmore (Pyper, 1985, pp. 72–81). At this point, defenders of the 'leakers' usually introduce the examples of Desmond Morton and Ralph Wigram, who were among the twenty or so leading civil servants who 'leaked' secret material to Winston Churchill in the 1930s, without which his campaign criticising the National Government's provision for defence would have been less effective. Churchill told Morton: 'No thought ever crossed your mind but that of the public interest' (Gilbert, 1976, pp. xxi–xxii). Whether or not Churchill was right, the same could not be easily said of Ponting, Tisdall or Willmore, whose disloyalty towards the Thatcher Government seemed to owe at least something to bureaucratic self-interest of the kind analysed by Selznick. Further, the behaviour of those who 'leaked' documents to Churchill does not have to be seen as admirable. Appeasement was a complex matter. After all, Churchill's official biographer, Martin Gilbert, managed to be the co-author of one book condemning appeasement (Gilbert and Gott, 1963), and then to write another book sympathetic to appeasement (Gilbert, 1966). There seems no necessity to concur with the view that the career Civil Service is the better for the presence in its ranks of licensed, pensioned rebels prepared to betray a trust for what they deem to be a 'good cause'. Clive Ponting's behaviour in 'leaking' material about the *Belgrano* incident merited the observations sometimes ascribed to Talleyrand: '*C'est plus qu'un crime, c'est une faute.*' Ponting's 'mistake', natural enough in the confusion invited by the behaviour of so many of the recent Governments, was to act as a 'political gospeller' and, thus, to fail to appreciate the essentially subordinate position of the official.

In February 1985, in the wake of the Ponting case, Sir Robert Armstrong, as Head of the Home Civil Service, in consultation with other Permanent Secretaries, thought it appropriate to issue a note of guidance on the duties and responsibilities of civil servants in relation to Ministers. Its message was straightforward:

Civil Servants are servants of the Crown. For all practical purposes the Crown in this context means and is represented by the Government of the day. There are special cases in which certain functions are conferred by law upon particular members or groups of members of the public services; but in general the exeuctive powers of the Crown are exercised by and on the advice of Her Majesty's Ministers, who are in turn answerable to Parliament. The Civil Service as such has no constitutional personality or responsibility separate from the duly elected Government of the day. It is there to provide the Government of the day with advice on the formulation of the policies of the Government, to assist in carrying out the decisions of the Government, and to manage and deliver the services for which the Government is responsible. Some civil servants are also involved, as a proper part of their duties, in the processes of presentation of Government policies and decisions.

Sir Robert emphasised that 'the British Civil Service is a non-political and disciplined career Civil Service, and those civil servants who could not accept the consequences of these arrangements should resign, while continuing to respect the confidences obtained during their work in the Civil Service' (HC 92-II, 1985–6, pp. 7–9).

The Armstrong Memorandum was unique. Never before in quite this manner had a civil servant of comparable status publicly set down in such detail what he believed to be the constitutional position regarding the relationship between Ministers and civil servants. That the Head of the Home Civil Service felt the need to issue a document of this kind was evidence of the controversy which had come to surround the subject. As if to confirm this, the Memorandum was given a generally unfavourable reception not only by outside commentators, who as a breed seem afflicted by compulsive reformism, but also by the First Division Association (FDA), representing many leading officials within the Service. The disquiet which the FDA had felt about the implications of the Ponting case for the relationship between Ministers and officials had led it earlier to promote the idea of a code of ethics for civil servants (*FDA News*, December 1984, pp. 1–3), in direct contrast with the sentiments expressed in paragraph 4060 of the Establishment Officers' Guide for the Civil Service, which explicitly denied the need for such a code. In its way, of course, the Armstrong Memorandum was a code of ethics of a kind, as was recognised at the time of its publication by the then General Secretary of the FDA, John Ward, who wrote:

the F.D.A. draft Code was designed to give a degree of liberalization and, most important, was to be set in the context of the repeal of Section 2 of the Official Secrets Act and the introduction of a Freedom of Information Act. In other words our draft took account of the problems highlighted by recent events and looked forward. Sir Robert's looks backwards. (*FDA News*, March 1985, p. 3)

Yet, when we come to the first general statement of principle in the FDA's draft code, it was stated that:

Civil Servants in the United Kingdom are servants of the Queen in Parliament. Executive government as a function of the Crown is carried out by Ministers who are accountable to Parliament. Civil Servants therefore owe to Ministers the duty to serve them loyally and to the best of their ability. (*FDA News*, December 1984, p. 3)

This seemed to be much the same position as that taken in the Armstrong Memorandum's second paragraph, where it said that 'civil servants are servants of the Crown' and that 'for all practical purposes the Crown in this context means and is represented by the Government of the day'. According to the textbook on constitutional law published by E.C.S. Wade and Godfrey Phillips, 'it is usual to refer to . . . "the Crown" as the collective entity which in law may stand for central government' (Wade and Phillips, 1977, p. 216). In the opinion of Wade and Phillips, 'the responsibility of Ministers to Parliament consists of a duty to account to Parliament for what they and their departments are doing', which means that the Minister 'must answer before parliament for anything that his officials have done under his authority' (*ibid.*, pp. 108–9). It could be noted too that Lord Croham, who as Sir Douglas Allen was Head of the Home Civil Service between 1974 and 1977, said much the same thing as Sir Robert Armstrong when lecturing on 'open government' in 1984: 'Civil servants are servants of the Crown with defined duties to the Government of the day, in which to all intents and purposes the concept of the Crown is embarked.' Lord Croham added:

> The duties of civil servants to Parliament are discharged through Ministers, with very limited expectations. The duties of Ministers are not supervised by civil servants. It is true that the Accounting Officer of a department, usually the Permanent Secretary, has a definite duty to inform the Comptroller and Auditor General, which implies immediate information to Parliament, if he is instructed by his Minister to make payments from public funds which have not been authorised by Parliament. This duty has very rarely had to be exercised. It is very tightly defined and is to enable a Permanent Secretary in specified circumstances both to obey his Minister but still have defence against a charge that he permitted an improper use of funds. It does not enable the official to overrule the Minister, it is specific to the duties of an Accounting Officer and it lays down who should be informed. Over and above this, civil servants have an implied duty not to mislead Parliament and to answer all questions put to them by a Parliamentary Committee as fully and frankly as they can, but they are entitled to reserve the position of their Ministers and are not expected to offer an independent commentary on the validity of the Government's position. (Croham, 1985, pp. 11–12)

It was, though, the 'independent' status of the career Civil Service which was at the heart of the debate about the Armstrong Memorandum. Like the position of Wade and Philips, that Memorandum was organised around the constitutional convention of ministerial responsibility, and, hence, effectively denied that the Service could or should have an 'independent' status in relation to the activity of governing. Those observers who considered the doctrine of ministerial responsibility to be a myth were naturally out of sympathy with the Memorandum, tending to prefer arrangements to be established which reflected what they saw as the reality of extensive Civil Service influence over Ministers, even control of them. The FDA also wanted these arrangements to be compatible with 'open government', and for civil servants to serve Ministers subject to explicit conditions, and informed the House of Commons Treasury and Civil Service Committee of this (HC 92-II, 1985–6, pp. 59–67). That Committee's Report on *Civil Servants and Ministers: Duties and responsibilities,* published in May 1986, failed to address fully the core issues it was charged with reviewing, preferring to adhere uncritically to the reforming agenda of the time. At one point, the Committee declared that 'the evidence that we have received does not suggest that the Government has made a convincing case against some form of Freedom of Information Act' (HC 92-I, 1985–6, para. 6.5). It was incumbent upon those advocating change to argue for it, and this sort of observation invited the dismissiveness with which the Thatcher Government felt able to treat the Committee's Report (Cmnd 9841, 1986).

The Westland affair 'dramatically exposed the difficult nature of the relationships between Ministers, civil servants and Parliament', the Treasury and Civil Service Committee believed (HC 92-I, 1985–6, p. vii), though the affair primarily involved personal rivalry between two members of the Thatcher Government, namely Michael Heseltine, the Secretary of State for Defence, and Leon Brittan, the Secretary of State for Trade and Industry. These two Cabinet Ministers differed over what would be the best arrangements for safeguarding the future of the Westland helicopter company, which was in financial difficulties, Heseltine wanted Westland to be taken over by a European consortium, and Brittan favoured the company being taken over by American controlled interests. Matters came to a head in early January 1986, when Brittan authorised the disclosure of confidential material from the Solicitor General, which cast doubt upon the accuracy of a statement made by the Secretary of State for Defence. Heseltine resigned from the Government because his preferred solution to Westland's difficulties seemed to him to be being frustrated. Brittan was then forced to resign shortly afterwards, having seemed to mislead the House of Commons about events relating to the publication of the Solicitor General's letter. Whether or not the Prime Minister knew of, and, hence, condoned the leaking of the letter became a matter of contention. That six civil servants were involved was also a subject of controversy. The six civil servants were Bernard Ingham, the Prime Minister's Chief Press Secretary, Charles Powell, Private Secretary (Overseas Affairs) in the Prime Minister's Office, Collette Bowe, Head of Information, John Mogg, the Private Secretary to the Secretary of State, and John Michell, Under Secretary in charge of Air Division – all of the Department of Trade and Industry – and the now familiar figure of Sir Robert Armstrong. The Defence Committee of the House of Commons investigated the Westland affair, and in July 1986 it produced two Reports on the subject, together with a substantial volume of evidence. That Report, called *Westland plc: The government's decision-making*, examined the affair in detail, and it discovered nothing that was either novel or exciting. The Defence Committee sought to explain the uninteresting nature of its Report by pointing to the fact that, while it was able to summon Sir Robert Armstrong and another Permanent Secretary, Sir Brian Hayes of the Department of Trade and Industry, to appear before it, the Committee had been denied the opportunity to cross-examine Messrs Ingram, Powell, Mogg, Michell and Miss Bowe. The Committee recommended that the situation in which such exclusions were possible should be changed (HC 519, 1985–6, pp. lxv–lxviii). The Government's initial response to this proposal was one of rejection (Cmnd 9916, 1986, para. 44), and its attitude came under attack from some of its own supporters when the relevant Reports were debated in the House of Commons in October 1986. Two months later, the House of Commons Liaison Committee reinforced the calls for a relaxation of restrictions (HC 100, 1986–7, para. 19), and the Government had earlier hinted at concessions. It was difficult to see what form such concessions could take which would not be undermining of the type of career Higher Civil Service that was essential to the running of British central government as currently organised. The most that the Conservative Government was likely to do was to make minor modifications to the Osmotherly Rules of 1980, the guidelines which state that civil servants who appeared before or who submitted papers to Parliamentary committees did so 'on behalf of the Minister' (Civil Service Department, Gen. 80/38, 1980, para. 7), and a White Paper, published in February 1987, did no more than that (Cm. 78, 1987, p. 4).

The peculiar character of the British career Civil Service and of the system within which it worked was exposed to further publicity in the Peter Wright secrets case. This the British Government pursued in the New South Wales Supreme Court in the latter weeks of 1986 and into 1987 in an attempt to prevent the publication in Australia of what it defined as officially secret material contained in a book called *Spycatcher*, the memoirs of Wright, a former senior intelligence officer. Students of bureaucracy noted that one of Wright's motives for publication was to make money in order to compensate for what he believed to have been inadequate pension arrangements. As the writ of the British Official Secrets Act did not extend to Australia, and as the gist of Wright's revelations had already been published in 1981 in the book by Chapman Pincher called *Their Trade is Treachery*, which must have appeared with the Government's connivance, the Thatcher Government's objective in pressing the case, thus giving *Spycatcher* priceless publicity, was unclear. The British Government was always likely to look foolish in expecting a foreign court to respect its esoteric form of politico-administrative behaviour. At home, operating within those conventions, Sir Robert Armstrong had dealt as comfortably with the inquiries of the House of Common's Defence Committee as he had done with those of its Treasury and Civil Service Committee. In New South Wales, treated with less respect, the Head of the Home Civil Service had a more difficult time, famously stating in response to cross-examination that he had not lied but that he had been 'economical with the truth'. Edward Heath condemned the Prime Minister's humiliating and 'improper' use of the Secretary of the Cabinet to put the Government's case in Australia (Campbell, 1993, p. 760), but Mrs Thatcher never did seek to match Heath's level of deference.

The Armstrong Memorandum was dismissed as a 'Yes, Minister Code' by 'liberal' opinion (*The Guardian*, 27 February 1985), but this invited the question of what else it could be. For it to be believed that, in principle, the career Service could say 'No, Minister' would be to accord that Service a constitutional veto of the kind once enjoyed, for example, by the House of Lords in relation to the Liberal Governments of Campbell-Bannerman and Asquith, which had the effect of negating the electoral verdict of 1906, and which was removed in 1911. Certainly, as Sir Douglas Wass observed:

> the Civil Service cannot be thought of as an in-built safeguard against what some people might call the excesses of a radical or reforming Government. The only effective safeguards . . . have to be found in the political and judicial processes, or in the force of circumstances themselves. (Wass, 1984, p. 53)

In constitutional terms, agents of Ministers more accurately summed up the role of civil servants than notions that officials should either fight for the policies that they believed in, or against those which they opposed, or that they should act like watchdogs armed with machinery other than that which existed through which to alert 'the public' about ministerial policies or behaviour they deemed undesirable. If the Armstrong Memorandum raised major constitutional questions, the answers were determined by structure. Civil servants were responsible to Ministers. Their relationship with the Crown was an indirect one, unlike that of the armed forces, which were organisations of a different kind, not least in disciplinary arrangements and ordinarily in roles. Unlike leading civil servants, officers in the armed forces hold the Queen's Commission, so there was a direct link with the Crown which was not commonly present in the Civil Service, and where there was such a link, as in the case of HM Inspectors of Schools, it was a matter for note. More generally, civil servants did not seem to have a direct responsibility as servants of the Crown in addition to their role as servants of the Government of the day. The constitutional lawyer Geoffrey Marshall did detect a potential area of such direct responsibility using the example to be found in the Franks report on Falkland Islands policy which revealed that in March 1982 officials of the Foreign and Commonwealth Office, after consultation with the Permanent Under Secretary of State, informed the Foreign and Commonwealth Secretary, Lord Carrington, that in November 1977 the previous Labour Government had covertly sent a small naval task force to the South Atlantic (Marshall, 1984, pp. 75–6). A potential role, though, differed from an actual one. Normally, the confidentiality of the views of Ministers in previous Governments, and of the advice tendered to them by civil servants, was protected by means of incoming Ministers being denied access to the papers of earlier Governments of a different political party. When this practice actually began seems not to be known, but Marshall recorded an opinion that the first time may have been 1951 (*ibid.*, p. 74). If so, the timing was interesting. For, although the Churchill Government of 1951–5 proved to be as innocuous in its dealings with the career Civil Service and as wedded to the Keynesian Welfare State as its Labour predecessor, the Conservatives did come to office armed with slogans about the evils of bureaucracy, and the leading civil servants might have felt that their precise relationship with the Attlee Government needed to be protected. Whether this was so or not, higher civil servants could not aspire to act as guardians of the Constitution in the same manner as some saw the Crown as doing in a political crisis or national emergency. They did not have any comparable responsibility for the continuity of the state and, besides the massive gulf in status, the Civil Service never enjoyed anything remotely like the popular authority of the Monarchy. Civil servants did not have a prior responsibility to Parliament. Except in the case of Accounting Officers, they had no direct relationship with Parliament at all. Thus, there was no useful purpose served by suggestions that civil servants appearing before Parliamentary Select Committees should have more freedom to answer questions on policy matters. So, the Armstrong Memorandum only stated the constitutionally obvious, given the structure of British central government at the time. A structure having greater resemblance to, say, the Swedish arrangements could be a different matter, of course, and the Next Steps of the Thatcher Government were in that direction.

4 The Thatcher Government, the Financial Management Initiative and the career Civil Service

The Civil Service is a career Service, i.e. its staffing policy is primarily based on recruiting people as they leave the education system and retaining them in the Service until they retire. The Civil Service is not alone in this. Most large organizations recruit in a similar way and offer a career to the majority of managerial employees. The career principle in the Civil Service should remain. But an inflow of new people and ideas is also needed. This can be achieved by making a number of temporary or permanent opportunities; and by encouraging civil servants to spend time gaining experience in other organizations.

This was the framework within which management development in the Civil Service was going to take place in the 1980s, as anticipated in 1983 by the Management and Personnel Office, the rump of the Civil Service Department (CSD) left behind in the Cabinet Office (Management and Personnel Office, 1983, para. 18). There seemed to be little fear of a Thatcher-inspired 'revolution' in this pronouncement. There was no sense that the Financial Management Initiative launched the year before threatened the existing arrangements unduly. Indeed, the sentences seemed to bear out the remarks of Lord Rayner, the original managerial 'revolutionary', who regarded the Civil Service as 'a mixture of superb talent and commitment to the public good on the one hand, and of an able coterie of cynics on the other'. Rayner detected

> two strands of thought in the Higher Civil Service. One is wholeheartedly committed to the policy of reform. Indeed, I drew repeatedly on the ideas and thoughts of officials. The other is frankly disposed to play things long, to ride out the storm, to wait for the outsider to go away and for Ministers to change. (Rayner, 1984, p. 16)

Individual Ministers did change, of course, though not always to the benefit of the Civil Service's self-interest, given the Government's economic liberal agenda, and that for eleven years there was the presence of Mrs Thatcher as Prime Minister, ill-disposed towards the maintenance of a large-scale career Civil Service of the type that she had inherited. Lord Soames, as Lord President of the Council, was a Minister responsible for the Civil Service Department before being dismissed by Mrs Thatcher after seeming to be less than enthusiastic about achieving an outright victory in the Civil Service strike of 1981. James Prior recalled:

> The strong advice of Christopher [Soames] and myself was to settle. But when the matter came to the full Cabinet, it was clear that Margaret had lobbied

intensively. Willie Whitelaw said afterwards she had told him she would resign if she didn't get her way. . . . The debate was one of the most acrimonious I have ever experienced. The Cabinet was completely split down the middle. In the end, the Prime Minister got her way.

Prior and Soames had been concerned about the immediate financial costs of the Civil Service strike (Prior, 1986, pp. 142–3), but this missed the point that a signal defeat for what she called the 'increasingly politicized' unions was essential if Mrs Thatcher's ambitions for Civil Service reform were to be realised. As the then Prime Minister saw things, 'the pursuit of new and more efficient practices' in government departments 'were being held up by union obstruction' (Thatcher, 1993, p. 47). That had costs too. Mrs Thatcher had no faith in the Civil Service Department's ability to carry out her reforming programme. The abolition of the CSD had been effectively decided several months before a House of Commons Treasury and Civil Service Committee Report in December 1980 had recommended that department's retention (HC 54, 1980–1), and a Prime Ministerial statement (997 HC Deb. 5s.c. 1970) and a White Paper (Cmnd 8170, 1981) had seemed accepting of this. In January 1980, Mrs Thatcher had visited the CSD, and later recorded that 'many of my worst fears about the Civil Service were confirmed . . . the only real question in my mind was whether responsibility for the CSD's work should be redistributed to the Treasury or the Cabinet Office' (Thatcher, 1993, pp. 47–8). Upon the CSD's abolition in November 1981, the role of the central management of the Home Civil Service was shared by the Treasury and the Management and Personnel Office, until the latter was replaced in August 1987 by the Office of the Minister for the Civil Service, also located in the Cabinet Office. Though the Headship of the Home Civil Service remained with the Secretary of the Cabinet, having only returned to the Treasury for a matter of months after the demise of the CSD and then on a joint basis, the various changes from 1981 onwards more generally had the appearance of a reassertion of Treasury control over the Civil Service. Central management in that form had its rationale, given the importance that the Thatcher Government attached to the containment of public expenditure. Contrastingly, the Financial Management Initiative, which that Government had come to require individual departments to adopt, emphasised the delegation of managerial authority within departments. Plainly, further structural and allied changes had to follow, but until they did, the Financial Management Initiative no more than threatened the relative coherence of the career Civil Service, the pattern of activity within which largely continued as if tangential to the Initiative.

I RAYNERISM, MINIS AND THE FINANCIAL MANAGEMENT INITIATIVE

One of the Thatcher Government's first acts was to appoint Sir Derek (later Lord) Rayner from Marks and Spencer, and a small supporting team, to advise it on the promotion of efficiency and the elimination of waste in government departments. The Financial Management Initiative was derived from these programmes, together with MINIS (Management Information System for Ministers) arrangements which Michael Heseltine first pioneered when he became Secretary of State for the Environment in 1979. Of Lord Rayner, Margaret Thatcher later wrote:

> The two of us used to say that in politics you judge the value of a service by the amount you put in, but in business you judge it by the amount you get out. We were both convinced of the need to bring some of the attitudes of business into government. We neither of us conceived just how difficult this would prove. (Thatcher, 1993, pp. 30–1)

As Mrs Thatcher had previous experience as a Minister and Sir Derek Rayner had worked inside Whitehall for the Heath Government, it was hard to see quite why the size of the task ahead was not appreciated, certainly in broad terms, especially as both the incoming Prime Minister and her Efficiency Adviser plainly had been influenced by Leslie Chapman's book about waste in the Civil Service. Indeed, during Sir Derek Rayner's initial briefing for the scrutiny exercises, he distributed copies of *Your Disobedient Servant*, and one official involved in the Rayner team recorded that Leslie Chapman's efficiency reviews in the Ministry of Public Building and Works were in several ways a model for the later Rayner scrutinies (Bray, 1987, p. 12).

'The environment in which I set to work was mixed', Lord Rayner later recalled, observing:

> The Prime Minister provided in 1979, and has done so since, a unique political imperative. She was and has stayed determined that there should be a radical change in the quality of management. Without this, my work and that of my successor could not have been effective. Support for the initiative was not extensive among other Ministers or at the higher echelons of the Civil Service. 'Management' seemed small to politicians, while to the latter it looked like yet another turn round a familiar buoy for which political enthusiasm would fade as quickly as it had done before. (Rayner, 1984, pp. 4–5)

Lord Rayner revealed that 'no one at the time of my arrival in Whitehall knew in financial management terms how much it cost to run government.' This was a consequence of a situation in which 'Ministers, politicians and officials have been mesmerized by the glamour of "policy"; and the costs of administering the policies were regarded as the candle ends of public expenditure' (*ibid.*, p. 2). Once identified in a detailed form, as they could not be in 1979, the 'candle ends' proved to amount to truly formidable sums of public money. For instance, gross running costs for the Civil Service during the financial year 1985–6 were some £12.3 billion, or about 3.4 per cent of GDP. The main element in these running costs was the pay bill, which was some £5.8 billion (*Civil Service Statistics 1986*, p. 4). Given that, broadly, every £1 billion extra on the Civil Service pay bill at the time added another penny to the basic rate of income tax (*The Economist*, 30 August 1986, p. 19), a Conservative Government committed to cuts in direct taxation was not as unreasonable as it was sometimes portrayed in wishing to cut Civil Service numbers and to limit its pay increases. The sheer scale of departmental running costs invited economies too.

The Rayner scrutiny programme made a start on this work. It was important to the Prime Minister and those few in the Government who took the matter seriously to start early on, and useful ground was broken. Nevertheless, in relation to the size of the task the symbolic value of Raynerism was always likely to outweigh its practical achievements. Some of the civil servants involved took a different view. Alan Bray wrote:

> The speed with which Derek Rayner began to act showed the extent to which the details of his strategy had been long prepared in advance. . . It consisted of a large number of close, searching studies of areas of activity, the 'scrutinies' as they came to be called. These were carried out not by Derek Rayner's own staff, which he kept very small, but by teams of 'scrutineers': civil servants drawn from the departments involved, usually of about Principal grade (the basic level for the young administrator in the Civil Service) and often very bright. The energies of his personal staff were put rather into sustaining the impetus in the studies begun by the scrutineers. Their brief was sharply focused. It was for each to examine in depth a clearly marked out part of a department's activities; this was usually an area proposed by the department involved and then agreed by Derek Rayner. The conclusions they came to were to be their own, but their methods of working were narrowly laid down from the onset by Derek Rayner himself. . . . None of the scrutineers could have left these meetings in doubt as to what they were expected to do. They were to ask radical questions. In his Note of Guidance he told his scrutineers to ask questions 'to the point of challenging the activity's very existence'. (Bray, 1987, p. 2)

Another official, Norman Warner, described the aim of the Rayner scrutinies as being 'to persuade organizations to review their activities and reform themselves from within' (Warner, 1984, p. 7). Alan Bray saw the Rayner exercises as 'in many ways . . . working with the existing culture of the Civil Service' (Bray, 1987, p. 36) and the Rayner approach as having permanence (*ibid.*, p. 65). Another former scrutineer, Clive Ponting, seemed to see Lord Rayner's departure in 1983, to be replaced by Sir Robin Ibbs, as marking the effective end of this particular initiative. Ponting considered that 'some small victories had been won, but Whitehall had absorbed Raynerism, as it had all the other schemes for reform and improving efficiency' (Ponting, 1986, p. 216). Leslie Chapman, who had wanted a much more centralised and ambitious programme, understandably treated the Rayner programme dismissively: 'The most important weakness was that Rayner had no right of entry into departments. He could investigate by invitation only, and even then only in areas selected by the departments themselves' (Chapman, 1980, p. 13; 1982, p. 37). Scepticism also characterised the attitude of *The Economist* (21 November 1985, p. 33):

Most of the Rayner/Ibbs team's bright ideas are made to wither by the bureaucracies at whom they are aimed. Standard practice in government departments has been to welcome them nicely, to give them tea, and delegate their conclusions to a long term committee. The Treasury, which ought to have been helpful, has preferred chopping items of spending to the greyer business of waste disposal. It has been cross that some of its own satellites, like Value Added Tax Offices, have received unflattering attention.

Those who had minimalist expectations about the effectiveness of the Rayner exercises had this assessment borne out by a review of them published by the National Audit Office in 1986. Between 1979 and 1983, the scrutiny exercises involved the completion by departments of five programmes comprising a total of 155 scrutinies which had identified potential savings of £421 million a year (using price levels ruling when individual scrutinies were undertaken). As at March 1985, recommendations relating to savings of £112 million a year had been rejected by Ministers or found to be unattainable, which sometimes meant their implementation would conflict with Government policies. Recommendations relating to savings of £38 million were awaiting decisions by Ministers. Of the remainder, recommendations valued at £171 million a year had been implemented by 1983–4 and others, valued at £100 million a year, were in the process of implementation. When the National Audit Office examined progress in the Department of Health and Social Security in November 1984 it found that decisions remained to be taken on major recommendations arising from a scrutiny exercise undertaken in 1980 on the Payment of Benefit to Unemployed People (National Audit Office, 1986a, pp. 1–8, 16, 28). A review by the Efficiency Unit of the Rayner exercises, which was published in 1985, said of departments that 'in contrast to the ninety days allowed for doing a scrutiny there is little continuing sense of urgency, once a scrutiny report arrives.' One headquarters manager wrote to his operational manager: 'I have cleared the action plan. I think it is the minimum we are likely to get away with, and I hope you will feel it is something you can live with' (Efficiency Unit, 1985, p. 4).

Incoming Conservative Ministers in 1979 had been regaled with documents known in Whitehall apparently as 'horror comics', which told them that if staff cuts were implemented on even the most modest scale the departments affected could not hope to function as effectively, with fairly obvious consequences for ministerial reputations. Michael Heseltine, believing that, as Secretary of State, he had inherited a stiuation in which the management arrangements in the Department of the Environment were hopelessly inadequate, resolved to do something about this and, at the same time, to reduce the number of officials, intervening in recruitment in order to do this. Heseltine later wrote:

Four years later, the DOE was 29 per cent smaller, employed 15,000 fewer people, and remained in my view one of the most impressive and creative departments in Whitehall. . . . Looking back, it seems incredible that a department which was supposed to be efficiently managed could lose a quarter of its manpower and still in other respects be the same department. The only possible explanation was deeply disturbing: that the system of management was nowhere near equal to the task.

Heseltine's approach from the outset had been that

> I must find out what was happening in my department and who was responsible for making it happen; who had set the targets, what the targets were and whether they were being monitored. Nobody could answer these questions for me. Nobody could recall them being asked before. Nobody had even the means of gathering the information. Frequently, the information did not exist. (Heseltine, 1987, pp. 16–20)

The task was certainly a formidable one, as the Secretary of State appreciated, recognising that the DOE was the fourth largest department in Whitehall, and only thirty-one British private companies had more employees and only two had a larger turnover (Heseltine, 1980, p. 63). In the spring of 1980, Michael Heseltine launched the Management Informtion System for Ministers which he derived from his private sector experience and from being Minister for Aerospace in the Heath Government, when his own ideas were 'built on dramatically with the help of civil servants and Derek Rayner' (HC 236-II, 1981–2, evidence q. 443–558). It was Heseltine's belief that 'all the information tools of management should be available to politicians and to civil servants' (Heseltine, 1980, p. 67), and he recalled that

> In creating the MINIS . . . system we looked, first of all, for the man in charge of a definable and recognizable unit of activity. . . . The head of each of the D.O.E.'s 57 directorates became the responsible officer. Usually each was close enough to the front line, the centre of activity, to know the names of his subordinates and the nature of their work. He was told the costs of the people working under his direct authority, and he analysed the time and cost devoted to each task. The result was a book which set out his management structure, his objectives and the costs of the work in hand, and set targets for six months ahead. . . . MINIS yielded a wealth of information and . . . revealed how little authority and therefore accountability even civil servants had. Too few were answerable. Before its introduction too many responsibilties were undefined. Technical experts advised administrators. Progress slipped between the two. Numbers were set by staff inspection. Pay was negotiated separately. People, especially the fast streamers, changed posts in the private office manner. (Heseltine, 1987, pp. 20–1)

Complementary to MINIS, a Rayner scrutiny conducted by an official, Christopher Joubert, later led to the DOE being divided up into 120 cost centres based on functional units within the department, each covering one or more of the activities identified in MINIS. The system was designed to provide, in addition to the personnel information already supplied by MINS, data on the actual expenditure incurred by each unit in comparison with the unit's budget (HC 236-III, 1981–2, pp. 156–7). Geoffrey Chipperfield, formerly a higher civil servant at the DOE, considered that the Joubert system was one which 'bites more deeply into the undergrowth of the department' than MINIS. He acknowledged Michael Heseltine's contribution, but stressed that the Secretary of State's ideas had been 'flowing with the tide, not against it' (Hardcastle *et al.*, 1983, p. 26). Another view would be that, prior to Heseltine, the scale of change in terms of management information and control had seemed more like a trickle than a tide.

There was support for Michael Heseltine in Downing Street, Mrs Thatcher finding his commitment to 'introducing new management systems into govern-ment' to be 'a most commendable interest'. She recalled: 'I encouraged him, arranging at one point a seminar with other Ministers to discuss it' (Thatcher, 1993, p. 424). The date seems to have been in late February 1982, and the other Ministers appear to have been uninterested (Likierman, 1982, p. 141). Michael Heseltine's recollection was that:

> on one memorable occasion, I was asked by the Prime Minister to give my colleagues an account of how MINIS was helping the DOE to put its house in order. My fellow Cabinet Ministers sat in rows while I explained my brainchild, each with his sceptical Permanent Secretary behind him muttering objections, or so I suspected. Any politician knows when he is losing his audience's attention, and I knew well enough. When I had done, there were few takers and absolutely no enthusiasts. (Heseltine, 1987, p. 22)

Asked by the House of Commons Treasury and Civil Service Committee in 1981 in effect why MINIS was not being copied in other departments, the then Head of the Home Civil Service, Sir Ian Bancroft, said:

> A great deal depends on the personal commitment of a Minister in charge of a department as to the amount of time and energy that he is going to give to putting very deep probes down into the tasks and the manning of his depart-ment. There are not all that many Mr Heseltines around. (H.C. 236-II, 1981–2, evidence, q. 363)

In response, in May 1982, the Conservative Government launched the Financial Management Initiative, the aim of which was as follows:

> to promote in each department an organization and system in which managers at all levels have:
> a.   a clear view of their objectives and means to assess and, whenever possible, measure outputs or performances in relation to those objectives;
> b.   well defined responsibility for making the best of their resources including a critical scrutiny of output and value for money; and
> c.   the information (particularly about costs), the training and the access to expert advice that they need to exercise their responsibilities effectively. (Cmnd 8616, para. 13)

The Government insisted that progress reports would be required and these were published in September 1983 (Cmnd 9058) and July 1984 (Cmnd 9297). Michael Heseltine, having moved to the Ministry of Defence by then, recalled that

By 1984 most departments had, at last, adopted management information systems with some or most of the features of MINIS, and were using them to improve financial control. To quieten any suggestions of vulgar imitation, and to maintain understandable *amour propre*, departments found different names and different acronyms: thus the Department of Trade and Industry introduced ARM (for activity and resource management); Agriculture sprouted both MINIM and the rustic sounding MAIS; in the Home Office there is APR, and in the Health Department DMA. By 1985, the Lord Chancellor's Department had devised something which sounds a little more lordly: it is called LOCIS, for Lord Chancellor's information system. (Hesletine, 1987, p. 23)

'The development of top management systems in departments within the last year has been noticeably dynamic. The evidence is that it is likely to continue to be so', the Financial Management Unit, established by the Treasury and the Management and Personnel Office to centrally monitor the progress of the FMI, reported in 1984 (Treasury, 1984b, para. 2.2). In 1985, the Financial Management Unit found the situation to be 'dynamic' once more, while emphasising how much the top management systems needed to 'mesh smoothly' with arrangements for budgetary control and programme management as well as the Public Expenditure Survey and Estimates processes (Treasury, 1985a, paras 1.1–1.2). While underlining the importance of the role played by the Principal Finance Officer in the overall allocation of resources within departments (Treasury, 1985b), the Financial Management Unit also sought to establish budgetary control systems in departments which reflected the delegation of responsibilities to line managers envisaged under the FMI (Treasury, 1984a paras 1.1–1.11). Following up on an earlier review by J.S. Cassels of the Management and Personnel Office of running costs (Cassels, 1983a), the Financial Management Unit examined the possibilities of extending the FMI to policy work (Treasury, 1985c), a matter taken up in the *Multi-Departmental Review of Budgeting* published in 1986 (Treasury, 1986a). The Comptroller and Auditor General, noting the Review's observations, commented:

> To the extent that the process of budgeting is a means for securing delivery of value for money against a background of aims, objectives and targets, it is clearly right that it should extend as widely as possible across direct central government expenditure (about £100,000 million in 1986–87) not only gross running costs (£13,000 million). Different approaches will be necessary for the management of programmes, according to whether they are administered directly, by sponsored bodies, or by independently elected local authorities . . . the identification and formulation of aims, objectives and targets for programmes is evidence that departments are aware of the need to ensure that programmes are effective as well as to secure efficiency and economy in administration. I observe, however, that setting conventional financial budgets for policies which are delivered through demand related expenditure is of doubtful value except, perhaps, for cash planning purposes. (National Audit Office, 1986b, p. 9)

What success, if any, the Thatcher Government had in its overall pursuit of greater efficiency in government departments was difficult to assess. In June 1985, Sir Peter Middleton, the then Permanent Secretary to the Treasury, stated that 'there is little doubt that productivity improvements in the public services have been at least as good as those achieved in the private service sector.' Taking up this observation, the former Treasury official, Sir Leo Pliatzky estimated that between 1979 and 1984:

> the Treasury can probably make a claim for growth in productivity in the Civil Service of between two per cent and three per cent a year, which is comparable with the productivity growth in those private service sub-sectors for which measures of productivity are relatively reliable.

Pliatzky cited in support of his estimate a report on productivity in central government commissioned by the National Institute for Economic and Social Research which made comparisons between systems and performance in several large private sector organisations and those of some parts of the Department of Employment, the Department of Health and Social Security and the Board of Inland Revenue. As far as systems were concerned, the report found that 'best practice' in the government departments concerned compared favourably with private sector practices. The approaches adopted by private companies differed considerably, but in some of them continuous precise work measurement and costing was more sophisticated than in the government departments. To the extent that the actual improvements in productivity could be measured the report did appear to substantiate the Treasury's belief that substantial progress had been made (Levitt, 1985; Pliatzky, 1986, pp. 28–9). Other case studies bore out this general picture: for instance, cost savings resulted from the Home Office's introduction of a monitoring system called CONACEQUN (completed naturalisation case equivalent unit) which cut by a quarter the time taken to claim British citizenship; and similar savings followed from the Department of Transport's application of a computer program QUADRO2 (queries and delays at roadworks) to motorway and trunk road maintenance contracts (Lewis, 1986; Durham, 1987).

These developments seemed admirable at least in principle, and the same could be said of what the Treasury in 1986 called the innovation of running costs controls for departments (Cmnd 9702-I, 1986, p. 26). These controls meant that, in future, government departments would be subject to cash limits for their running costs and therefore unable, as in the past, to move money from their programme expenditure or capital items to cover them without coming to the Treasury, getting the approval of the Chief Secretary, and notifying Parliament. Plainly, as a Treasury official, C.D. Butler told the Treasury and Civil Service Committee, such an innovation worked 'with the grain of the delegated responsibility for budgeting and for management which is part of the Financial Management Initiative' (HC 192, 1985–6, q. 97). The development of the FMI had been welcomed by the Comptroller and Auditor General, who recorded that:

departments consider that the visible benefits of their F.M.I. systems have included greater cost consciousness at all levels of management and the Multi-Departmental Review of Budgeting cites many examples of administrative cost savings from management action inspired by the improved information and the constraint on resources imposed by a tightly drawn budget. This emphasizes the need to hasten the extension to programme expenditure of those features of budgeting systems which will assist achievement of improved efficiency and effectiveness. (National Audit Office, 1986b, pp. 10–11)

There was a rather different tone to a mangement consultancy report on arrangements in Whitehall with which Michael Heseltine was associated when out of office. That report observed:

The establishment of effective Top Management Information Systems has so far eluded most departments. The systems started in the early days of the F.M.I. have not so far been developed to achieve that. A few departments have evolved their own systems: most have retained a basically standardized, all embracing system based upon early work in the Department of the Environment. We believe that the current systems are of little continuing value for the purposes of top M[anagement] I[nformation] S[ystems] and should be radically rethought.

The existing arrangements were characterised by too much information being made available, leading to 'overload' and the suggested remedy was that 'most executive work, and other areas, such as the "shadowing" of statutory bodies or regulating functions, should be made the clear responsibility of agencies or middle management, with the introduction of appropriate information systems to meet their needs.' The role of top management would then become, firstly, 'the management of the political process'; secondly, 'the provision of policy advice and programme design'; and thirdly, 'the monitoring of executive tasks'. The first two roles were 'essentially not susceptible to standard techniques of management evaluation', and 'the last, new role will require new techniques of monitoring and evaluation systems and the capacity to use them', and the report looked to higher civil servants with experience in both the public and private sectors to do this work (Mothio, 1989, pp. 26–7). The character of the career Civil Service, though, had not changed that much by that stage, and not always in the favoured direction when it had done, as a review of its structure, pay, recruitment and training arrangements will illustrate. At this stage too, in important respects, even the much publicised cuts in Civil Service numbers tended to be a subject for exaggeration.

II THE BID TO REDUCE THE SIZE OF THE CIVIL SERVICE

'If we were to channel more of the nation's talent into wealth creating private business, this would inevitably mean reducing employment in the public sector', Margaret Thatcher later wrote, adding:

Since the early 1960s, the public sector had grown steadily, accounting for an increased proportion of the total workforce. . . . The size of the Civil Service reflected this. In 1961 the numbers in the Civil Service had reached a post war low of 640,000, by 1979 they had grown to 732,000. This trend had to be reversed. Within days of taking office . . . we imposed a freeze in recruitment to help reduce the Government's pay bill by some 3 per cent. Departments came up with a range of ingenious reasons why this principle should not apply to them. But one by one they were overruled. By 13 May 1980 I was able to lay before the House [of Commons] our long term targets for reducing Civil Service numbers. The total had already fallen to 705,000. We would seek to reduce it to around 630,000 over the next four years. (Thatcher, 1993, pp. 45–6)

This form of behaviour was that of 'die-hard opponents of public service', the Union Side of the National Whitley Council declared, predicting that as a result of these 'further arbitrary cuts' in the numbers of civil servants all that would survive in four years' time would be 'the skeletal remains of the Civil Service'. The Union Side believed that 'the size of the Civil Service is hardly a worthwhile political issue, but the effectiveness of the Service is' (*Whitley Bulletin,* June 1980, p. 85). The unions were to find that, as we have seen, the Thatcher Government had ideas about that matter too. That the Conservative Government had 'an ideological hatred of the public sector' was the reason advanced in 1983 by Alistair Graham, as General Secretary of the Civil and Public Services Association, to explain its discriminatory and antagonistic attitude towards the Civil Service (*Red Tape,* December (1) 1983, p. 1). The Service was believed to be being singled out in the name of ideology for de-privileging and for ruthless cuts in numbers. William McCall, the General Secretary of the Institution of Professional Civil Servants, complained in 1983 that 'it is like being squeezed by a boa-constructor – only more so' (*IPCS Bulletin,* no. 14/86, p. 1).

Any expectation that economic liberal ideologues would be pleased with progress, however, would have been confounded. Even the attainment of the target first set in 1980, and the announcement, by Nigel Lawson as Chancellor of the Exchequer in his Budget Statement of 1984, that there would be a further reduction in the number of civil servants to 593,000 by April 1988 (56 HC Deb. 6s. c. 292), did not seem to placate the Radical Right. When Mrs Thatcher suggested in 1985 that 'our Civil Service is now smaller than at any time since the War', *The Economist* (2 March 1985, p. 45) was swift to point out that the cuts in numbers had mainly fallen on the industrial Civil Service, nearly all of whose members worked in dockyards and Royal Ordnance Factories, and observed:

Turn to real civil servants and Mrs Thatcher's claim is wide of the mark. There were 499,000 in 1945, with departments staffed on a full war footing. Mrs Thatcher this year apparently needs more than Churchill did to win the War; she has 504,000.

When compared with the scale of change that took place in the private sector during the Thatcher years, and in some other parts of the public sector too, such as British Steel, where the number of employees fell by 56 per cent between 1979 and 1982/3 (Abromeit, 1986, p. 142), the career Civil Service might be said to have got off lightly. Given the tendency to cite past statistics, one notes the Government Statistical Service's observation that:

> The main feature of the historical series is the expansion of the Civil Service during the two World Wars. In each of the wartime periods staff increased threefold: numbers of non-industrial staff rose to 221,000 in 1918 and the total to an all time maximum of well over 1 million in 1944. By 1947, nearly 400,000 staff (mainly industrial staff in military establishments and Royal Ordnance Factories) had been shed. The total number declined slowly from 1947 (784,000) to 1960 (643,000) but rose to 748,000 in 1976 – the highest for over twenty years. Since 1976, staff numbers have fallen almost continuously. *(Civil Service Statistics, 1989–90, p. 5)*

The number of non-industrial civil servants actually marginally increased in 1977 and the relevant figure was only 3,000 down by 1 April 1979, but if one includes the reductions in the number of industrial civil servants there had been an overall fall at that date of about 2 per cent since 1 April 1976. That still left a 14 per cent overall increase between 1960 and 1979, and of 49 per cent in non-industrial numbers during that period. In thousands as at 1 April each year, the statistics for the Thatcher era were broadly as shown in Table 4.1 *(ibid., p. 41)*.

So, Radical Right criticisms of the Thatcher Government's approach had some substance in that the number of industrial civil servants had been reduced by 60 per cent between 1979 and 1990, whereas non-industrial numbers had only fallen by 13 per cent, thus giving an overall reduction in the size of the Civil Service of 23 per cent. The translation of Royal Ordnance Factories into a public limited company and the introduction of commercial management at the Royal Dockyards at Devonport and Rosyth could hardly be objected to by economic liberals. As regards the numbers of 'real civil servants' compared

Table 4.1 *Civil Service Numbers*

Year	Non-industrial	Industrial	Total
1979	566	166	732
1980	547	157	705
1981	540	150	690
1982	528	138	666
1983	519	130	649
1984	504	120	624
1985	498	101	599
1986	498	96	594
1987	507	90	598
1988	507	73	580
1989	500	69	569
1990	495	67	562

with the immediate post-war period, the important point that was missed was that of changes of status. There were 107,685 *permanent* non-industrial civil servants employed on 1 April 1946, and 344,001 *temporary* ones (separate figures were not kept in 1945). Over the next twenty-five years, the totals were more or less reversed. So that, by 1 April 1971 there were 366,758 permanent non-industrial civil servants and 131,667 temporaries (*Civil Service Statistics 1971*, p. 14). The Treasury had told the Fulton Committee in 1966 that 'the distinction between established and unestablished staff should be retained', not least because to do otherwise 'would add considerably to the cost of Civil Service superannuation' (*Fulton Evidence*, vol. 4, p. 378). The Fulton Committee took no notice. With characteristic superficiality, the Committee objected to and wanted abolished the term 'establishment', because it had 'overtones of comfort and complacency'. Furthermore, it made recommendations to extend what had been 'established' status to almost all non-industrial civil servants, with all that meant in terms of security to tenure and pension rights (*Fulton Report*, 1968, pp. 48–9, 199). Official evidence to the English Committee of 1976–7 later showed that these recommendations had been implemented (HC 535-II, 1976–7, p. 10).

'An established civil servant – unless he makes a complete fool of himself – has a job for life', stated one of the few books written about the main body of the Civil Service, published in the tranquil 1950s (Dunnill, 1956, p. 67). Once past the probationary period (which, by the 1980s, was usually of one year's duration) non-industrial civil servants were relatively secure. The cuts in numbers during the Thatcher era were very largely achieved by natural wastage. That, to take one example, 'there were five hundred non-industrial redundancies in 1985 and nearly two thousand amongst industrial staff' in the Civil Service (*Civil Service Statistics 1986*, p. 8) would not seem unduly harsh to economic liberals, and possibly to others too in the context of continuing job losses elsewhere. Traditionally, though, 'a job for life' had been one of the prime characteristics of at least the non-industrial Civil Service, and any policy of cutting staff numbers would be bound to be alarming to civil servants and their unions. In 1987, it was announced that, from April 1988 onwards, personnel targets would be dropped, thus placing sole reliance on running cost limits with the intention of giving 'individual Civil Service managers greater flexibility to make best use of the resources available to them' (110 HC Deb. 6s. c. 933–4). The room for manoeuvre, though, was bound to be severely restricted, not least because, as will be seen, the essentials of the career Civil Service remained in place.

III THE CHANGING STRUCTURE OF THE CIVIL SERVICE AND ITS PAY AND PROMOTION SYSTEM

As in all developed bureaucratic hierarchies, for most of its members a career Civil Service and its structure inevitably has the character of a pay and promotion system. This was bound to be so among the broad mass of civil servants. As one experienced official put it many years ago:

> The hope, and indeed expectation, of promotion is . . . something the civil servant, more than most men, lives with throughout his working life. The Service is so graded and its salary scales so adjusted that failure to cross a particular promotion bridge at more or less the expected time may well represent a serious setback, not only financially, but socially and personally. (Dunnill, 1956, p. 61)

The old saw that whenever three or four civil servants are gathered together, the subject under discussion will be promotion and at least one of those present will be saying 'now take my case' (*ibid.*, p. 60) rings true of publicly funded bureaucracies with their commonly standardised rewards and relatively regularised promotion procedures. Apart from 'restructuring' exercises and the necessarily occasional windfalls of 'back pay' from a salary settlement, normally it was only through promotion that the civil servant could obtain sustained advances in his or her standard of living. The prestige that might accompany high status in the Civil Service, at least within the machinery of central government, was not available to the broad mass of civil servants, who could not be unaware of popular contempt for their calling, and it was a natural reaction to seek material compensations (cf. Walker, 1961, pp. 254, 261). The sentiments of public service may always have been less widespread than was once believed. H.E. Dale (1941, p. 77) wrote of the inter-war Higher Civil Service that 'a few enter the Service from idealistic motives: most have no particular desire to be government officials, apart from the material inducements; but for various reasons they have a negative feeling towards the other possible callings.' Dale was clear that few of his contemporaries would have entered certainly the Home Civil Service if they had possessed the private means to avoid that fate. Forty years on, Lord Rayner found the higher civil servants that he dealt with to be 'a mixture of superb talent and commitment to the public good on the one hand; and of an able coterie of cynics on the other' (Rayner, 1984, p. 16).

The 'material inducements' that Dale talked about seem to have been quite modest in the inter-war period, when, of course, economic liberalism ruled, and they remained so until the 'Priestley formula' for Civil Service pay, born of Keynesianism, promised civil servants relatively higher rewards. The promise of Priestley was often denied by incomes policies, but the main practical objection to the implementation of the fair comparison principle and the 'relativities' that went with it, was the substantial overall cost of the resulting salary settlements. In much the same spirit as it hacked away at the career hierarchy, and it attempted to remove index-linking provisions from Civil Service pensions, the Thatcher Government tried to cut the Gordian knot of Civil Service pay in 1980. The Government explicitly declined to implement the latest findings of the Civil Service Pay Research Unit as regards the broad mass of civil servants, and then abolished the machinery concerned. The Megaw Committee of 1981–2 was appointed to review Civil Service pay, with the implication that it ought to try to turn the clock back before Priestley (Fry, 1974, pp. 319–33; 1985, pp. 96–121).

The expectations and attitudes that the Priestley era had fostered were not easily disposed of. The Thatcher Government did not help its own cause when, inconsistently, it allowed the Review Body on Top Salaries to survive. Established in 1971 by Edward Heath's Conservative Government, then supposed to be in its economic liberal phase, the Review Body had since then periodically made recommendations about the salary levels of the highest grades of the Civil Service and those of other public sector groups, based on outside comparisons. According to Christopher Monckton, formerly in the Prime Minister's Policy Unit:

> When the Review Body on Top Salaries recommended a large increase in the salaries of top civil servants in 1985, all the papers relating to the report were given a national security classification as though the matter was a military secret which could, in the wrong hands, endanger the safety of the State. Members of the Prime Minister's Policy Unit are cleared to see papers classified up so far as Secret. We were, therefore, unaware of the existence of the Report or of any papers relating to it until we saw the Cabinet Minute recording that the Report had been agreed. At this point we at once protested at this scandalous abuse of the classification system and made enquiries which eventually revealed that the Prime Minister had taken our silence on the matter as acquiescence. It is no secret that since the review the Prime Minister has realized that the wrong decision was taken. (letter to author, 11 February 1987)

If this account is accurate, it would be difficult to present the behaviour of the higher civil servants concerned as being compatible with any serious notion of public service.

As there was 'strong evidence' that 'grade drift upwards' had taken place in the Civil Service in the 1970s, as Sir Frank Cooper, the then Permanent Under Secretary at the Ministry of Defence, had observed (Cooper, 1981, p. 13; cf. Fry, 1985, p. 148), a natural accompaniment to the setting of targets for reductions in numbers was for the Thatcher Government to review the structure of the Civil Service. This activity was concentrated at first at or near the top of the Service. The formal task of a team led by Sir Geoffrey Wardale appointed in January 1981 was:

> To examine the contribution of different management levels to work involving staff of the Open Structure (excluding those in purely specialist hierarchies); to consider in the light of that examination the case for shortening the chain of command both by abolishing grades and by restricting the number of management levels in particular areas of work; and to make recommendations. (Wardale Report, 1981, para 1.1)

The Economist (17 May 1980, p. 10) thought that it had 'first put forward' the idea 'since adopted by Sir Derek Rayner' that 'the entire Under Secretary grade should be abolished as an aid to speed and efficiency.' In actual fact, Sir Alexander Johnston, the then Chairman of the Board of Inland Revenue, had suggested to the Fulton Committee in his oral evidence in 1966 that the Under Secretary grade was 'superfluous' and retained for career purposes (PRO: BA 1/3; Fry, 1993, p. 175). The Under Secretary grade had only become a permanent feature of the then Administrative Class immediately after the Second World War, having been developed, largely in place of the previous Principal Assistant Secretary grade on the grounds of the increased volume and complexity of the work (Cmd 9613, 1955, para. 48). As, at the beginning of 1981, the Under Secretary grade accounted for 591 of the 784 posts in the post-Fulton Open Structure (Wardale Report, 1981, para. 21), its survival was predictable. The Wardale inquiry concluded that 'there are . . . a number of Open Structure posts [that] can be removed and should be' (*ibid.*, para. 6.2), but that:

> There are chains of command in which all existing levels, using all available Open Structure grades, are needed, and where there would be a risk of serious damage if a level was removed. Therefore, no Open Structure grade should be abolished. (*ibid.*, para. 6.1)

What was unexpected was that extensions of unified grading, in the form of expanding the Open Structure, would take place under the Thatcher Government. The most prominent of the recommendations of the Fulton Committee that had not been implemented had been its proposal that unified grading should be introduced from the top to the bottom of the Home Civil Service. Obstruction on the part of the then Head of that Service, Sir William Armstrong, was blamed by some, and there was certainly opposition from the representatives of the former Executive Class, whose members' prospects would be disproportionately and adversely affected by a change to unified grading, which would primarily benefit members of specialist groups. When the Open Structure was established in 1972, unified grading was only taken down to Under Secretary level. Sir Robert Armstrong later observed that the further extension of unified grading had not been ruled out by his predecessor. It was something to be achieved by stages, and that plans had been made to take such grading down to Principal level (Fry, 1993, p. 272–5). The extension of the Open Structure down to Senior Principal and equivalent grades in 1984 encompassed some 5,600 staff previously organised in approximately 100 grades (*Civil Service Statistics 1984,* p. 6), and its further extension down to Principal and equivalent levels in 1986 involved another 5,500 staff previously organised into approximately 60 grades (*Civil Service Statistics 1986,* p. 6). Numbered grades having been introduced at the top of the Service in 1984, the Open Structure from 1 January 1986 onwards had the following appearance:

Grade 1   Permanent Secretary.
Grade 1A   Second Permanent Secretary.
Grade 2   Deputy Secretary.

Grade 3   Under Secretary.
Grade 4   Executive Directing Bands and corresponding Professional and
            Scientific grades.
Grade 5   Assistant Secretary and corresponding Professional and Scientific
            grades.
Grade 6   Senior Principal and corresponding Professional and Scientific
            grades.
Grade 7   Principal and corresponding Professional and Scientific grades.

The rationalisaiton of salary scales seemed to be more in the spirit of the
Fulton Committee than that of the FMI, although a more radical approach was
indicated, as will be seen, by experiments with performance-related pay, which
the Prime Minister made clear in April 1987 were being made permanent (114
HC Deb. 6s. Written Answers, c. 656).

There was little sign of radicalism, though, in the restructuring of the lower
grades of the Administration Group. This followed from the Government's plans
to introduce new technology into departments and its recognition of the need for
the co-operation of the staff concerned, who in some instances would need to be
redeployed. The main elements of the deal were as follows. The Clerical Assistant and Clerical Officer incremental pay scales were shortened with effect from
1 January 1986. The staff in the Clerical Assistant and related Data Processing
grades were absorbed into a new grade of Administrative Assistant with effect
from 1 January 1987. With effect from the same date the existing grades of
Clerical Officer and Senior Data Processor were combined to form the new
grade of Administrative Officer, involving a general additional increase in the
salary maximum six months later. Data Processing staff retained their existing
allowance. While the Local Officer II grade in the Department of Health and
Social Security remained a separate departmental grade, its members also received the same pay increases as the new Administrative Officer grade, with the
result that its relative position was enhanced (*Red Tape*, April (1) 1986, pp. 1–
2). Grade renaming, especially when it attached the famed Civil Service designa-
tion 'Administrative' to routine clerical work, raised suspicions that a classic
pseudo-restructuring exercise had been engaged in, raising costs and rewards all
round. Less contentiously, the most important point about the deal, and why it
was worth exploring in detail, was that it was very much an across-the-board
settlement of the traditional kind. As a similar sort of settlement was obtained
for what could still be described as the Executive part of the Administration
Group (*Opinion*, March 1987, pp. 1, 4) little seemed to have changed, but, also
in the first part of 1987, a deal was concluded between the Institution of Professional Civil Servants and the Treasury which that department plainly considered
represented its first serious breakthrough in its bid to establish 'a new pay regime
in the Civil Service' (Treasury, 1987a, p. 1).

'The difficulties of introducing pay rates' in the Civil Service 'related to merit
proved immense', Margaret Thatcher was later to write, recalling that 'we

made progress, but it took several years and a lot of pushing and shoving' (Thatcher, 1993, p. 46). The appointment of the Megaw Committee in June 1981 had been almost predictable. There was a 'dreadful symmetry' about the setting-up of outside bodies to review Civil Service pay arrangements at roughly twenty-five-year intervals, Peter Jones of the Council of Civil Service Unions was to observe. Whether or not Nietzche's theory of eternal recurrence was at work, Jones wrote of the Megaw Committee:

> This is the fourth major inquiry into Civil Service unions pay this century, and its arrival was bang on time, with its predecessors being launched in 1912, 1929 and 1953. Each previous inquiry plumped for a system based on comparability with outside rates of remuneration, but with a successive degree of sophistication which found its apogee in the pay research method advocated by the last, the Priestley Royal Commission. Cynics may say that the Megaw Inquiry will follow the established pattern and 're-invent the wheel' (*CCSU Bulletin*, November 1981, p. 137)

When the Megaw Report on Civil Service pay was published in July 1982, *The Economist* detected 'signs of relief' on the part of the Prime Minister, observing:

> The last time Mrs Thatcher commissioned an inquiry intended to chip away at Whitehall privilege, Sir Bernard Scott's findings on inflation proofed pensions recommended the extension of index linking, not its abolition. Sir John Megaw, former Lord Justice of Appeal, did not so signally fail her this time. On only one point – regional variations in pay, which he found against – did he waver from what Mrs Thatcher thinks is her line. . . . Mrs Thatcher hoped that he would inject a strong market element into pay determination while building in incentives for high performance and productivity.

The Economist argued, as it had done over several decades, that 'the only sensible guiding principle of any wage system is to pay enough to recruit when you want, judged day to day' (*The Economist*, 10 July 1982, pp. 20–1). The Anderson Committee had said more or less the same in 1923 (Anderson Report, para. 3) without the Tomlin Commission feeling the need to follow suit, and if that body had not chosen to adopt a simple market principle in 1931 of all years, the majority of the members of the Megaw Committee were always unlikely to act differently fifty years later.

So, while the sole trade unionist on the Committee, John Chalmers, issued a Minority Report (Cmnd 8590, 1982, pp. 102–15) which kept the Priestley flag flying, the recommendations in the Megaw Committee's Majority Report represented a compromise with the market (Fry, 1983, pp. 90–6; 1985, pp. 115–19). Thus, the Majority Report declared that:

> The governing principle for the Civil Service pay system in the future should be to ensure that the Government as an employer pays civil servants enough, taking one year with another, to recruit, retain and motivate them to perform efficiently the duties required of them at an appropriate level of competence. (Cmnd 8590, 1982, para. 91)

Inevitably also, though, the Majority Report embraced the comparability principle:

> Civil Service pay increases and level of remuneration, including fringe benefits, should in the longer term broadly match those available in the private sector for staff undertaking jobs with comparable job weight. . . . The main comparisons used in the system would be of the trends of percentage increases in comparator pay rates in the current pay round. This information would be supplemented as soon as possible, and thereafter every fourth year, as a check, by information on levels of total remuneration. . . . The data collection analysis would be carried out under the supervision of an independent Board. (*ibid.*, para. 101)

This Civil Service Pay Information Board (*ibid.*, para. 125) was to consist of five 'independent minded persons' appointed by the Prime Minister (*ibid.*, para. 128) and 'to maintain demonstrable independence from the Civil Service management and unions, surveys, data collection and analyses should be undertaken by management consultants on behalf of the Board' (*ibid.*, para. 129). What was termed 'informed collective bargaining' (*ibid*, para. 9) was to be engaged in when the Board presented the negotiating parties with its findings. The limits within which a pay settlement could be researched would be 'the inter quartile range', meaning the middle ranges of outside pay. Though the parties would need to give weight to management needs' (*ibid.*, para. 102), the majority of the Megaw Committee believed that 'the Government should regularly make it clear, as it has done to us, that the cash limit system does not necessarily imply a completely rigid control of pay increases on the basis of the initial assumptions' (*ibid.*, para. 219).

The majority of the Megaw Committee recommended too that more emphasis needed to be placed on internal relativities than had been the case under the Priestley system (*ibid.*, para. 195), involving discussions of them between management and unions against the background, where appropriate, of job evaluation information (*ibid.*, para. 103). It was these observations that aroused the interest of the Institution of Professional Civil Servants, representing specialist groups, which, unlike the other unions, saw 'the Megaw Report as the foundation on which a new pay system can be built', not least because of the prospect it offered of 'resolving long standing internal anomalies' (*IPCS Bulletin*, 10/82, October 1982, p. 1), meaning, of course, those which disadvantaged specialists. Another recommendation was that the Civil Service Arbitration Agreement should be revised to put the Government and the unions on a more equal footing (Cmnd 8590, 1982, paras. 269–70). The Megaw Majority Report favoured too 'arrangements to encourage more active departmental and line management involvement in relating pay to management needs and efficiency, and measures to relate performance directly to pay' (*ibid.*, para. 104). Incremental scales were only to be retained for grades below Principal and its equivalent (*ibid.*, para. 335) and even then related to performance as measured in annual reports (*ibid.*, para. 339). For grades from Principal to below Under Secretary, incremental pay should be replaced by merit ranges, again on the basis of annual reports (*ibid.*, para. 344). The salaries of civil servants at Under Secretary level and above should continue to be settled without negotiation, after the receipt of the report of the Review Body on Top Salaries (*ibid.*, para. 355). As for index-linked pensions, the Megaw majority did not feel the need to replicate the work of the Scott Committee, and restricted itself to recommending the civil servants' pension contributions should be made more explicit (*ibid.*, paras. 163–4).

Both the Majority and the Minority Reports of the Megaw Committee were essentially conservative in that they acted as if centralised pay determination and grading for the Civil Service as a whole, which the Treasury dated from the days of the Tomlin Commission (Treasury, 1991, p. 45), could and would continue in broadly the same form, whereas decentralised arrangements of the type encouraged by 'business methods' were already in the offing. The Megaw Majority Report did seem to make a concession to business philosophy in embracing merit pay, and *The Economist* (10 July 1982, p. 21) credited this idea to Sir Derek Rayner. There are, in fact, few new ideas in the world of Civil Service pay. Though it came to be largely forgotten later, the Fulton Committee, for instance, had recommended the introduction of performance pay, while at the same time endorsing the Priestley system (Cmnd 3638, 1968, paras 226–9). The intellectual coherence of the Priestley Report was attributed to Barbara Wootton, who had a clear, socialistic position she believed to be 'rational' (Wootton, 1955). Her alarm at the variations in public sector pay later detected by her disciple Hilda Kahn, and expression of the need 'to bring order out of the present chaos' (Kahn, 1962, p. 10) leaves one in little doubt about the condemnation that pay on 'business methods' lines would attract. What the Thatcher Government needed was to draw a line under the Priestley era and its 'rationality'. Inevitably, there was not to be a clean break. That the Review Body on Top Salaries survived the Megaw Majority Report underlines the Report's conservatism. As for the Pay Information Board idea this seemed redolent of the 'three wise men' approach to pay determination of the 'fair wage' era, of which the Priestley Commission was a part (Williams, 1956, pp. 621–34). Not surprisingly, the Board was never established. Naturally enough, *The Economist* (10 July 1982, p. 21) welcomed what it described as the privatisation of pay research while casting doubt upon the professional integrity of the management consultants to be employed in much the same manner as that journal had done that of the Civil Service Pay Research Unit. That comparability was to be resorted to at all rather than sole reliance on a simple market rule was, of course, because a career Civil Service did not exist on a 'day-to-day' basis, and, while one response would be to break up that Service, in the meantime, the centralised form of pay determination persisted.

The Civil Service's pay arrangements developed in a complex manner during the 1980s, but the Council of Civil Service Unions at least found them to be capable of a straightforward interpretation, as it made clear in a paper submitted to the TUC Public Services Committee in 1989:

Since the Government unilaterally abandoned pay research in 1981, the Treasury's pay strategy has been to continue to screw down Civil Service pay in the interest of containing public expenditure. In effect, annual pay reviews since 1981 had been cash limit driven at the expense of meaningful negotiation. As chronic problems of recruitment and retention and low morale emerged the Treasury resorted to the pursuit of flexibility, through ad hoc arrangements such as Special Pay Additions and Local Pay Additions, and ill fated performance bonus schemes, generally with little or no consultation. These ad hoc pay arrangements failed to solve the problems and Treasury was forced to discuss implementing long term pay determination. The Treasury's general approach to the non-industrial Civil Service's emerging pay system is to promote a more selective approach, whereby pay is targeted at groups and areas where it considers there are problems, that is grades where there are recruitment and retention difficulties, or skill shortages.

As the objective of the Civil Service unions was to secure 'a settled, orderly and fair national pay system for all non-industrial civil servants', the conclusion of long-term pay agreements was preferable to 'the haphazard and disjointed arrangements' that had preceded them, especially as the agreements involved union participation. All the agreements reached included a spinal pay structure (which was a series of incremental points incorporating pay scales), performance pay, and a system for pay determination in the long term based on annual pay movements surveys and also surveys conducted at least every four years of the levels of pay and benefits of jobs outside the Civil Service. All the arrangements also contained provisions for extra pay to be accorded to posts where there were recruitment and retention difficulties (*CCSU Bulletin*, May 1989, p. 69).

It was in the autumn of 1985 that the Treasury produced outline proposals for a long-term Civil Service pay agreement, nearly three years after the then Chancellor of the Exchequer, Sir Geoffrey Howe, had announced both the Government's acceptance of the Megaw Report and the intention to seek an agreement (34 HC Deb. 6s. Written Answers c. 12). The delay seemed mysterious to the Council of Civil Service Unions because all the proposals seemed to amount to were 'a watered down version of the Megaw Committee's majority recommendations'. What the Treasury proposed was that pay increases should be negotiated between itself and the CCSU so as to lead to an overall percentage increase for the non-industrial Civil Service as a whole lying between the upper and lower quartiles of pay settlements in the private sector. So long as this overall framework was respected, different groups could receive different increases above or below the negotiating range. For 1986, as had been the case in 1984, the negotiating range was to be established by the Office of Manpower Economics. For 1987 and later the method of establishing the negotiating range would be agreed between the two sides. Either side could introduce into the bargaining process such factors as they wished, including recruitment, retention and motivation. The Treasury's aim was for the Civil Service pay system to develop flexibility on the basis of joint consultation. In the case of a dispute, and if both sides agreed, this could be referred to the Civil

Service Arbitration Tribunal for resolution. The Tribunal's decision would be binding, though it could not lead to a settlement outside the negotiating range and it would also be subject to public expenditure constraints. The agreement was intended to be a lasting one, subject to both sides accepting its continuance and, as the Chancellor of the Exchequer had stated in December 1982, the Government reserved the right to suspend the operation of the agreement to safeguard the public purse or public policy. The CCSU, while envisaging further discussions, dismissed the Treasury's outline proposals as 'seriously flawed' (*CCSU Bulletin*, November 1985, pp. 149–50).

In the immediate period after its defeat in the Civil Service strike of 1981, the Service's union movement had held together remarkably well, but after four years of joint action 'the difficulties involved in formulating a common claim covering grades from cleaner to Assistant Secretary' proved to be too many. As Peter Jones of the Council of Civil Service Unions explained:

> Prior to 1981, central involvement in pay by the Council and its predecessor, the National Staff Side, was limited to determining the *system* under which Civil Service pay was settled. Before the days of annual pay research, and in times of incomes policy, we did pursue central claims, but these were supplementary activities and were never a regular feature of Civil Service pay determination. Pay bargaining has always been primarily a matter between our constituent unions and management. After all, direct involvement in pay bargaining is the main function of any trade union, and it is natural for the Council's constituent unions to wish to reassert their rights in this respect in 1985. (*CCSU Bulletin*, December 1984, p. 149)

The unions were displeased by the outcome, as their leaders made clear in the marvellously extravagant style perfected by the legendary W.J. Brown in which few forms of exaggeration need be spurned. According to Alistair Graham of the Civil and Public Services Association, the Treasury's pay offer for 1985 was 'low and vindictive' (*Red Tape*. April (1) 1985, p. 2). Graham believed the offer to be 'a monstrous insult to the workhorses of the Civil Service at the sharp end of Thatcher's Britain' (*CSSU Bulletin*, April 1985, p. 49). Campbell Christie of the Society of Civil and Public Servants found the offer that they received to be 'totally inadequate in the sense of any equity, any fairness, and any justice' (*Opinion*, May 1985, p. 1). The General Secretary of the Institution of Professional Civil Servants, William McCall, considered the offer that the union received to be 'completely unacceptable' adding that 'the Government's claim that the 3 per cent cash limit is not an overriding factor is once again exposed for the sham that it is' (*IPCS Bulletin*, 4/85, p. 1). The IPCS, together with the Society and the First Division Association, the other unions most closely involved, had also objected to the Government's performance bonus scheme for civil servants between the ranks of Principal (Grade 7) and Under Secretary (Grade 3) which was introduced on a three-year experimental basis from April 1985 onwards (69 HC Deb. 6s. Written Answers C. 192–3). The titles of the pamphlets that the objecting unions jointly issued in 1986, *Performance Pay: The first year of failure* and *Performance Pay: A mis-*

conceived experiment, encapsulated their attitude. The latter pamphlet cited American experience as part of the case against this development.

None of this seemed likely to make any difference. The Government had a different agenda from that of the unions and one which had the aim of eventually moving away from undifferentiated, across the board Civil Service pay settlements. The interests of the mass of civil servants, the 'half million galley slaves' as Peter Jones picturesquely called them (*CCSU Bulletin*, February 1985, p. 17), were by no means uniform, and the specialist groups had been conventionally located to one side of the main structure. Specialists, and thus commonly members of the IPCS, had been prospectively the main beneficiaries of the extension of unified grading down to Principal level completed in 1986, as we have noted, and this had obvious implications for pay. Breaking ranks with the Council of Civil Service Unions had also led the IPCS to obtain a pay settlement in 1986 which was 'nearer the going rate than any settlement since 1980' (*IPCS Bulletin*, 6/86, p. 1). The IPCS had not been as dismissive of the Treasury's one-term pay agreement proposals as other unions had been. The headline 'Perfection is not our business' in an *IPCS Pay Special* published in November 1985 seemed to sum up General Secretary William McCall's pragmatic attitude towards the Treasury's scheme, which the IPCS's National Executive Committee shared, and the majority of the membership came to do so too.

Thus the union and the Treasury, on behalf of the Official Side of the National Whitley Council and the departments generally, eventually signed the *Agreement on the Pay, Pay System, Organization and Personnel Management Arrangements for Grades and Groups Represented by the Institution of Professional Civil Servants* dated 7 May 1987. The new system was designed to link pay and personnel management arrangements; to provide incentives for improving and maintaining efficiency; to reward sustained high performance; to provide greater flexibility in the management of the staff concerned and better opportunities for career development; to maintain the openness of all the rules and provisions of the pay, promotion and career management arrangements; to provide for equity of treatment while also providing for flexibility to deal with particular pay problems; to secure the confidence of the public in the system for determining the pay of the staff in the non-industrial Civil Service covered by the Agreement by providing that their pay shall be enough, taking one year with another, to recruit, retain and motivate the civil servants concerned to perform efficiently the duties required of them; to secure the confidence of these civil servants that their pay will be determined fairly; and to enable the Government to reconcile its responsibilities for the control of public expenditure with its responsibilities as an employer. The new system involved the introduction of the pay spine and of pay spans. The pay spine was a sequence of pay points, arranged to provide suitable incremental progression, on which all staff covered by the Agreement were to be paid with effect from 1 September 1987. A pay span consisted of a number of consecutive pay points on the pay spine which were available for paying staff occupying posts within that span. Post were to be allocated to spans according to their job weight and there was to be one span for each grading level thus determined. Categories, classes and grades as such were to be abolished and occupational groups were to be redefined. Pay spans would be divided into scales and ranges. A pay scale or scales would form the lower part of a pay span, and, provided they were efficient, staff would normally progress in annual steps up to the spine to the maximum of their scale. Staff who received a 'Box 1 – outstanding' marking for overall performance in their annual report and who were below the maximum of the scale were to be eligible to receive an immediate extra increment. They would then receive their normal increment on their incremental date. This provision was to apply within the limit of the maximum of the scale. Increments could also be withheld or withdrawn in accordance with the arrangements set out in paragraphs 1247 and 1248 of the Civil Service Code. The pay range was to consist of at least three points on the spine. Progression up the range was to be discretionary in the sense that it would not be automatic, but it would be in accordance with clearly defined rules and criteria. Increments in the pay ranges would depend on performance as assessed in annual reports over a period of time. Staff would be eligible for consideration for an increment in the range in accordance with the following criteria. One would be following receipt of at least one Box 1 ('outstanding') marking after reaching the maximum of the scale. Another would be following receipt of at least three consecutive Box 2 ('performance significantly above requirements') markings after reaching the maximum of the scale. Another would be following receipt of at least five consecutive markings at Box 3 ('performance fully meets normal requirements') or above after reaching the maximum of the scale and if in the view of management they merited such an award for consistently producing valuable and effective work. Further increments could be awarded after the elapse of further similar periods. It was expected that if reporting and marking criteria were properly observed the staff who received range points would constitute no more than 25 per cent of the staff at each grading level in each department. Range points could be withdrawn on a mark time basis where performance was deemed to have fallen off over a prolonged period. After consultation between the parties, central control and monitoring arrangements would be introduced. Additionally, range and scale points could also be used for other purposes:

> where, for example, particular and special difficulties of recruitment and/or retention arise they may be dealt with by identifying the group of posts concerned on the basis of function and/or discipline and/or location, and advancing pay for the staff occupying these posts up the span. Their pay scale will be adjusted accordingly. Exceptionally other arrangements may be made to deal with particular problems when the other provisions of this Agreement are unsuitable or inappropriate.

There was to be an appeals procedure in accordance with paragraph 9973 of the Civil Service Code. The remainder of the Agreement was concerned with matters such as fluid grading and the future of occupational groups in relation to career management, and details of the implementation of the new pay arrangements, with the Office of Manpower Economics being assigned the fact finding role (Treasury, 1987b).

Even the prospect of the above being done provoked the opposition of the Society of Civil and Public Servants, not least because 'the integration of various occupational groups is a very real threat to Administration Group jobs and promotion avenues. The Agreement raises the possibility of unified grading down to EO level with specialists competing for administrators' jobs thereby worsening the promotion prospects for Society grades' (*Opinion*, March 1987, p. 8). The Agreement with the IPCS, the Society believed, gave the Treasury what it wanted in terms of 'total flexibility' because it 'allows for individual pay rates as well as different pay rates for the same grades in different parts of the country or even on different sites in the same geographical area'. The Society recorded Treasury sentiments as being that 'we want to avoid situations where we have to pay 5,000 civil servants in order to retain or recruit six.' The emphasis on performance pay led the society to fear for the future of 'normal increments' which 'until now have been seen as a right' (*ibid.*, p. 1). What was being sidestepped, the Society considered was 'the central problem of paying competitive salaries for all' (*ibid.*, p. 5). When the Society's General Secretary, Leslie Christie, circulated similar material to his membership, his counterpart at the IPCS, William McCall, accused him of engaging in 'mischief and misinformation', and rebutted some of the detailed criticisms of the Agreement (*IPCS Bulletin*, 4/87, p. 2). Essentially, the Society, together with some of the other Civil Service unions, thought that confrontation with the Government would exact better pay arrangements than those then on offer from the Treasury, and the IPCS did not, preferring to take advantage of arrangements, which were adopted from the Megaw Report, that provided for 'annual increases to be settled with the interquartile range of pay movements outside', together with in 1988 a levels survey which would represent 'a comprehensive, job for job, pay comparison exercise for the first time since 1980' (*IPCS Bulletin*, 2/87, p. 1).

The confrontational strategy could not easily survive the re-election of the Conservative Government with a substantial majority a matter of weeks after the IPCS Agreement was finalised. One outcome of lengthy and detailed negotiations was the *Provisional Agreement between H.M. Treasury and the Board of Inland Revenue (on behalf of the Official Side) and the Inland Revenue Staff Federation* of November 1987. This was plainly modelled on the IPCS Agreement having similar opening paragraphs, and the same number of objectives, though differently ordered and, in some cases, worded. A double pay spine was established of which had thirty-three pay points, with spine A covering the main IRSF grades and spine B the remainder. Advancement up the scale was by annual increments up to the maximum, after which there were three range points attainable on the basis of performance. There were also arrangements for accelerated incremental progression for individuals below the maximum who obtained the best performance ratings. The spine also included pay spans, with posts allocated within them according to grading levels and job weight (Treasury, 1987c). Then, in July 1988, came *New Pay Arrangements for Grades 5, 6, and 7*, meaning the former Assistant Secretary, Senior Principal and Principal grades and their equivalents. These arrangements resulted from an agreement between the Treasury and the FDA, the IPCS and the National Union of Civil and Public Servants (as the Society had become). This pay spine was a single one with twenty-two points involving annual increments, together with the now familiar pay span and accelerated increments arrangements and four range points above the scale maximum (Treasury, 1988). Then, in April 1989, came the *New Pay Arrangements for Executive, Office Support and Related Grades* agreed between the Treasury and the NUCPS (Treasury, 1989a) and the *New Pay Arrangements for Clerical and Secretarial Grades* agreed between the Treasury and the Civil and Public Services Association (Treasury, 1989b). Each agreement included a pay spine which was a sequence of full and half pay points. In the case of the agreement with the NUCPS, this took the spine to point 29, and in that with the CPSA to point 22.5, and both had the now common provisions for range points and accelerated increments and so forth.

By the end of the 1980s, at first sight and in some contrast with the intervening years, the Civil Service seemed to have developed a coherent pay system to take the place of that bequeathed by the Priestley Royal Commission. The Review Body on Top Salaries, a link with the earlier arrangements, had been one advocate of the introduction of performance pay in the Higher Civil Service (Cmnd 9525-I, 1985, pp. 48–50). The long-term pay agreement that the Treasury had secured for Grades 5, 6 and 7 had involved over 20,000 staff. The agreement made with the IPCS had covered 60,000 civil servants as had that with the IRSF, while the agreements with the NUCPS had embraced 100,000 civil servants, and that with the CPSA approximately twice as many. The Council of Civil Service Unions observed:

> All five agreements make provision for performance pay. In all five cases, however, the agreements have preserved existing pay scales and normal incremental progression. Performance criteria have been introduced only in respect of additional payments above the old scale maximum, and any pay achieved by performance is extra money on top of existing scales. The agreements have also been successful in eliminating many unacceptable features of the Government's earlier experiments in performance pay in the Civil Service. In particular in place of a wholly discretionary system – with the dangers of favouritism and abuse – the agreements tie the performance pay to annual markings under the established Civil Service staff reporting system. The agreements also provide for an appeals system and for joint monitoring and review.

Quotas constrained the award of performance pay in order to limit the overall cost. The Council also noted that:

Regional pay variation is not a feature of any of the agreements. Indeed, for the unions concerned, the agreements provide a framework for a measure of control over the Treasury's recent propensity to impose non-negotiable flexibility, for example, Local Pay Additions. (*CCSU Bulletin*, May 1989, pp. 69–70).

Though London weighting was familiar enough, being a nationally negotiated feature of Civil Service pay, Local Pay Additions had been unilaterally introduced by the Treasury in 1988 to enable departments to meet recruitment and retention difficulties in London and the South East. The extent of departmental discretion and the resulting variations in the pay of officials of the same grade in differing towns and sometimes the same ones had alarmed the Council of Civil Service Unions, which described the outcome of this 'sorry saga' as a 'dog's breakfast' (*CCSU Bulletin*, July 1988, p. 97). More dispassionately, the National Audit Office later concluded that 'on the available evidence from [the] Treasury and the Department of Trade and Industry, Local Pay Additions are an effective, cheap and flexible response to staff recruitment problems', but that 'this is not so strongly the case for retention' (HC 259, 1991–2, p. 3).

'The future long term pay of non-industrial civil servants will be determined by a system of informed collective bargaining', the Council told the TUC Public Services Committee in May 1989, believing that 'provisions on pay flexibility do not run counter to agreements providing for a *national* framework for bargaining and the preservation of *national* pay rates' (*CCSU Bulletin*, May 1989, p. 70). Regional pay, though, was not the only threat to the coherence of the Civil Service pay system. From that perspective, performance pay had merited the unions' early antagonism, and, with provisions for its award reaching all the way up the service to Grade 2 (Deputy Secretary) and Grade 3 (Under Secretary) levels, its further application seemed more likely than any return to greater uniformity in rewards.

IV RECRUITMENT, TRAINING AND THE CAREER CIVIL SERVICE

The belief that 'as between two able men, the specialist is less likely to become a successful administrator in the modern State than, say, one who has been trained in the Honours school of *Literae Humaniores* at Oxford' might be said to have been the Civil Service's traditional attitude towards the direct entry recruitment of adminstrators ever since Macaulay pronounced on the matter in the 1850s. Macaulay certainly implied that 'at its best, a humanistic training produces greater flexibility and greater open-mindedness than is the case with a specialist training.' Macaulay, though, was not the author of those words. Nor were those sentiments penned by a First Civil Service Commissioner in a mood of what, in another context, Stanley Baldwin once called 'appalling frankness'. The words were those of Harold Laski (1938, p. 323). They did not stop him from writing later that the Civil Service was 'much too convinced that a man who could get a First in Greats at Oxford could see all the problems of his time with an insight and imagination less likely to be available to other men' (Laski, 1951, p. 162). Laski was the populariser, if not always the originator, of many of the familiar criticisms of direct entry recruitment to what used to be called the Administrative Class, and of much else about the Civil Service, not least 'the narrow social class from which the highest civil servants are drawn' (Laski, 1938, p. 324), an observation better directed at the Diplomatic Service than the Home Civil Service. Laski proposed opening up the Civil Service to late-entry recruitment, not least from other areas of the public service, and, as part of a substantial extension of post-entry training provision, he advocated the establishment of 'a Staff College for the Administrative Class, and for promising recruits from the lower grades' (Laski, 1942, pp. 10–11). Laski's fellow authority in the academic study of public administration, W.A. Robson, kept what became the Fabian reforming agenda up to date in the 1950s, most obviously in the form of admiration for the training and professionalism of the French Higher Civil Service (Robson, 1956, p. 58), and the Fulton Committee took up this agenda in the 1960s, as did the English Committee in the 1970s and the Treasury and Civil Service Committee later. When John Garrett of that last-named Committee was told in 1993 by the First Civil Service Commissioner that in the recruitment of fast-stream administrators 'we dot not actually keep [details of] school background any more' (HC 390-II, 1992–3, evidence, q. 746), Garrett did not resist observing 'how convenient!' (*ibid.*, q. 747).

'It would be fanciful to suggest that perhaps some of the world-wide reputation which British civil servants had acquired for integrity might not unfairly be credited to the body which selected them', wrote the official historian of the Civil Service Commission about its centenary (Reader, 1981, p. 49). In translation, this meant that the Commission did deserve some of the credit, and few would deny this. That the Civil Service Commission developed into a detached, schoolmasterly institution was entirely unsurprising, given that it was required to be a disinterested examining body, conducting open competitive examinations, and, certainly down to 1939, when the Civil Service as an employer could still command its potential market, the Commission was well fitted for its role. The changed market situation of the post-war years eventually altered that. The talented had less need to wait upon the Civil Service Commission to take what seemed to be its time to recruit them. That the Commission handled nearly 300,000 candidatures for various posts in the immediate post-war reconstruction competitions, and that as early as 1948, under the aegis of Sir Perceval Waterfield, it had developed the Method II means of entry to the then Administrative Class (*ibid.*, pp. 47–8; Chapman, 1984) was not suggestive of an institution unable to come to terms with a changed recruitment situation, at least initially. In the longer run, full employment took its toll and, by the 1960s, the Commission's traditional role as an academic examining body was being undermined, with the literary style open competitions for the Clerical,

Executive and Administrative Classes either being abandoned or soon likely to be dispensed with. In 1965, the Civil Service Commission came poorly out of a review of Civil Service recruitment conducted by the Select Committee on Estimates (HC 308, 1964–5). In a chapter called 'The end of the Ancien Régime,' the official historian observed that:

> The Commissioners' annual reports during the last years of the Commission's existence as a separate and independent government department make depressing reading. So much so that *The Guardian* on one occasion commented that it detected in them a note of despair. At a time when the sphere of government activity was expanding and more and more tasks were laid on the Service by successive Administrations, circumstances could hardly have been more unfavourable for recruitment to almost all classes, generalists and specialists alike. Industry and local authorities, much more than hitherto, were in the market for graduates and also for those with the professional qualifications the Service was seeking in larger numbers. . . . Even in years which saw some increase in unemployment and economic uncertainty there was almost no improvement in recruitment to many of the professional and specialist fields. . . . The failure to fill posts was not the only disturbing factor. There was a failure to attract a sufficient proportion of entrants to the specialists classes who in the opinion of the selection boards were of really high quality and anxiety was expressed about who within the Service would prove capable of filling the senior professional posts in the future. (Reader, 1981, p. 51)

That the Civil Service Commission was made part of the Civil Service Department in 1968, as a result of the Fulton Report, was an important change in status, although it did not affect the Commissioners' independence in selection. In 1969, the traditional Administrative Class examination, which had long been called Method I, was dispensed with. The Fulton Committee had been divided on the matter and it was the Civil Service Commissioners themselves who had pressed for abolition (PRO: BA 1/5; Fry, 1993, pp. 221, 225). The Fulton Committee had been less than admiring of what had been called Method II, or rather, K.A.G. Murray, the Chairman of the Civil Service Selection Board (CSSB) at the time, believed, 'two or three like minded members' of the Committee had this outlook. He blamed them for the Fulton Report containing 'disgracefully ill informed comments on selection' which were little more than 'generalized criticism unsupported by evidence'. Murray observed that 'as CSSB professionals . . . it was difficult not to resent the amateurish Fulton views.' Help was at hand in the form of the Davies Committee, which conducted 'a full scale external review of CSSB procedures', the results of which were 'comforting'. Murray recalled:

> The leader in *The Times* on the publication of the Davies Report [in 1969] hit a note not often found regarding inquiries into the Public Service: 'Seldom has a piece of public administration come so well out of so searching an inquiry.' This bucked me up no end, although it was saddening that it took several weeks for the Highest Ones in the then Civil Service Department to indicate satisfaction. (Murray, 1990, pp. 22–3)

The Davies Committee had accorded Method II as much praise an any recruitment process run by human beings could reasonably bear. The Committee found 'no evidence of bias in Method II itself either in the procedures or on the part of the assessors'. The Committee described Method II as 'a selection system to which the Public Service can point with pride'. This did not stop the Committee from producing twenty-three recommendations for changes, which were implemented in whole or in part. However, these proposals were framed on the assumption of Method II continuing to be used for selecting 'graduates with the qualities of Assistant Principals'. The Committee recognised that 'if and when the wider graduate entry discussed in the Fulton Report is introduced or other changes occur, consequential change in the selection system may well be needed' (Cmnd 4156, 1969, pp. iv, 82–6).

When the wider graduate entry was introduced in 1971 it took a differentiated form, with the Administration Trainee grade replacing that of Assistant Principal, and ten years later the Civil Service Commission announced that 'from 1982 we shall be reverting to an exclusively "fast stream" entry for a smaller number of Administration Trainees' (115th Report, 1982, p. 9). What had not changed was the continuing criticism of the Civil Service Commission for displaying preferences for Oxbridge graduates, former pupils of fee-paying schools and arts rather than social or natural-science graduates in recruitment to the Administration Trainee grade. Norman Hunt, having been a leading light on the Fulton Committee, aired these criticisms in evidence to the English Committee in1977 (HC 535–II, 1976–7, evidence, q. 1051–65; HC 535–III, 1976–7, evidence, pp. 1090–124). The then First Civil Service Commissioner, F.H. Allen, subsequently set up a committee to defend the Commission's selection procedures against these familiar criticisms, and, as long as it was a general entry to the Administration Trainee grade that was under review, there was little danger of it losing the argument, and so it proved when the relevant research was published (Allen Report, 1979). For one thing, it was the written qualifying examination that finished off most of the non-Oxbridge competitors. The detail need not detain us (see Fry, 1985, pp. 56–62), not least because in any general competition at this level among the products of the higher-education system it would be surprising, even to those of us with no connection at all with either institution, if Oxford and Cambridge graduates were other than disproportionately successful. Similarly, although not remotely from that background myself, that those with middle-class origins fared disproportionately well in competition at this level and of this type, in what, beyond the initial stage involved much in the way of extended interviews, ought not to be surprising. In what proved to be an unwise attempt at 'demystifying our procedures', the Commission agreed to the BBC making television programmes about the selection of fast-stream administrators, which were broadcast on 4 and 11 December 1986. The Commissioners found that the manner in which the work of CSSB and the Final Selection Board was portrayed was unsatisfactory:

The impression [was given] that background was more important than ability in determining whether a candidate was successful. This is not the case. There would be little point in using an expensive extended selection process if this were so. As it is, we have devised such a process precisely because our exclusive concern is to assess in depth a candidate's ability and potential against highly specific selection criteria which have been validated against the needs of the job to be done. (120th Report, 1987, pp. 14–15)

The Civil Service Commission was guilty of being naive. So was K.A.G. Murray in writing of the personnel at CSSB that 'the bulk would have been content to be seen as "liberal", with or without the capital' (Murray, 1990, p. 7) as if this was not evidence of the holding of a political position. One notes studies which suggest that the extent of social mobility in Britain has tended to be understated (Heath, 1981; Rubinstein, 1986, pp. 163–207; 1993), and if the Higher Civil Service of the 1980s – as represented in one study of Permanent Secretaries – still seemed to exhibit a considerable degree of social homogeneity, this seemed less so than half a century before and certainly the upper-class contingent was much reduced (Theakston and Fry, 1989, p. 145). Though concern about the social composition of the Higher Civil Service, which has increasingly tended to move away from being primarily a matter of class, seems inevitable even in the British form of political democracy, the Civil Service Commission's task was not supposed to be that of engaging in essays in social engineering, but to observe the principle of recruiting administrators solely on the basis of merit, and thus to seek 'the brightest and the best'. It was consistent with this approach that the European fast-stream entry for administrators was introduced in 1990, and that the fast-stream principle had been extended to specialist groups.

While, certainly by the 1980s, the Civil Service Commission had translated itself into a highly professional central recruitment agency, the fact was that 90 per cent of direct-entry recruitment was not done by the Commission at all, but by government departments themselves. The 10 per cent of recruitment that was carried out directly by the Commission was to the grade of Executive Officer and above and to equivalent grades in other occupational groups and classes. Writing in 1981, the then First Civil Service Commissioner stressed that departmental recruitment was subject to at least formal Civil Service Commission supervision (Allen, 1981, pp. 22–3). Following the Civil Service Order in Council of 1982, this was no longer the case (Civil Service Commission, 116th Report, 1983, pp. 19–30). In 1985 and 1986, experiments were made in the local recruitment of Executive Officers by the Board of Inland Revenue and the Department of Health and Social Security (Civil Service Commission, 119th report, 1986, p. 15; 120th Report, 1987, p. 17). Departmental recruitment would seem to be promotive of greater flexibility, and, in the economic climate of that time, it could be expected that national pay scales would enable government departments with offices in the relatively depressed parts of Britain to locally recruit potentially very able people, even of university entrance standard as then defined and sometimes with the basic qualifications already attained, for even routine clerical work. In the more prosperous regions, the Civil Service was less well placed. There was a high wastage rate in the clerical grades in such areas, and the reason for the local recruitment experiments mentioned earlier for the Executive Officer grade was that 'the biggest problem in filling vacancies remains in London and the South East where unemployment is relatively low; the cost of living, particularly housing, relatively high; and competition from employers at its fiercest' (Civil Service Commission, 120th Report, 1987, p. 14).

Few outsiders seem much interested in the career Civil Service below its higher grades, despite the need to get the work done efficiently, and despite the fact too that, in modern times, the Civil Service has always placed great emphasis on promotion from below. In 1985, the Management and Personnel Office conducted a review containing no fewer than forty-one recommendations about identifying and developing internal talent in the Civil Service (Eland Report, 1985). The Civil Service Commission emphasised two years later that 'we remain anxious to develop in-Service talent to the full; the aim is for 50 per cent of the fast stream to come from internal sources' (120th Report, 1987, p. 16). This was at the same time that the Commission was turning down literally thousands of outside applicants for the fast stream. It seems not entirely unreasonable to doubt whether, this side of the Second World War, what was a much-expanded career Civil Service ever had the depth of talent which would justify except to itself and its interest groups, the scale of promotion from below into the higher grades which seems to have occurred; and, to look at another source of talent, one notes too that many of the specialist groups have been in recruitment difficulties throughout the post-war period. The eye of the outsider naturally tends to be drawn to direct-entry recruitment, but the Executive Officer grade, for instance, while attractive to some graduates by the 1980s and traditionally the entry point for those with at least basic university entrance qualifications, was mainly composed of former members of what used to be called the Clerical Officer grade, which over the years had struggled to attract recruits, and continued to do so outside the less-favoured regions. Whether abandoning the wider graduate entry was such a good idea for the Civil Service could be doubted, although the conventional wisdom about the Service has tended to be that it contains massed ranks of untried talent, and, of course, there could be no definite evidence that this was not the case. It also flies in the face of such wisdom to add that, while it was worth noting – as the Civil Service Commission felt the need to do twice – that 'for the first time Oxbridge candidates made up a minority of those appointed' to the fast stream when the results were declared in 1986 (120th Report, 1987, pp. 14, 16), this need not necessarily be a welcome development. It might well be a worrying sign that in the competition for the ablest graduates, the severity of which showed no sign of abating, as the Atkinson inquiry testified (Atkinson Report, 1983, p. 6), the career Civil Service was losing out. No recruitment system can be better than the men and women presenting themselves for appointment, but it was evident that 'research in the 1970s established that the CSSB method had effectively predicted long-term potential for senior posts in the Civil Service', and a further statistical study of candidates selected between 1972 and 1981 and recorded as 'fast streamers' and still in post at the beginning of 1992 came to the same, documented conclusion (Clements-Bedford Report, 1992, pp. 2–4).

'In practice the new entrant to the Administrative Class is inducted rather than trained' was how C.H. Sisson described the traditional attitude towards the post-entry training of higher civil servants which persisted into the first part of the 1960s. Sisson approvingly quoted the observation of what he called an authoritative Treasury source that

> This practice is in accordance with the long established tradition of regarding members of the Administrative Class as intelligent amateurs who form their judgements on the basis of experience rather than as a result of a prescribed course of theoretical training. (Sisson, 1966, pp. 35, 37)

A quarter of a century before, another insider, H.E. Dale, had gone to some trouble to rebut academic sniping about the supposed 'amateurism' of higher civil servants (Dale, 1941, pp. 212–23). Besides academics, early advocacy of a form of professionalism had come from the Society of Civil Servants, representing the Executive Class, who had hoped to model the Institute of Public Administration, when it was first established in 1922, on the British Medical Association and other professional bodies. To this end,

> It would develop a technique of administration and encourage all civil servants to treat themselves not as a promiscuous horde of clerks, with pension privileges, but as men, with expert training and technical knowledge, as clearly qualified for the special task of public administration as chartered accountants for accountancy. (Nottage and Stack, 1972, p. 281)

This analysis did not impress the Treasury in the person of Sir Russell Scott, who seemed to see a professional Institute as 'a glorification of the bureaucracy'. A Treasury colleague suspected that the Institute was 'a forced growth under the benign warmth of Mr Sidney Webb and his admirers' (*ibid.*, pp. 284–5). The Institute eventually became very respectable, being translated into the Royal Institute of Public Administration in 1954, but it never became a professional body, and pressure for the professionalisation of post-entry training for administration in the Civil Service took other forms. This was primarily for the establishment of a Civil Service College of some kind. Laski was insistent that such an institution should not degenerate into 'a kind of superior business college' (Laski, 1943, p. 19). W.A. Robson wanted a British equivalent of the *Ecole Nationale d'Administration* (ENA) in Paris. It made no difference. For many years, nothing happened.

From the Plowden Report on the Control of Public Expenditure of 1961 onwards, though, the talk in and about the Civil Service was of management and, even if the working reality was much the same, the Dale–Sisson style of administrator was deemed to be out of fashion, and so, too, was the notion that the British Civil Service had a monopoly of wisdom about how to conduct the higher levels of public administration. The French Higher Civil Service tended to be ascribed that role and academic pressure for something resembling the ENA to be established in Britain was stepped up. The British career Civil Service did not do this, but, in 1963, the Treasury established the Centre for Administrative Studies (CAS) at which, following the successful completion of their probation, Assistant Principals were required to follow courses of instruction in economics and related subjects, the scale of which eventually became more ambitious. A Treasury Working Party in 1967 envisaged the CAS being translated into a Civil Service College under a different name (Fulton evidence, vol. 5(1), p. 83) and, as is well known, the Fulton Report of 1968 advocated the establishment of the Civil Service College (Cmnd 3638, pp. 35–40), which duly took place in 1970. While, of course, bearing in mind that departmental provision always dominated post-entry training in the Civil Service, it could be suggested that, if centrally provided post-entry training in the Civil Service ever had a golden age in Britain, and it was debatable if it ever did, then the Centre for Administrative Studies era of 1963–70 was it. The former Director of Training and Education at the Treasury, Desmond Keeling, was understandably proud of the CAS, and, for instance, at the time took the present writer to task for allegedly solely attributing 'the decision to give the main course in the third year, rather than pre-entry as in some countries, to a wish not to waste resources on training those who would leave the Service at the end of their two year period of probation'. Keeling insisted that:

> The decisive factors were in fact the greater effectiveness of training given to those with experience of work in departments, and the preference for basing decisions at the end of probation on performance over the full two years in jobs, rather than partly on performance on courses. (Keeling, 1971, p. 63)

Although Keeling did not say so, whatever the intentions, such a structure minimised the departure from the traditional arrangements. Training remained unimportant in career terms. C.H. Sisson could still feel comfortable about things. 'There has been some elaboration of the training of the young administrator and a Centre for Administrative Studies has been set up', Sisson wrote, but 'unaccompanied by any change in the method of recruitment' it 'has certainly not changed the character of the Service nor was it meant to' (Sisson, 1966, p. x11).

Predictably, the Civil Service College was soon in difficulties. A Civil Service Department review team identified one reason in 1974:

> The College, unlike the justly esteemed *Ecole Nationale d'Administration*, is not an elitist institution. If it had been, it might have found it easier both to establish its repute with some of its more demanding critics and to fulfil the research and promotional roles proposed for it. On the contrary, it was proposed by the Fulton

Committee and accepted by two successive Governments, that it should be a large scale and broad based institution. As such, it has been expected to provide a very widely assorted range of courses, more varied, probably, than those of any comparable institution in this country and of such a divergent nature as to generate not a little ambiguity, and even some inner contradictions, in its role. All this for a very large and constantly changing body of trainees of very widely varying abilities, experience and degrees of commitment and enthusiasm. (Heaton–Williams Report, 1974, p. 14)

So, the Civil Service College was supposed to cater for everybody and in its early years at least it ended up pleasing very few people, including its first Principal, who was drawn from academic life and who wanted an elitist institution rather like, ironically, the London School of Economics of Laski's time, and to which the Civil Service unions were opposed. As performance at the College was not important for their careers, the training provision for the Administration Trainees attracted criticism (Fry, 1993, pp. 267–72).

The post of Principal went to senior civil servants from 1976 onwards, and the Civil Service College gradually established a role for itself as an efficient provider of Civil Service training. In terms of overall provision, it was a minor role as, for instance, the College's Report for 1982–3 made clear:

Departments rightly continue to provide the great bulk of Civil Service training from their own internal resources. Most have their own training centres and they were responsible . . . for 75 per cent of the total training (measured in trainee days). A further 20 per cent was provided by external institutes – local authority night schools, further education institutes, polytechnics and universities, and business schools. The remaining 5 per cent was the College's share. (13th Report, 1982–3, p. 3)

As for efficiency, in 1986, Noel Moore, the College's Principal, was able to write:

Compared with the 1980/81 academic year we had in 1985/86 almost three times as many students on more than twice as many courses although we had each student for a shorter time. We ran 40 per cent more course days and 47 per cent more student days. . . . The total teaching and directive staff remain much the same; support staff are fewer. (16th report, 1985–6, p. v)

The same official emphasised elsewhere that fast stream training in 1982/3, for instance, had accounted for only 3,300 trainee days out of a total of 72,000 (Moore, 1984, p. 98). Outside interest remained centred on provision for the high fliers, inevitably, and John Thompson, responsible at the time for running fast-stream courses at the Civil Service College, wrote in 1984:

During the 1970s, fast stream training was based on two long courses of eight to fifteen weeks taken between postings. The courses comprised a mix of the disciplines fashionable at the time – economics, statistics, public administration, social/industrial policy, finance and staff management. However, by 1980 conditions in the Civil Service began to make it difficult for departments to release staff for long courses. This, together with decreased recruitment, made for poor use of College resources. A change was needed.

From September 1981, a modular system was introduced to meet formal training needs of the different phases of the early career of those in the Administration Trainee and Higher Executive Officer (Development) grades. The induction courses were concerned with Communication Skills, with Parliament, Government and the Civil Service, and with Finance and Control of Public Expenditure. There were six modules available at the next level, including Essential Quantitative Skills and also Economics, Government and the Administration, and later still, further modules were presented, notably Staff Management (Thompson, 1984, pp. 48–54). The continued prominence of economics and its related subjects reflected the subject matter of most administrators' work, and the supposed flexibility of modularisation did not disguise the lesser commitment of resources.

Training in the non-industrial Civil Service in the late 1980s was reviewed by the National Audit Office (NAO), which observed of its provision:

> This compares favourably with the volume of training per person in the private sector. But a review of good practice in the private sector, carried out by the NAO in parallel with the Civil Service study, showed that in a sample of leading firms the training is differently distributed, with senior staff and high fliers receiving most training. In the Civil Service, junior and middle managers receive the most. (National Audit Office, 1990, p. 1)

This was despite the Coster Report of 1984 and the resulting Senior Management Development Programme for staff broadly between Principal (Grade 7) and Assistant Secretary (Grade 5) introduced in September 1985 because 'formal training had been neglected' and intended to be on a scale 'well above the average for British managers' (Coster Report, 1984; Coster, 1987, p. 293). Earlier in 1985, a six-week Top Management Programme for newly appointed Under Secretaries (Grade 3) had been established (Civil Service College, 15th Report, 1984–5, p. 5). The Senior Professional Administrative Training Course (SPATS), designed for specialists transferring to administrative work, dated from as early as 1972 (Fry, 1985, pp. 49–50, 67–8). Sixteen weeks of early career formal training for administrators, though, never was going to impress those aware of the ENA arrangements and that institution's type of direct entrant. The Fultonite view, at least as presented by John Garrett twenty-five years on, was that the Civil Service College had become 'gentrified' in 'the way that educational institutions in Britain always go in that they always begin as technical colleges for ordinary people and end up as universities' (HC 390–II, 1992–3, evidence, q. 647). Garrett described the Civil Service College as having facilities that were 'gold plated' (*ibid.*, q. 668) and as being like 'Oxbridge with rhododendrons' thus reinforcing 'the mandarin image' (*ibid.*, q. 666). While the ENA might well aspire to a social status comparable with that of, say, Christ Church or All Souls, Oxford, the Civil

Service College has never been in this league, and, though definitions of what constitutes a university keep changing, for most of its existence the College has had more in common with a technical college. The Fulton Committee neither sought such status for the Civil Service College nor did it do much to prevent it. Some of the Committee's members were interested in the ENA, presumably with a view to importing it, but this did not amount to advocacy, and the Fulton Report itself was dependent on the Treasury's Osmond Report for the main body of such ideas as it had on post-entry training (Fry, 1993, pp. 207–14, 221–5). Sir William Armstrong's reported observation that 'a week at Sunningdale could be the crown of a Messenger's career' (Kellner and Crowther Hunt, 1980, p. 93) was indicative of the type of college that the then Head of the Home Civil Service wanted, let alone many of the Service's unions. Far from having 'a mandarin image' then or later, the Civil Service College always seemed forlorn in its early years, before carving out for itself a role that seemed of utility in the eyes of the Service, to which was added the self-conscious commercialism that the Thatcher Government required even in the College's dealings with the Service.

The Fulton Committee certainly wanted the career Civil Service to persist, but it also believed that it needed to be opened up to more later recruitment than had been common, which has occurred, and also to secondments with the private sector. The formal scheme for secondments was introduced following the Fulton Report in 1968. The next marked shift was in 1977, when the then Government decided to seek a 'sharp and significant increase' in the number of civil servants seconded to business organisations. In March 1989, Lord Young and Richard Luce, as members of the Thatcher Government, initiated the Bridge Programme 'to build more bridges between government and industry', the aim of which was to further encourage secondments and job exchanges between civil servants and business people, the scheme being run by individual departments. Prior to this programme, targets were set for the Civil Service as a whole (250 outwards and 200 inwards). Under the Bridge Programme, an overall doubling of secondments took place (Gosling and Nutley, 1990, p. 3). A follow-up study found that civil servant secondees were regarded by private sector organisations as being 'excellent ambassadors for their departments', and that, while the Bridge Programme might well lead to the formalisation of procedures, previously these had been haphazard (*ibid.*, p. 92). As far as civil servants' careers were concerned, the study concluded:

> There was evidence from line managers and other departmental representatives that the idea of a lifetime career was changing. The 'velvet drainpipe' was leaking at all levels, through secondment, and through early leaving (sometimes as a result of secondment). This was not regarded as a particular problem as a well trained and informed civil servant would benefit the private sector. However three large companies were very concerned lest the civil servants might be 'testing the water' before taking the plunge into the private sector. They saw their role as training bureaucrats for the Government. (*ibid.*, p.91)

Greater movement in and out of the Civil Service had long since become a familiar part of the reformers' agenda. Yet when Peter Levene was brought into the Ministry of Defence from private industry in 1985 at a salary twice that of his Civil Service counterparts (*FDA News*, April 1985, pp. 1–2), there was unease, which the Civil Service Commission expressed in the truly British form of needing to get the procedures right (119th Report, 1986, pp. 7–9), an outlook also present in several antipathetic House of Commons reports about higher civil servants taking up outside appointments (HC 216, 1980–1; HC 302, 1983–4; Cmnd 9465, 1985; HC 392, 1987–8; HC 622, 1987–8; Cm. 585, 1989; HC 383, 1988–9; HC 14, 1989–90; HC 269, 1990–1; HC 48, 1991–2).

V 'FRANKENSTEIN'S MONSTER' AND THE 'OLD CIVIL SERVICE'

The Thatcher era was a traumatic one for the career Civil Service. The Conservative Government's policy of cuts in numbers recalled the reductions of the inter-war years, when economic liberalism also reigned, which had meant that only in 1939 did numbers of officials pass the level attained in 1920 (*Civil Service Statistics 1971*, p. 14). The across-the-board nature of the cuts embarked on in 1979 was a crude one, thus having much the same character as the financial arrangements in departments which the Government found. Behind the supposed sophistication of the Public Expenditure Survey Committee system, in its heyday admired as much by academic observers (e.g. Heclo and Wildavsky, 1974) as by the civil servants involved (e.g. Goldman, 1973; Clarke, 1978), and PAR, as ambitious in conception as it was feeble in application, lay a total ignorance of what the Civil Service's running costs were. Before 1979, such costs seem to have been dismissed as mere details. Now, they were known. The FMI was put in place, and, at least to the casual eye, efficiency studies appeared to be reaching into the darkest corners of government departments (e.g. Management and Personnel Office, 1984, 1985; Efficiency Unit, 1984), their findings sometimes prefaced by a stern message from the Prime Minister herself. It was not surprising that there was talk of a 'new Civil Service'.

The sheer scale of the operations of government departments, as well as the still substantial numbers of staff involved, continued to make attempts at the close control of activity into a formidable task. For example, the Defence Estate of the time, even on a restrictive definition, occupied 222,000 hectares in the United Kingdom alone, and included some 3,000 establishments and 137,000 married quarters. 'The Estate's market value has never been properly assessed', the Comptroller and Auditor General revealed in 1987:

> In 1982–83, after a very broad brush desk exercise, the Property Services Agency estimated the saleable value at some £6,900 million and the replacement cost at

possibly £50,000 million. Net annual expenditure on the Estate, about 8 per cent of the Defence Budget in recent years, was estimated at £1,400 million in 1986–87. (National Audit Office, 1987, p. 1)

The order of the sums put the scale of the Thatcher Government's economising arrangements into a more modest perspective.

In deriding the FMI as being 'like Frankenstein's monster, made up of bits and pieces of other people's management philosophies, waiting for a spark of life', Peter Jones of the CCSU, presumably unwittingly, emphasised the FMIs limitations in relation to the Government's aims:

> The spark of life missing from this forlorn creative is of course, the allocation of real money to managers. . . . But giving them real money would, of course, mean giving them real power down the line – the last thing that the central departments, or, for that matter, department level managements, would contemplate. So we are left with the usual half baked Civil Service compromise. Civil Service managers are to have all the rigours and disadvantages of devolved power, without being allowed to exercise that power. (*CCSU Bulletin*, February 1985, p. 17)

But if Civil Service managers had 'devolved power' to decide the terms and conditions of service of officials in their cost centre (instead of, subject to some developments in performance pay, having to accept that salaries, the major element in costs, were beyond their control) it was difficult to see why the unions would be pleased about this or what role might eventually be left to them to play. Without such 'devolved power' for managers, the impact of the FMI was bound to be a relatively restricted one. If there had been a 'compromise', whether 'half-baked' or not, it still seemed to be weighted in favour of the conventional arrangements. This was why Mrs Thatcher welcomed the IPCS deal of 1987 in terms of 'a major step forward in the management of the Civil Service' (114 HC Deb. 6s. Written Answers c. 656) because it opened up the prospect, though no more at the time, of movement away from the conventional pay format.

To the extent that the Thatcher Government followed a consistent policy towards the non-industrial Civil Service during its first two terms of office, the most common perception of its approach was encapsulated in the title of a multi-departmental review published by the Treasury in 1986, *Using Private Enterprise in Government*. The Rayner scrutinies and the White Paper on Efficiency (Cmnd 8293, 1981) and the associated personnel targets, the FMI and the universalisation of MINIS and the controls on running costs, and the preaching of the contracting out of departmental services whenever possible, could be cited as evidence of consistency. The conversions to contracting out were initially few, an indication that the changes wrought had been as limited as would be expected in the short run. The multi-departmental review of competitive tendering and contracting for services in government departments found in 1986 that 'there has been substantial progress in contracting out the basic ancillary services. 84 per cent of cleaning, 82 per cent of maintenance, and 73 per cent of laundry services have been contracted out.' Momentum for further action in the remainder of departments' work was being lost, the review stated, not surprisingly adding that the Government wanted it to be recaptured (Treasury, 1986b, pp. 5, 15). That ancillary services had been subjected to competitive tendering at all was a break with the past, but core services in the non-industrial Civil Service remained largely intact. This reality was not obscured by 'pointing up the responsibility of Permanent Secretaries as senior line managers in their departments' (National Audit Office, 1986a, p. 6), or by references to the Permanent Secretaries and their Deputy Secretaries as 'top management', or by treating 'the middle tier of Under and Assistant Secretaries and Principals who organize the implementation of policy' as 'headquarters management' (Efficiency Unit, 1985, p. 1), or by referring to, say, Executive Officers as 'line managers'. Further, while the developments which had led to the FMI continued to evolve, as was evident, for example, from the dropping of staff targets in favour of sole reliance on running cost limits, the maintenance of a career bureaucracy could not easily co-exist with the pursuit of greater managerial efficiency. As one economic liberal put it: 'Bureaucrats have every inducement and incentive to spend rather than economize or save, since there are no rewards for not spending' (Hartley, 1986, p. 84). Uniformity of the kind which suited a career Civil Service was the enemy of the FMI. While performance pay represented a potentially important incursion into traditional arrangements, at the end of the second Thatcher Administration it was still the case that the 'old Civil Service' survived, and, as the present writer observed in 1987, it remained to be seen whether or not the Conservative Government had sufficient political enthusiasm to move to the next stage, which would be to establish something akin to a Swedish-style division between policy Ministries and administrative boards (HC 358-I, 1986–7, p. 117). The political will proved to be there.

5 The Next Steps Report and 'radical reforms of the Civil Service'

It was only towards the end of my time in government that we embarked upon the radical reforms of the Civil Service which were contained in the Next Steps programme. Under this programme much of the administrative – as opposed to policy making – work of government departments is being transferred to agencies, staffed by civil servants and headed by chief executives appointed by open competition. The agencies operate within frameworks set by the departments, but are free of detailed departmental control. The quality of management within the Public Service promises to be significantly improved. (Thatcher, 1993, p. 49)

Thus wrote Margaret Thatcher in her memoirs. The official history of the Next Steps programme recorded that when, in the autumn of 1986, her Adviser on Efficiency, Sir Robin Ibbs, presented a critical review of progress in Civil Service reform since 1979,

the Prime Minister . . . was disappointed to discover that, after seven years of effort to improve management in the Civil Service, so much still needed to be done. She commissioned Sir Robin to find out why, and to suggest how to move matters on.

So, 'at the beginning of November 1986, Sir Robin Ibbs and the Efficiency Unit – a small team of civil servants and people from industry – began an intensive fact finding exercise' (Goldsworthy, 1991, pp. 3–4). The Efficiency Unit presented its report *Improving Management in Government: The next steps* to the Prime Minister in the spring of 1987 (*ibid.*, p. 8). In February 1988, the report was published under the same title, and Kate Jenkins, Karen Caines and Andrew Jackson were named as its authors. Sir Robin Ibbs tended to get the credit, or the blame as ascribed by Nigel Lawson, the Chancellor of the Exchequer at the time, who considered Ibbs to be an inadequate successor to Lord Rayner. Certainly, at first, Lawson saw little virtue in what he called the 'Ibbs initiative' of hiving off executive functions of departments to agencies. 'There was no-one more zealous for privatization than I was', Lawson declared, and his preferred solution was to take privatisation deep, instead of marginally, into the areas of activity conventionally assigned to government departments (Lawson, 1992, pp. 390–3), thus anticipating the later *Competing for Quality* policy. Meanwhile, Lawson had welcomed the IPCS pay deal of 1987, and the imitative agreements with other unions that followed, because they represented 'the weakening of the idea that all civil servants should be treated in the same way, and the introduction of market forces into Civil Service pay negotiations, was a triumph of sorts' (*ibid.*, pp. 393–4). If Lawson, and the economic liberals who thought like him, had a chilling message for the Civil Service, it was at least matched by one emanating from within its own core. For, as we shall see, the proposals contained in the Mueller Report of 1987 struck at the heart of the whole notion of there being a large-scale career Civil Service.

I THE MUELLER REPORT: A PROGRAMME FOR CHANGING CIVIL SERVICE WORKING PATTERNS

> Examination of working patterns outside the Civil Service shows that many people do not work from 9am to 5pm, 5 days a week with the prospect of a lifetime's employment and career advancement. Non-standard and alternative working patterns are increasing and becoming more widespread. The most significant trends are the wider and more imaginative use of part-time work, varieties of temporary work, shiftworking and sub-contracting, and the reduction of systematized overtime. The primary reason for this development is the economic pressure to reduce running costs by matching staff costs with work as closely as possible. The secondary reason is the availability of labour prepared, and sometimes demanding, to work non-standard patterns. Managers at local level have generally had the freedom and incentive to respond by developing individual schemes which, taken cumulatively, amount to a significant change in employment practices.

In this way, in a report called *Working Patterns*, a study team from the former Management and Personnel Office, led by Anne Mueller, summarised some recent developments in outside employment (Mueller Report, 1987, paras 2.1– 2.2) in a document dated September 1987 and circulated by the Treasury within the Civil Service and its unions two months later. For the Mueller team's examination of 'alternative patterns of work being evolved by business and industry' was accompanied by a consideration of 'what benefits these might have for the Civil Service and for the customers of the various services which are provided' (*ibid.*, para. 1.2).

What was proposed in *Working Patterns* was what in effect would be a two-tier Civil Service, with a core Civil Service that would enjoy job security and career prospects, and a peripheral Civil Service that would be employed on a wide range of conditions of employment. These contracts would permit the introduction on a large but unspecified scale of recurring temporary contracts; nil-hours contracts, which would mean people being available for work but with no guarantee of it; annual-hours contracts, involving restoring shift work a year in advance; widespread part-time employment; part-time work for individual senior staff; fixed-term contracts; and provision for home working (*ibid.*, para. 7.1). The benefits that followed from new working patterns of this kind were said to be the opportunities given for the better use of new technology (*ibid.*, para. 3.14), the greater ability to respond to fluctuations in workload and the enhanced capacity to adopt to new demands in the labour market (*ibid.*, para. 2.4), notably by recruiting staff with scarce skills (*ibid.*, para. 3.21). The study team recognised that:

> Some outside employment conditions and practices that are favourable to altern-ative working patterns are at odds with those that are generally regarded as essential elements of the Civil Service employment/career package or as distinct-ive characteristics of a 'good employer'. (*ibid.*, para. 6.9)

In the Civil Service as currently organised, the study team said, 'some regu-lations, such as those covering shift disturbance allowance, travel and sub-sistence, superannuation and maternity leave can constrain the efficient management of working time', adding that 'the rules of annual leave, overtime and substitution may not always operate to make sure that the needs of the work take precedence' (*ibid.*, para. 4.9).

Essentially, what the study team which produced *Working Patterns* were saying was that the career Civil Service with its implication of permanency tends to make for staff costs to be effectively treated as if they were fixed costs, while the philosophy of the FMI was to treat them as running costs. The FMI and the career Civil Service on anything like its existing scale were inherently incompatible, given the severely restricted scope for managerial initiative that the career Civil Service's substantial bundle of employment rights dictated. Hence, given the Conservative Government's wish to persist with the FMI, the scale of the career Civil Service had to be considerably reduced, eventually down to a core. The study team objected to the use of the terms 'core' and 'periphery' on the grounds that 'in general successful outside firms do not have one set of terms and conditions from which all alternative working patterns are seen as derogation' (*ibid.*, para. 7.8). The career Civil Service, though, did have possibly as much standardisation as its necessarily complex structure could sustain, and the Mueller team recognised that retaining the core of the career Civil Service and eventually developing alternative working patterns elsewhere risked

> creating two classes of employee – the 'haves' and the 'have nots'. In Civil Service terms any such move would be redolent of the worst features of established and unestablished service before the 1971–72 pension reforms and would rightly be resisted. (*ibid.*, para. 7.7)

The establishment issue, though, was to do with security of tenure and associ-ated rights and the *Working Patterns* reforms were directed towards restricting tenure and rights. If the norm was substantially changed, then appeals against aberrations lost their force.

'*Working Patterns* is a programme for revolutionary changes in Civil Service conditions of employment', declared the IPCS, accompanying its analysis with a picture of 'the original nil hours contract – dockyard labourers waiting to be offered work "on the stones" in London Docks in 1931'. The IPCS observed:

The *Working Patterns* programme of 'reforms' would spell the death knell for the role of government as a 'good' employer. In pay terms that has already been the case since 1980. The Cabinet Office report would now kill off any remaining pretension that the Government's own employment policies should set an acceptable standard for the rest of the community.

While the 'overriding concern' behind the Mueller proposals was 'to cut costs', the IPCS thought that 'a vast new workload' would be imposed on 'departments and line managers with scant prospect of cash savings at the end of the day' (*IPCS Bulletin*, 2/88, pp. 8–9). The unwillingness to consult the unions before the circulation of the Mueller Report seemed to offend the FDA as much as that document's 'emphasis on cost cutting'. The FDA could not see how adopting alternative working patterns that had the effect of diminishing job security would attract people to the Civil Service, but it saw merit in some of the Mueller proposals because 'we have a long standing commitment to the extension of part-time work which can play an important part in helping a civil servant to combine a career with domestic responsibilities; and we favour flexible working hours.' The FDA then issued a set of guidelines for negotiators which seemed designed to negate the exercise (*FDA News*, March 1988, p. 7). The NUCPS and the CPSA issued a pamphlet which described the Mueller Report as 'a major threat to the career Civil Service, to our jobs and conditions of service, and to our rights as workers and trade unionists'. These unions dismissed any idea that the proposals would improve the position of those with domestic commitments which presently impeded their careers. The strategy behind *Working Patterns* was the cutting of costs and thus the numbers of permanent civil servants, and the creation of 'a large tier of second class civil servants with few rights, poor pay, and no career opportunities' (CPSA/NUCPS, 1988). The Council of Civil Service Unions, in its response to the Mueller Report sent to the Treasury in March 1988, carefully used research findings to challenge the evidence of changing working patterns outside the Service on which the Mueller proposals in part rested, before going on to give details of 'a real alternative', meaning the further improvement of conditions of service (*CCSU Bulletin*, July 1988, pp. 101–11). Meanwhile, the main attention had turned to the Next Steps Report, in which proposals akin to the Mueller approach found a place.

II THE NEXT STEPS REPORT OF 1988

When the Efficiency Unit's report, *Improving Management in Government: The next steps* was published early in 1988, its authors were anxious to locate the document as part of a tradition of enquiry into the Civil Service by citing earlier reviews by Northcote and Trevelyan and by the Fulton Committee (Efficiency Unit, 1988, pp. 31–2). In fact, the Ibbs Report emphasised its distinctiveness early on by firmly stating:

The Civil Service is too big and too diverse to manage as a single entity. With 600,000 employees it is an enormous organization compared with any private sector company and most public sector organizations. A single organization of this size which attempts to provide a detailed structure within which to carry out functions as diverse as driver licensing, fisheries protection, the catching of drug smugglers and the processing of Parliamentary Questions is bound to develop in a way which fits no single operation effectively. (*ibid.*, para. 10)

So, in marked contrast with the Fulton Commitee, which recognised that the work of government departments might be better organised if each department employed its own staff independently, and constructed its own grading system, but then went on to endorse a unified Civil Service (Fulton Report, 1968, para. 196), the Efficiency Unit was prepared to envisage the breaking up of the career Civil Service. 'At present the freedom of an individual manager to manage effectively and responsibly in the Civil Service is severely circum-scribed', the Ibbs Report correctly observed.

There are controls not only on resources and objectives, as there should be in any effective system, but also in the way in which resources can be managed. Recruit-ment, dismissal, choice of staff, promotion, pay, hours of work, accommodation, grading, organization of work, the use of IT equipment, are all outside the control of most Civil Service managers at any level. The main decisions on rules and regulations are taken by centre of the Civil Service. This tends to mean that they are structured to fit everything in general and nothing in particular. The rules are therefore seen primarily as a constraint rather than as a support; and in no sense as a pressure on managers to manage effectively. Moreover, the task of changing the rules is often seen as too great for one unit or one manager or indeed one department and is therefore assumed to be impossible. (*ibid.*, para. 11)

So, like the National Audit Office and the Public Accounts Committee be-fore it, the Efficiency Unit had come to the conclusion that the FMI had only scratched the surface. In pursuit of the fuller realisation of the objectives of the FMI not much more could be done as long as the career Civil Service persisted in its present form. The Efficiency Unit reported that, to judge from the discus-sions that it had engaged in during its investigations:

it was clear that the advantages which a unified Civil Service are intended to bring are seen as outweighed by the practical disadvantages, particularly beyond Whitehall itself. We are told that the advantages of an all-embracing pay struc-ture are breaking down, that the uniformity of grading frequently inhibits effec-tive management, and that the concept of a career in a unified Civil Service has little relevance for most civil servants, whose horizons are bounded by their local office, or, at most, by their department. (*ibid.*, para. 12)

Although the Unit found that the pressures on departments were mainly on expenditure and activities, and that there was still too little attention paid to the results to be achieved with the resources (*ibid.*, para. 8), the management and staff concerned with the delivery of government services, which involved some 95 per cent of the Civil Service, were generally convinced that the developments towards more clearly defined and budgeted management had been both positive and constructive (*ibid.*, para. 3).

At the higher levels of the Civil Service, though, 'senior civil servants inevitably and rightly respond to the priorities set by their Ministers which tend to be dominated by the demands of Parliament and communicating Government policies', the Efficiency Unit unsurprisingly observed (*ibid.*, para. 6); and most Ministers, feeling overloaded already, had told the Unit that, provided no major political risk was involved, they would welcome the divesting of managerial tasks. As things stood, Ministers thought that 'better management and the achievement of improved performance is something that the Civil Service has to work out largely for itself.' The Efficiency Unit thought that it would be 'unrealistic to expect Ministers to do more than give a broad lead' (*ibid.*, para. 7). What had to be doubted, though, was whether their experience fitted higher civil servants to do more than this themselves. As most civil servants were well aware, 'senior management is dominated by people whose skills are policy formulation and who have relatively little experience of managing or working where services are actually delivered.' One Grade 2 official told the Unit, 'the golden route to the top is through policy not through management', and this was reflected in the early experience and training of fast-stream recruits. As the Unit observed, 'this kind of signal affects the unwritten priorities of a whole oganization, whatever the formal policy may be' (*ibid.*, para. 4) and added that:

> managing large organizations involves skills which depend a great deal on experience; without experience senior managers lack confidence in their own ability to manage. Although, at the most senior levels, civil servants are responsible for both policy and service delivery, they give a greater priority to policy, not only because it demands immediate attention but because that is the area in which they are on familiar ground and where their skills lie, and where ministerial attention is focused. A proper balance between policy and delivery is hard to achieve within the present framework. (*ibid.*, para. 5)

So, the Efficiency Unit concluded, the framework needed to be changed:

> The aim should be to establish a quite different way of conducting the business of government. The central Civil Service should consist of a relatively small core engaged in the function of servicing Ministers and managing departments, who will be the 'sponsors' of particular government policies and services. Responding to these departments will be a range of agencies employing their own staff, who may or may not have the status of Crown servants, and concentrating on the delivery of their particular service, with clearly defined responsibilities between the Secretary of State and the Permanent Secretary on the one hand, and the Chairmen or Chief Executives of the agencies on the other. Both departments and their agencies should have a more open and simplified structure. (*ibid.*, para. 44)

The Unit said that it was essential to appoint a Project Manager at senior level to ensure that the programme of change took place (*ibid.*, para. 45); and in making a statement to Parliament about the Unit's recommendations and the Conservative Government's response to them, Mrs Thatcher as Prime Minister said that a Permanent Secretary in the Office of the Minister for the Civil Service, the successor to the Management and Personnel Office, would be responsible, through the Head of the Home Civil Service, to her for managing the process of change needed to implement the recommendations (127 HC Deb. 6s. c. 1149). The Efficiency Unit (1988, para. 46) had stated that 'within two years at the most, departments should have completed identification of areas where agencies are the most effective way of managing and should have changed their own internal structures to implement this change'. The first candidates for agency status, with the number of civil servants involved in parentheses, were as follows: the Vehicle Inspectorate (1,600); the Driver and Vehicle Licensing Directorate (5,400); the Companies Registration Office (1,100); the Employment Services part of the Department of Employment, including job centres and unemploy-ment benefit administration (35,600); the Meteorological Office (2,600); six Non-nuclear Research Establishments of the Ministry of Defence (15,000); the Passport Office (1,000); Her Majesty's Stationery Office (3,245); the historic Royal Palaces (300); the Royal Parks (600); the Queen Elizabeth II Conference Centre (65); and the Department of Health and Social Security Resettlement Units (600) (Goldsworthy, 1991, p. 11).

The Radical Right was never going to be impressed by the Next Steps initiative. 'Mrs Thatcher has produced a timid list of organizations that could be early candidates for agency treatment', *The Economist* (20 February 1988, p. 29) complained, adding:

> Another Cabinet Office report prepared by Sir Kenneth Stowe recommends a more radical approach, freeing up whole departments from Treasury control and giving them supervisory boards. Sadly, that report languishes, unpublished, in a Whitehall pigeon hole. Mr Peter Kemp, who is moving from the Treasury to oversee implementation of the Ibbs Report, should dust it down. He should also consider an even bolder approach, hinted at but not developed in Mrs Thatcher's statement on the Ibbs report: competitive tendering. Many government bodies charged primarily with executive functions could easily be made to tender regu-larly for their business. Imagine what that might do for the efficiency of the Inland Revenue or Customs and Excise.

Mrs Thatcher's statement indicated that the Government had 'not excluded the possibility' of locating agencies outside the Civil Service (127 HC Deb. 6s. c. 1155), believing herself that 'it would be best to deal in that way with [agencies] that are essentially commercial services', and specifically mentioning the Property Services Agency and that there was 'a review of that agency and how best to reform its activities' (*ibid.*, c. 1156). The appointment of Peter Kemp as a Second Permanent Secretary in the Cabinet Office as Project Man-ager and Head of the Office of the Minister for the Civil Service was one of the few aspects of the Next Steps programme that met with the approval of Nigel Lawson, the then Chancellor of the Exchequer. 'Kemp was an unusual official, an accountant by training who had joined the Treasury from the private sector', Lawson wrote, adding that when Kemp had previously been a Deputy Secretary in the Treasury in charge of Civil Service pay, 'it was largely through his efforts that I was able to effect a major change in Civil Service attitudes and practice.' Lawson was unadmiring of Sir Robin Ibbs, as we noted earlier, and of his plans, and considered that having 'an autonomous agency, whose head was, according to the original Ibbs blueprint, effectively accountable to no-one' was one of the principal problems of the Next Steps proposals. Another was that of 'maintaining effective control of the agencies' expenditure, in which Ibbs showed no interest'. Lawson recalled persuading the Prime Minister that this problem had to be addressed, and 'a long battle ensued, resulting in a lengthy written concordat negotiated by Peter Middleton on behalf of the Treasury and Robin Butler on behalf of Number 10', a consequence of which was that 'the chief executive of the agency and his "board" would be set stiff financial targets which would have to be agreed with the Treasury in the first place and monitored by the Treasury thereafter.' Lawson thought that Peter Kemp proceeded to do 'a remarkable job' in developing the Next Steps programme, but Lawson himself remained unenthusiastic, seeing 'the main practical advantage' of agencies to be that 'by creating accounts, boards of directors and saleable assets, future privatization may prove less difficult' (Lawson, 1992, pp. 392–3).

'The Civil Service unions are predictably (and unthinkingly) hostile to the plan', *The Economist* (20 February 1988, p. 28) wrote of the Next Steps proposals, but the reaction was by no means uniform. The Prime Minister had given an assurance that 'the Civil Service unions will be consulted about the setting up of particular agencies', and that 'they will also be consulted if any change in terms and conditions of civil servants is contemplated' (127 HC Deb. 6s. c. 1149). Though 'time alone will tell what will be the eventual fate of the Ibbs Report', the Council of Civil Service Unions responded cautiously, the scope accorded to joint consultation was welcomed, and it was noted that Peter Kemp's 'track record' at the Treasury in this regard was 'a good one'. The Council welcomed too what it perceived as the prospective diminution of the Treasury's 'central control of resources', believing that 'any real devolution of managerial responsibility (as opposed to the "Monopoly-money" approach of the FMI) is bound to loosen this control' (*CCSU Bulletin*, April 1988, p. 49). The FDA recognised that 'the changes proposed by Ibbs are potentially far reaching' not least because they sought to 'break up traditional arrangements on pay and personnel', adding:

> Nevertheless leaving aside the buzz words used in the report like 'chief executive' and 'project manager', the immediate changes stemming from the report are less dramatic than many expected from earlier Press speculation. . . . This is probably because the Government has failed to resolve the inherent tensions between its wish to give Civil Service managers more 'personal responsibility' and its desire to retain central control over expenditure. (*FDA News*, March 1988, p. 7)

The Vice-Chairman of the IPCS, John Gibson, told its 1988 annual conference that the Ibbs proposals should be treated with 'considerable unease' because under them 'the Civil Service would ultimately become a cadre of policy makers and everything else would be done outside the Civil Service proper. This is certainly radical, it is certainly dramatic, but is it sensible? Is it even realistic?' (*IPCS Bulletin*, 7/88, p. 6). In his speech to the annual conference of the CPSA, the General Secretary, John Ellis, took a different line:

> What we face with the Ibbs Report is an alternative to privatization. The fact that it was given so much credit by the Prime Minister was the reason for my and others' relief when the announcement was made on February 18. If Ibbs had been rejected, the alternative with this Government was not inaction, it was privatiza-tion. It is absolutely vital, therefore, that the Civil Service trade unions do all they can to make the agency concept a success because, if it fails, privatization will be the next step for large parts of the Civil Service. (*Red Tape*, June 1988, p. 6)

In stark contrast, the NUCPS denounced 'the Ibbs plan' as 'the first step towards privatization', and its General Secretary, Leslie Christie stated:

> Our first priority will be to defend the terms and conditions of civil servants and at the same time win the public debate about the future of the Civil Service. The Government's 'hidden agenda' poses the most serious threat to civil servants' terms and conditions yet faced. National rates of pay, job security, career oppor-tunities, even the Civil Service pension scheme – all these things are on the line. Government assurances that all staff in departmental agencies will remain civil servants mean nothing when fragmented pay and pension arrangements, wide regional variations in pay, and new powers to 'hire and fire' replace established Civil Service conditions. (*NUCPS Journal*, March 1988, p. 5)

By the early months of 1988, with the Ibbs proposals added to those in the Mueller Report, there was good cause to take a bleak view of the career Civil Services' immediate prospects, and there was worse to come.

III THE IMPLEMENTATION OF THE NEXT STEPS PROGRAMME

Out of a total of approximately 600,000 civil servants, the immediate imple-mentation of the Ibbs Report only involved about 70,000, some of them engaged in what could be seen as marginal activities. This seemed to convince many commentators not only that the original proposals of the Efficiency Unit had been scaled down considerably, because of Treasury opposition of the kind that Nigel Lawson later made public (Lawson, 1992, p. 392) and of the centre generally fearing loss of power; but also that those proposals that were published were of little consequence, which was not necessarily the case. All depended on political will and commitment. 'The Government will develop a continuing programme for establishing agencies, applying progressively the lessons of the experience gained', Mrs Thatcher told the House of Commons on presenting the Ibbs Report (127, HC Deb. 6s. c. 1149). With a continuance of the political dynamic for change, there was the prospect of the eventual emergence of a structure of British central government which resembled Swedish arrangements.

Whether or not the Swedish model did influence the preferred Ibbs structure, one problem common to both involved political accountability. 'The most striking difference between Britain and Sweden is the absence of a concept of ministerial responsibility', one student of the Swedish arrangements has written:

> In Sweden, a Cabinet Minister is not held responsible for administration, for he is not the head of a hierarchy whose duty is the administration of government policy. Before the advent of 'popular' government, administration was a matter for the King, who appointed his own Ministers and administered in accordance with the law. It is the latter concept of responsibility to the law which has been the central pillar of Swedish theory concerning the responsibility of both Ministers and State employees. The development of Parliamentary Government in Sweden did not lead to a subordination of administration to Parliament. The 1809 Constitution recognized the separation of powers, and although this effectively ended with the completion of Parliamentary democracy in 1918, the institutional framework and the culture derived from an earlier period persisted.

This 'independence' of administration is reflected in the fact that the Ministries are small, with some 2,000 employees in total, and the Central State Boards, which carry out administration, are staffed by the bulk of the Civil Service. The 'independence' of the Boards is circumscribed by the fact that their budget is determined by the Government, which can also require them to adopt 'good administrative practice' and inspect them to ensure that this is done; and there is the further link that the Heads of Boards are normally of the same political persuasion as that of the Government, which makes for informal co-operation (Robertson, 1982, pp. 162–5). One observer of Swedish government compared the relations between Ministers and Boards to those conducted in the twilight zone of Minister–public corporation relationship in Britain (Elder, 1970, p. 72). Of the many reasons why enthusiasm for the public corporation form of organisation in Britain had considerably diminished compared with when Stanely Baldwin pioneered the modern form of corporation with the Central Electricity Board in the 1920s or when Herbert Morrison played a major role in establishing a range of such corporation in the 1940s, the relevant one of concern here was that restrictions on the Parliamentary scrutiny of the activities of those organisations freed them from the detailed investigation of administration that ministerial departments always had to be prepared for. Experience did not seem to have borne out Morrison's prediction that by establishing a range of public corporations, Britain would 'get the best of both worlds' with a form of organisation which combined 'business management' and 'public accountability' (418 HC Deb. 5s. c. 969).

The Efficiency Unit explicitly cited the nationalised industries as examples of central government functions already carried out at arm's length from Ministers (1988, Annex A, para. 4) and drew attention to the fact that the Boards of Customs and Excise and of Inland Revenue were non-ministerial departments which had defined statutory responsibilities; and that the Property Service Agency, and the Defence Procurement Executive, and the National Health Service Management Board were agencies within departments; and that the Manpower Services Commission and the other main bodies in the employment group were non-departmental public bodies (*ibid.*, para. 5). The Efficiency Unit pointed out too that of the 76 Accounting Officers appointed by the Treasury, only 18 were Grade 1 Permanent Secretaries. So, 'the modification of accountability' that the Unit was proposing was not going to radically change relationships with the Public Accounts Committee (*ibid.*, para. 7). Further than this, as was currently the case, officials with operational responsibility would be liable to appear before other Select Committees of the House of Commons (*ibid.*, para. 8) and the powers of the Parliamentary Commissioner for Administration would continue to apply to agencies (*ibid.*, para. 9). The Efficiency Unit added:

> Quite apart from the issue of improving Civil Service management, there is a good case for trying to reduce the degree of ministerial overload that can arise from questions about operations, as distinct from policy. For example, Social Security Ministers receive about 15,000 letters a year from M.P.s, many of which are about individual cases. In the future, M.P.s could be asked to write about operational matters directly to the Chairman of the Board or the local office manager. Arrangements of this sort could be promulgated by a letter from the relevant Minister or the Leader of the House to all M.P.s. In the past the Chancellor of the Exchequer has written to all M.P.s asking them to refer questions about constituents' tax to local tax offices, and the Secretary of State for Social Services has written similarly about referring social security cases to D.H.S.S. local office managers. If an M.P. writes to an operational manager about matters which are essentially political, it is already normal practice for the manager to refer the letter to the Minister. (*ibid.*, para. 10)

Nevertheless, when the Labour MP John Garrett, in response to the Prime Minister's statement on the Ibbs Report, expressed the view that its proposals would 'inevitably lead to a lessening of ministerial accountability to this House because our constituency cases will be the responsibility of the heads of quangos – some private – rather than the responsibility of Ministers' (127 HC Deb. 6s. c. 1155), the disquiet expressed anticipated what was, understandably, a recurrent theme in the interchanges between the Conservative Government and the Treasury and Civil Service Committee as the reforms got under way.

'I am Central Department Project Manager', Peter Kemp informed the Treasury and Civil Service Committee during the first of a succession of inquiries on that body's part into the Next Steps programme (HC 494-II, 1987–8, evidence, q. 9), and he had 'a very small team – initially only three people – to help him'.

In addition to this Project Team, and the benefit of informal discussions with people from business and academic life and other professions, the Project Manager had the aid of two other groups:

> Closest at hand was the Project Executive, a small working group from the central departments – the Treasury, the Efficiency Unit, and the O.M.C.S. – which met weekly to think through some of the across the board issues as they came up, and to make sure that there was agreements about the way that progress was being made. The Project Manager also met informally each month with the Project Liaison Group composed of senior representatives from the main departments. Here, ideas could be exchanged before they were worked up into firm principles. This helped to involve departments in the process of developing Next Steps policy and to get endorsement of the Project Manager's ideas. The aim was to foster support for and a sense of purpose about Next Steps at senior level. (Goldsworthy, 1991, pp. 21–2)

'Although the Government was firmly committed to implementing Next Steps, the policy itself was not publicly set down anywhere in any detail', the official historian of the programme observed, adding: 'Indeed, Sir Robin Ibb's Report had described an idea, and sketched out – but no more – how it might be put into effect, so the policy had to be developed in the light of progress' (*ibid.*, p. 34). There was no lack of 'a sense of purpose' on the part of Peter Kemp. When asked by a member of the Treasury and Civil Service Committee in May 1988 what percentage of the Civil Service he expected would be in agencies in ten years' time, Kemp replied: 'I would be personally sorry if we did not get to at least three-quarters.' As the agencies only included '11 or 12 per cent so far' of the Service, Kemp recognised that realising his target meant that 'the very large battalions like the D.H.S.S., which has something like 90,000 people, come into the reckoning' (HC 494–II, 1987–8, evidence, q. 23). Kemp seemed to have clear ideas about where there was little scope for agencies. While 'the Foreign Office, like other departments, will be surveying their activities on that front', Kemp's view was that:

> It may very well be there are parts of the Foreign Service which would be inappropriate. I have just been to Stockholm talking to people who have a similar system to this and their residual Civil Service consists of about 2,000 people of which nearly half are the Foreign Office. The Swedish experience – and it goes back 300 years – seems to be that the approach has not proved successful in this area. I would not like to say that was the only area where it was unsuitable. (*ibid.*, q. 9)

In areas where Kemp thought agencies to be suitable he did not always find that his view was shared, at least at first. Nigel Lawson, the contemporary Chancellor of the Exchequer, later recalled that 'early on' he had 'volunteered three of my outlying departments, the Stationery Office (HMSO), the Royal Mint, and the Central Office of Information, as executive agencies', but that:

> I did not, however, support Kemp's desire to convert the Inland Revenue and the Customs and Excise into agencies. These politically sensitive departments, with a

small but important policy role, had long enjoyed a high degree of autonomy from political control so far as their executive functions were concerned, and converting them into agencies would have created no discernible advantage. Moreover, the only way in which it could have been achieved would have been to transfer their policy role to the Treasury, leaving them as purely tax collecting agencies. This was something to which the Chairmen of the two Revenue departments were implacably opposed, arguing with some plausibility that policy advice was improved if it was informed by practical experience on the ground. (Lawson, 1992, pp. 392–3)

Whatever the merits of such arguments, the Boards of Inland Revenue and of Customs and Excise were eventually drawn into the Next Steps programme, and, as early as June 1989, an official from the Board of Customs and Excise, A.W. Russell, made it clear to the Treasury and Civil Service Committee that, at least in its case, this was going to happen (HC 217, 1988–9, evidence, q. 116).

When appearing before that Committee in May 1989, Peter Kemp saw no reason to go back on his earlier 'guestimate' that three-quarters of the work of the Civil Service might eventually be carried out by executive agencies (HC 348, 1988–9, evidence, q. 5), even though the initial Next Steps target of sixteen agencies being set up by April 1989 had not been met. 'In fact about eight are now likely to be set up by July 1989', the Comptroller and Auditor General had commented in a report published on 6 June 1989 (HC 410, 1988–9, para. 58). When the Chairman of the Public Accounts Committee cited this observation, Peter Kemp, giving evidence the next day, replied:

The unpublished report, although obviously available to the National Audit Office, I made to the Prime Minister in July 1988 did suggest that we might have expected 16 to be set up. In fact only five were set up. We now have seven. We did one last month, the Resettlement Agency of the Department of Social Security, and only yesterday the Civil Service College was set up as an agency. I am hoping very much there will be one more: the QE II Centre will be set up before we get to the end of July. You are quite right that makes eight out of 16. (HC 420, 1988–9, evidence, q. 4016)

'We have not been able to go quite as fast as Peter Kemp had hoped', G.H. Phillips, the senior official at the Treasury with whom Kemp had most regular contact, said in evidence to the Treasury and Civil Service Committee, observing:

First of all, it is important when you are starting off a new enterprise – and here we agree completely with Peter Kemp – that you set yourself an ambitious target in order to get things moving, in the knowledge that you may not be able quite to meet it. Secondly, in the process of dealing with these first few agencies we have obviously come across a number of across-the-board issues which have needed to be settled in relation to these particular agencies but which might then have application across government. Therefore it has been right to take time over doing them.

In addition, 'in departments there has been a recognition that perhaps their timetables on some occasions were over-ambitious' (HC 348, 1988–9, evidence, q. 263). The Treasury and Civil Service Committee, displeased with progress in some areas, looked for 'an improvement in the pace at which executive agencies are created' (HC 348, 1988–9, para. 12).

'The Project Manager's judgement is that by next summer at least 20 agencies will have been established, with more to come', the Conservative Government stated in October 1989 in response to the Treasury and Civil Service Committee (Cm. 841, 1989, p. 3). 'There will be 30 agencies established by the end of next week', Richard Luce, a Minister of State involved, informed a Tory MP on 2 April 1990, adding that 'we expect more to be set up by the summer'(170 HC Deb. 6s. Written Answers c. 386). When it reported in July 1990, the Treasury and Civil Service Committee found that 'the situation this year is very different: 33 agencies have been established compared to eight a year ago' (HC 481, 1989–90, para. 8), and observed:

> Not only have more agencies been created: larger numbers of staff are now involved. The largest agency created in the first year of the programme was [the] H.M.S.O. with 3,250 staff. In the past few months the Employment Service (35,000) and the Land Registry (11,000) have been launched. The total number of staff now in agencies is about 80,000. (*ibid.*, para. 9)

The first Next Steps Review, published in October 1990, stated that 'there are now 34 agencies. . . . By next summer we expect that there will be around 50 agencies up and running covering 200,000 people' (Cm. 1261, 1990, p. 7). When Sir Peter Kemp, as he had become, gave evidence to the Treasury and Civil Service Committee once more on 24 June 1991, he informed them:

> We have got 50 agencies set up so far; in fact, we have got 51 and I commend to you the Social Security Agency in Northern Ireland which I was in Belfast this morning helping to launch . . . I hope . . . that at this time next year we can show you 20 more. That is our present estimate of what we are going to get to then. And there will be over half the Civil Service by then with (as we always say) more to come. (HC 496, 1990–1, evidence, q. 413)

As the second Next Steps Review, published in November 1991, made clear, the most important change that had taken place during the previous year had been the establishment of the Social Security Benefits Agency in April 1991, which had about 70,000 staff (Cm. 1760, 1991, p. 57). The Review also recorded that:

> Customs and Excise is moving towards full operation on Next Steps lines and since 1 April 1991 most of its work has been organized in 30 Executive Units. These include all 21 of the department's regional collections as well as the Investigation Division and a number of operational and service units formerly organized as headquarters divisions. About 95 per cent of the department's 27,500 staff work in Executive Units. (*ibid.*, p. 17)

Besides these Units, there were fifty-six Next Steps agencies, the Government stated in November 1991, in response to the Treasury and Civil Service Committee, and it noted that 'the Inland Revenue has published an action plan for moving towards full operation on these lines' (Cm. 1761, 1991, p. 1). The Valuation Officer of the Board of Inland Revenue had been launched as an agency on 30 September 1991, involving about 5,300 staff (Cm. 1760, 1991, p. 65). On 1 April 1992, thirty-four Executive Offices were established by the Inland Revenue and together with the Valuation Office Agency they accounted for about 96 per cent of the department's total staff of over 70,000 people (Cm. 2111, 1992, p. 44). In the third Next Steps review, published in December 1992, Richard Mottram, Sir Peter Kemp's successor as Project Manager, was able to record that:

> There are now 76 executive agencies, of which 20 have been launched in the last year together with 30 Customs and Excise Executive Units and 34 Inland Revenue Executive Offices working on Next Step lines. Between them, they employ just over 290,000 civil servants, or slightly more than half the total. (*ibid.*, p. 6)

In the fourth Next Steps Review, published in December 1993, it was stated that:

> Since the publication of the last Review . . . 16 new agencies have been launched. These include H.M. Prison Service, the third largest agency, whose Director General (Chief Executive) is responsible for managing a mix of directly managed and contracted out facilities, and the Child Support Agency and the Northern Ireland Child Support Agency [which were] the first official bodies to be established, from the outset, as agencies.

The Review recorded that

> There are currently 92 agencies. Together with the 31 Executive Units of H.M. Customs and Excise and the 33 Executive Offices of the Inland Revenue, working fully on Next Step lines, they employ 60 per cent of the Civil Service. (Cm. 2430, 1993, p. 6)

That the figures for the Inland Revenue and the Customs and Excise differed from before was explained by reorganisation. In the latter case, for instance, a Management and Consultancy Services Unit had been launched in July 1993 (*ibid.*, p. 33). The Review stated:

> Our aim has been to identify by the end of 1993 the principal areas of Home Civil Service activity which are potential candidates for agency status, and to ensure that most of those that are to become agencies should be up and running by mid-1995. (In Northern Ireland, because the Next Steps programme started later, the respective dates are end-1994 and mid-1996.) . . . Agencies and announced candidates for agency status in the Home Civil Service . . . represent 78 per cent of the total (*ibid.*, p. 10)

That 'most of the Chief Executives are still drawn from the Civil Service' was a further reason why Nigel Lawson had been sceptical about the Next Steps programme (Lawson, 1992, p. 393), and he had got his facts right. As the fourth Next Steps Review observed at the end of 1993:

> Chief Executives are normally appointed through open competition to get the best person – whether a civil servant or an outside appointee for the job. Of the 98 Chief Executive and Chief Executive-designate appointments made so far, 65 have been recruited via open competition. Of those, 35 have come from outside the Civil Service, from a wide variety of backgrounds including the private sector, local government, the National Health Service, and the academic world. (Cm. 2430, 1993, p. 8)

The Treasury and Civil Service Committee had stated early on that:

> If one of the objects of the Next Steps programme is to develop managerial talent within the Civil Service, we would expect a considerable proportion of future senior appointments to come from within the Civil Service, but to be appointed as a result of open competition. (HC 348, 1988–9, para. 29)

The Government did not agree about open competition always being resorted to, although it emphasised that 'the rules on propriety governing Civil Service appointments will be fully observed in agency appointments' (Cm. 841, 1989, p. 17). When the Committee repeated its opinion on open competition (HC 481, 1989–90, para. 28), the Government took the same line (Cm. 1263, 1990, p. 7), which was, as the Economic Secretary to the Treasury expressed it in a Parliamentary Answer in May 1990, that:

> The first priority in selecting Chief Executives and other key staff for agencies must be to get the right person for the job. . . . Open competition will be considered in every case as a potential means of attracting talented people from inside and outside the Service.

The Minister added that 'pay is usually based on normal Civil Service arrangements but more is offered if this is necessary to secure the right person' (173, HC Deb. 6s. Written Answers c. 192). The Treasury and Civil Service Committee was told in 1990 that 'the Chief Executive's job at the Social Security Benefits Agency carries a salary about half the going rate in a private financial institution with a network of high street outlets' (HC 481, 1989–90, para. 29). The Chief Secretary of the Treasury at the time, Norman Lamont, thought that 'the implication of creating Next Steps agencies is that some of these things will have to be looked at afresh', and recognised that recruiting from the private sector on the basis of higher pay might well have repercussions in the rest of the Civil Service (*ibid.*, evidence, q. 232). Chief Executives were appointed on the basis of fixed-term contracts, which were not the same in each case, and Peter Kemp emphasised that if major mistakes were committed by them the reaction should be their dismissal, 'to fire the people in charge' (*ibid.*, q. 162). Kemp saw Chief Executives and other key people in agencies as being appointed to particular jobs as such (*ibid.*, p. 85) adding that:

> These will be people with grades, because we are that sort of animal. There must be bench marks for pay and that sort of thing, but they are still not in the hierarchical

situation as they might previously have been. These are very special jobs and responsibilities delegated by the Minister personally . . . they will be individually graded posts, but they will be rather more loosely graded. (*ibid.*, q. 175)

'A key feature of Next Steps is the personal accountability of Chief Executives to their Ministers for the discharge of their responsibilities as set out in an agency's framework document and for the achievement of performance targets', the Treasury stated in 1989, adding that 'Chief Executives' authority is delegated to them by Ministers who are and will remain accountable to Parliament and its Select Committees' (Cm. 914, 1989, para. 5.3). The Treasury continued:

> The Government therefore believes that the general rule must continue to be that civil servants who give evidence to Select Committees do so on behalf of their Ministers. In practice, where a Committee's interest is focused on the day-to-day operations of an agency, Ministers will normally regard the Chief Executive as best placed to answer on their behalf. The Chief Executive will be able to inform the Committee how his agency has performed its responsibilities. Ministers themselves will remain fully accountable for all Government policies. Agency Chief Executives will in addition be appointed Accounting Officers or Agency Accounting Officers. . . . Where the agency has its own vote, the Treasury will appoint the Chief Executive as Accounting Officer under existing procedures . . . the Government has also accepted that where an agency does not have its own vote and is financed by one or more vote sub-heads the departmental Accounting Officer will designate the Chief Executive as Agency Accounting Officer. . . . Similarly, where an agency is a trading fund, the 1973 Act requires the Treasury to appoint an Accounting Officer and the policy will be to appoint the Chief Executive. (*ibid.*, paras 5.4–5.5)

Framework documents were reviewed at three-year intervals and more frequently if policy or other changes required it (Goldsworthy, 1991, p. 27). The Treasury's view in 1989 was that:

> The framework document for each agency is a new and key element in the accountability process. Objectives for units of Civil Service work have existed since the Financial Management Initiative, but they have usually been for internal management purposes. Framework documents, which are normally made available to Parliament and published more widely, set out explicitly for each agency its aims and objective, and the boundaries between policy and service delivery functions. They also describe the monitoring, accountability and reporting patterns between the agency and the parent department, the financial and the personnel management flexibilities that the agency will have, and the Accounting Officer status of the Chief Executive. They are essential to Next Steps, in that they publicly set out the respective roles of Ministers (and their supporting officials) in policy and strategic management and those of agencies in execution and delivery. They define clearly the tools that each will have and the measures for assessing agency performance; and they make transparent the resulting accountabilities within Government and to Parliament. (Cm. 914, 1989, para. 5.8)

Accountability in the form of Parliamentary questions about the activities of executive agencies proved to be matter for controversy which only began to be settled after the House of Commons Select Committee on Procedure, reporting in May 1991, recommended that 'in future replies from agency Chief Executive in response to Parliamentary questions referred to them by Ministers should appear in the Official Report' (HC 178, 1990–1, para. 125). The Treasury and Civil Service Committee supported this recommendation (HC 496, 1990–1, para. 82), but the Government responded with a holding answer (Cm. 1761, 1991, p. 11), and seemed to think in terms of a separate publication which would contain Chief Executives' replies to questions on operational matters (199 HC Deb. 6s. Written Answers c. 552). The Administration Committee of the House of Commons resolved that 'letters sent to Members by agency Chief Executives in response to Parliamentary questions should be printed among the written answers in the daily Official Report, beneath a standard form of reply given by the Minister with responsibility' (211 HC Deb. 6s. Written Answers c. 941) and the Government concurred three months later (212 HC Deb. 6s. Written Answers c. 286–8).

Though there were plenty of people who believed that the Next Steps initiative would falter, neither the Thatcher nor the Major Governments proved prepared to let this happen, and, in September 1990, the Prime Minister's Adviser on Efficiency, Sir Angus Fraser, the successor to Sir Robin Ibbs, and the Efficiency Unit were asked to lead a study:

> to investigate, in the context of the development of the Next Steps programme, the relationships between individual departments and their agencies, taking account of the responsibilities of the central departments [and] to consider how departments ought to adapt their structure, size and methods of working and to make recommendations. (Efficiency Unit, 1991, p. 29)

The Fraser Report, *Making the Most of Next Steps*, was published in May 1991, and it identified three areas in which more progress could be made. The first was in 'getting the context right' (*ibid.*, p. 2), and the Fraser Report recommended that:

> Departments and agencies must develop and maintain a clear and shared vision of what an agency is there to do and of what its priorities and objectives should be. This is particularly important at the three year review. The Project Manager should continue to monitor progress on these issues in his reports to the Prime Minister. (*ibid.*, p. 3)

The Report also stated:

> We would expect departments and agencies to give a high priority to improving target setting. The aim should be for each agency to have a handful of robust and meaningful top level output targets which measure financial performance, efficiency and quality of customer service, over and above whatever subsidiary performance indicators are required for the agency's internal management purposes. (*ibid.*, p. 3)

Further:

> There should be a firm timetable agreed between the agency, the department and
> the Treasury for ensuring that all agencies have, by the time of the three year
> review of their framework document, financial regimes suited to their business
> needs, including the associated accounting and financial management systems.
> The Project Manager should continue to monitor progress on these issues in his
> reports to the Prime Minister. (*ibid.*, p. 4)

The second area that the Fraser Report saw as one in which progress was
needed was in 'empowering the Chief Executive' (*ibid.*, p. 2) and it was recommended that:

> The objective should be to move to a position where agency framework docu-
> ments establish that, with the overall disciplines of the cash limits and targets set,
> managers are free to make their own decisions on the management of staff and
> resources except for any specifically reserved areas. The exclusion of any area
> from the Chief Executive's authority should be positively justified. In order to
> achieve further progress in delegation, a first objective should be to revise frame-
> work documents on these lines at the first three year review of each agency. This
> does not rule out an earlier review if the Chief Executive or sponsor department
> considers it timely. The Order in Council should be amended at the earliest
> opportunity to permit such delegation (*ibid.*, p. 5)

The Report also stated:

> Open competition should continue to be the conventional route for filling Chief
> Executive posts. Departments should develop for all Chief Executives, including
> those from inside the Service, schemes for remuneration which offer significant
> rewards for achieving results and clear and effective penalties for failure. (*ibid.*,
> pp. 5–6)

Further:

> All departments should examine the full range of internal services they provide
> (including consultancy, inspection and review services) and, in the context of
> their next annual plan, set out a timetable for moving to the provision and
> procurement of as many of them as practicable on a full cost basis. This would
> leave Chief Executives – and where appropriate budget holders within the depart-
> ment – free to decide where they can obtain best value for money. Where they
> continue to use H.Q. resources or expertise whether or not on a charging basis,
> costs and quality of service should be clearly specified. It would be primarily for
> the Treasury to monitor progress in this area in its discussions with departments
> on their plans. (*ibid.*, p. 6)

The third area in which the authors of the Fraser Report believed progress
needed to be made was in 'reappraising the role, organization and size of
departments' (*ibid.*, p. 2), observing:

> As the Next Steps initiative develops, departments should formulate a clear state-
> ment of their evolving role and the part their agencies play in the delivery of their

policy objectives. The statement of the agency's strategic purpose can then be expressed in the context of the department's aims and objectives and become part of a shared vision. (*ibid.*, p. 7)

The Report also stated:

Departments should consider how best they can support Ministers in their roles in relation to agencies and identify a focal point at senior level for their dealings with each agency. The arrangements adopted should be clearly set out in the framework document and their effectiveness evaluated as part of the three year review of the framework document. . . . The Accounting Officer Memorandum . . . should be amended to clarify the respective Accounting Officer responsibilities of Chief Executives and Permanent Secretaries. (*ibid.*, pp. 7–8)

Further:

Departments should agree with [the] Treasury a timetable for establishing target staffing levels, preceded, as necessary, by a detailed review of their headquarters functions, which needs to include the relevant posts in the Senior Open Structure. These reviews should be informed by wider advice from within the Service, including the Next Steps Project Manager, and by calling on experience from the private sector and other parts of the public sector. (*ibid.*, p. 9)

The Fraser Report said of the role and organisation of the central departments:

As the initial work demanded by the establishment of agencies declines, the central departments should review their changing roles in the light of the Next Steps and set new staffing levels for these functions. It will be even more important than in the past that the criteria for selecting people to staff these functions should include experience of working in other parts of government, including agencies directly concerned with the provision of services. (*ibid.*, p. 9)

It was the central departments, by that time the Treasury and the Office of Public Service and Science, that commissioned a study by a French official, Sylvie Trosa, to evaluate progress in implementing the Fraser Report, and this was circulated in February 1994, the same month which marked the sixth anniversary of the launching of the Next Steps initiative. The Trosa Report recognised that the Fraser inquiry had concluded that 'there was a need to make certain changes to the current arrangements' affecting the relationship between departments and agencies, notably 'avoiding day-to-day interference in management issues; defining a clear role for the centres of departments; enabling mobility of staff between the agencies and the departments; and planning the evolution of the human resources of the departments'. The Trosa Report observed:

Those recommendations are as relevant now as they were when the (Fraser) Report was issued. That raises the question of why very little progress has been made on these issues since the Report was published. Several hypotheses might be made but what seems clear is that one of the major reasons that relatively little has happened is that departments have not felt that it was in their interests to implement the changes. Given that part of the Fraser recommendations was for a 25 per cent reduction in departmental staff dealing with central functions, perhaps this is not too surprising. (Trosa Report, 1994, p. 72)

The Trosa Report found that the concept of the Fraser Figure, 'the focal point at senior level' within the department 'dealing with each agency' as the Fraser Report had put it, did not seem to be working well. This was:

mainly because the proper balance between representing the view of both the department and the agency has not been achieved . . . nor have most Fraser Figures been able to devote enough time to following the activity of the agency. Therefore, the Fraser Figure should be a very senior figure who will be respected by the department and agency. It would also be helpful if he had a small team helping him; this team should avoid any overlapping and also be independent from the policy divisions of the department to avoid any conflicts of interests, thereby being more free to promote the Next Steps process.

The Trosa Report saw a Ministerial Advisory Board as being 'the principal tool for advising' the Fraser Figure, who had 'a role which cannot be assumed by any other layer of management'. The Trosa Report observed:

There exists a considerable cultural gap on both sides with Chief Executives often believing that departments' management is a bureaucratic obstacle, and departments viewing agencies as little fortresses following their own aims regardless. Both viewpoints can be true. Too often senior managers in a department have no experience in man management. The fact is that many agencies buy fewer services from the centre and are more concerned with creating closer relationships with their clients. In that case, if a department does not make a special effort (such as an effective Advisory Board) to keep a certain unity, the divergence between agencies and parent departments can only grow. (*ibid.*, p. 6)

The Trosa Report's view was that:

Agencies are a compromise; they are semi-autonomous bodies within a department. As long as they are part of a department, it will be difficult to make a success of Next Steps (which means that everybody shares the values of output oriented activities, a more customer related attitude, greater responsibility and accountability) without extending the values of Next Steps to the whole department by: more interchange of staff through mobility (still minimal), common training, networking etc., and the extension of Next Steps principles to the remaining parts of a department (probably fewer financial targets but more quality and improvement targets). Otherwise the fact of having two categories of staff (Ibbs Report) and two completely different ways of working can only create resistance and inertia (to go back to Trevelyan, the intellectual and the executive functions will remain separate). (*ibid.*, p. 7)

Though the Trosa Report wrote in terms of 'the new role for central departments' and indicated what it should be (*ibid.*, pp. 69–70), the form that this would take depended on the future shape of the Civil Service. As the Report stated:

What will remain a common currency within the Civil Service? Financial, management and personnel rules will become more and more different; the only element of unity which will be left, besides ethical standards, will be the uniform tag of being a civil servant. (*ibid.*, p. 7)

IV MARKET TESTING, CONTRACTING OUT AND 'THE END OF THE NATIONAL CIVIL SERVICE'?

The Conservative Government's priorities in relation to the Civil Service were exemplified by the various stages by which the Next Steps agencies were established. The official historian later wrote of the process:

It is necessary, first, to take a fundamental look at the work in question and to decide whether it needs to be done at all. If not, it can be abolished. If the work is to continue, Ministers must decide whether it could be better done in the private sector or, if it is to remain in government, whether it would be carried out by a private firm under contract. If Ministers decide that none of these alternatives is suitable, and that the function must remain a government service, agency status is considered. There are no absolute rules about this. (Goldsworthy, 1991, pp. 22, 25)

There was a clear ordering of preferences, though, and, in October 1988, Margaret Thatcher as Prime Minister was to emphasise about the Next Steps programme that 'I cannot rule out . . . that after a period of years, agencies, like other government activities, may be suitable for privatization' (139 HC Deb. 6s. Written Answers c. 14). This statement recalled Mrs Thatcher's earlier observations about commercial services being transferred from the Civil Service to the private sector, and the Property Services Agency and Crown Suppliers Act of 1990 was an example of the pursuit of this policy. While such legislation did not directly threaten the interests of the main body of the non-industrial Civil Service, the Mueller Report allied to the Next Steps Report did have that prospective effect. A change of Prime Minister encouraged the Council of Civil Service Unions to anticipate that 'the end of the winter may be in sight' (*CSSU Bulletin*, February 1991, p. 17), but Mrs Thatcher's replacement by John Major in November 1990 did not diminish the Conservative Government's commitment to promoting change in the Civil Service. As we have seen, there was no slowing in the pace of the implementation of the Next Steps programme. Any expectation that the Higher Civil Service would escape unscathed into Next Steps-style policy Ministries was not to be borne out. The Radical Right was still hunting the Higher Civil Service as well as showing little sign of leaving the broad mass of civil servants in peace, and *The Citizen's Charter* of 1991 provided early evidence that this outlook was present in the Major Government.

'We believe that the process of buying public services from private contractors is still only in its infancy', *The Citizen's Charter* stated, adding: 'We propose to move the process decisively forward. There are great potential benefits to be had, both in improved quality and lower costs.' It was the Government's intention to 'remove remaining obstacles to successful contracting out' and to 'subject much more work each year to market testing than has ever been the case before' (Cm. 1599, 1991, p. 33). This was a clear threat to the maintenance of Civil Service numbers, pay levels and conditions, which was made even more evident when the promised follow-up White Paper, *Competing for Quality*, was published by the Treasury in November 1991, for it stated that:

> Market testing so far has been largely concentrated on traditional support services. The Government wishes to build on this by opening up to competition new areas, closer to the heart of government. Departments, executive agencies and non-departmental public bodies need to test the scope for a greater private sector contribution to the delivery of, for example, clerical and executive operations, specialist and professional skills, and a wide range of facilities and management approaches. (Cm. 1730, 1991, p. 12)

The Government wanted to give 'a new impetus' to market testing and to the contracting-out of function, and in future, departments and executive agencies were to have targets by which to measure progress in these areas. The targets were to be identified with the help of private sector advisers, and a continuing programme was envisaged which would be subject to central monitoring (*ibid*., pp. 8–9). The procedures for market-testing existing services were to be speeded up. After what it called 'a decade of efficiency reform', the Government believed that the existing practice of allowing time for the in-house operation to obtain maximum efficiency before competitive tendering could begin should be discontinued (*ibid*., p. 11). The Government anticipated that 'departments which achieve savings through market testing and contracting out' would be able to apply these savings for 'the benefit of their programmes'. It also recognised that:

> For competition to be possible, managers need to know the full cost of providing services in-house. Often overhead costs fall on central budgets and appear free to the user. . . . Where a manager's budget is fully charged for all the goods and services used, the incentive to increase efficiency is maximised for costs and savings directly affect the budget. Increasingly, services provided by one department to another are being charged for. The Government is also encouraging charging for services supplied within departments. (*ibid*., pp. 9–10)

To remove any disincentive to contracting out associated with the rights of civil servants to redundancy compensation after being transferred to the private sector, under the provisions of the Transfer of Undertakings (Protection of Employment) Regulations 1981, the Government promised legislation (*ibid*., p. 12), and the relevant change was part of the Trade Union Reform and Employment Rights Act of 1993.

'Competing for our own jobs?' was how the National Union of Civil and Public Servants greeted the White Paper, *Competing for Quality* (*Opinion*,

December 1991, p. 6), and the Council of Civil Service Unions interpeted the underlying policy as one which was 'determined to push the notion of competitive tendering to the limit in the Civil Service . . . the list of areas to be examined excludes virtually nothing – except perhaps the security services' (*CCSU Bulletin*, January 1992, p. 1). *Jobs for Sale* was the sub-title of a critical pamphlet that the CCSU published on the subject in 1992, which observed:

> The speed of this tendering drive is alarming . . . with little regard for the procedures for hiring consultants at huge costs to the taxpayer, and with no apparent safeguards against conflicts of interest. Private sector consultants invariably have clients with a keen interest in Civil Service work. Despite the rhetoric of the Citizen's Charter the Government emphasis is on cutting costs, rather than improving services. The hype of 'value of money' is a smokescreen for cuts. The Government concentrates on efficiency at the expense of effectiveness. They have shown no interest in any clear quality based criteria for market testing, preferring to concentrate on encouraging private sector involvement in setting both the Governent's agenda and its timetable. (CCSU, 1992, p. 3)

When *The Government's Guide to Market Testing* was published in 1993 (Efficiency Unit, 1993b), the CCSU soon responded with the line that 'the issue of full and proper consultation with the trade unions should be prioritized in the guidance' (CCSU, 1993, p. 1). Quality of service was not necessarily the Conservative Government's main consideration either. 'Competition does not mean invariably choosing the cheapest service', Francis Maude, the Financial Secretary to the Treasury, told the House of Commons in 1991, but the attraction was that 'market testing has typically cut the cost of providing services in central government by no less than 25 per cent' (199 HC Deb. 6s. c. 25). The second annual report on *The Citizen's Charter* recorded 'a step change in central government's market testing activity'. By the end of 1993, 389 individual market tests had been completed, and 'in most individual cases where comparisons are possible savings of over 25 per cent have been made' and 'the overall average saving' was 'over 22 per cent'. In-house teams had won 68 per cent of the work when they had been allowed to compete, which was not always because '113 activities were contracted out as a result of a strategic decision to employ an outside employer' (Cm. 2540, 1994, p. 93). The potential for market testing was further assisted by provisions in the Deregulation and Contracting Out Act of 1994, under which the principle established in *Carltona Ltd* v. *Commissioners of Works and Others* (1943, 2 All E.R., 560–4) that functions assigned to Ministers could be exercised by civil servants on the Ministers' behalf was prospectively extended to private contractors. Only the European authorities, though, could modify or replace the Acquired Rights Directive of 1977, to which the TUPE regulations of 1981, cited earlier, related. As the First Division Association suggested, it really was a matter of 'TUPE or not TUPE?' as far as contracting out was concerned (*FDA News*, February 1993, p. 1) because, under its provisions, those transferred out from the Civil Service had to be given comparable terms and conditions of service.

Meanwhile, the Conservative Government had continued to make changes in the Civil Service's pay arrangements. Long-term pay agreements displaying substantial levels of conformity over wide areas of the Service always did cohere uneasily with the Conservative Government's preference for the application of the principles of private business practice, and it was unsurprising that *The Citizen's Charter* emphasised that in future 'a larger proportion of pay would be linked to performance' and that 'we will encourage the drive towards greater delegation and flexibility in the Civil Service' (Cm. 1599, 1991, p. 35). The then Chancellor of the Exchequer, Norman Lamont, developed these themes in a statement on 24 July 1991 which indicated that the Civil Service pay arrangements needed to be renegotiated. The Chancellor proposed to introduce what he called

> three new elements into Civil Service pay structures. The first is to put in place a range of forms of performance related pay in order to achieve a closer link between performance and reward both for individuals and for groups of staff. This will be an important means of securing the objective of improving the quality of public services, which is at the heart of the Citizen's Charter Programme. Over time, performance will come to determine a larger portion of the pay bill without performance pay becoming a disguised way of providing unacceptably high increases in the pay bill. The second is further to enable responsibility for pay bargaining to be delegated to Civil Service departments or agencies, to allow them wider discretion in relation to their pay and grading regimes. Alternative pay and grading structures will be approved where they are expected to produce value for money benefits greater than through centrally controlled negotiation. The third is to give an option to those departments and agencies for which such extensive discretion is not appropriate to negotiate for themselves flexibilities of their own within the total of the overall central pay settlement agreed by the Treasury. (195 HC Deb. 6s. Written Answers c. 604–5)

The phrase in the Chancellor's statement that the Government was concerned 'to secure the confidence of the staff that their pay will be determined fairly' (*ibid.*, c. 605) recalled sentiments that were commonly a feature of the fifth clause of the various pay agreements negotiated since 1987. Notice of the Government's withdrawal from these pay agreements was to be accompanied in early 1992 by its further withdrawal from the agreement that dated back to 1925 which provided for arbitration in Civil Service pay and related matters. The Council of Civil Service Unions observed:

> Arbitration has been available in the Civil Service since Whitleyism was introduced in 1919, and the current agreement formalised these arrangements 66 years ago. Since then it has been endorsed by successive Governments of all political persuasions. It has served both the Civil Service and the country very well indeed, avoiding innumerable serious conflicts and providing the background to a fair and stable industrial relations regime. Over 500 cases have been dealt with by the Civil Service Arbitration Tribunal, some, like the 1962 and 1982 central pay claims, involving the pay of the entire Civil Service. In recent years, however, the present

Government, concerned only to ensure that its perception of what should happen must prevail, has refused access to arbitration on a number of occasions – most recently on the Council's 1991 London weighting claim. The agreement, which provides for unilateral access to arbitration, has been subverted by the device of the Secretary of State for Employment, who is the custodian of the agreement, refusing to carry out his obligations. No doubt the Government is fearful of a legal challenge, so it has followed on earlier precedent and has simply copped out of the agreement. Shades of 1981. (CCSU Bulletin, February 1992, p. 17)

A new Civil Service Arbitration Agreement was promulgated in October 1992 which 'does not provide for unilateral access to arbitration, as did the old one' (CCSU Bulletin, October/November 1992, pp. 148–9).

By the time that the first annual report on The Citizen's Charter was published in November 1992, its authors were able to record that 'new performance pay schemes have been put in place for half a million civil servants. These provide for an individual's pay to reflect his or her performance against objectives set each year' (Cm. 2101, 1992, p. 67). The headines in a pay bulletin which the Institution of Professionals, Managers and Specialists issued in July 1992 summed up the negotiations and some of their outcomes: 'Tough times, hard facts' – 'Pay revolution hits grades 5–7 hardest' – 'Performance pay shakes system'. The pay proposals for Grades 5, 6 and 7 were:

> dramatic evidence of the Government's ambitions for performance related pay. The scale max and all centrally determined spine points disappear to be replaced by a pay range. Between the min and the max of the range departments will be allowed to pay staff on intermediate points, negotiated with their trade union side. Range quotas and restraints are abolished.

As the document, New Pay Arrangements for Grades 5, 6 and 7, dated September 1992, stated, 'all increases will be performance related' (Treasury, 1992a). A similar statement was made in the Agreement on the Pay, Pay System, Organization and Personnel Management Arrangements for Grades and Groups represented by the Institution of Professionals, Managers and Specialists, dated October 1992 (Treasury, 1992b), and the New Pay Arrangements for Executive, Office Support and Related Grades (Treasury, 1992c) and New Pay Arrangements for Clerical and Secretarial Grades (Treasury, 1992d) took broadly the same form. What had survived all the various changes in pay arrangements was provision for levels surveys conducted every four years of the interquartile range of pay and conditions of relevant jobs outside the public sector. Although such surveys only informed rather than constrained negotiations, naturally enough they tended to be seen by the unions as a very important component of the pay determination system. Of course, Civil Service pay arrangements of whatever form necessarily had to be subject to considerations of wider economic policy, and in November 1992, the then Chancellor of the Exchequer announced that 'in the coming year pay settlements in the public sector should be restricted to a maximum of 1.5 per cent

. . . without exception, regardless of whether pay is negotiated, recommended by review bodies or subject to formula calculations' (213 HC Deb. 6s. c. 996). The IPMS commented:

> On November 12, Chancellor Norman Lamont turned the fastest U-turn yet by the Government. He suspended the Civil Service pay agreements along with the pay review systems of all five million public service workers. In the process he dishonoured the new I.P.M.S. Payspans agreement that the Treasury had signed 35 days before. (*IPMS Bulletin*, 11/92, p. 1)

Understandably, there were similar protests from the other unions. It was not strictly true that the new pay agreements had been suspended. Only the pay determination provisions were suspended until the end of the pay restraint period, in accordance with provisions contained in the agreements enabling the Government to take this course where necessary to safeguard the public purse or for reasons of public policy. The pay agreements themselves remained in place.

These developments were overshadowed by the Civil Service (Mangement Functions) Act of 1992, which made important changes in the relationship between the centre and departments and agencies. The Chancellor of the Duchy of Lancaster, William Waldegrave, stated:

> In the present organization . . . the Treasury is given the responsibility for determining pay, grading, expenses, allowances, holidays, hours of work, and other related personnel matters. The Minister for the Civil Service regulates the conduct of civil servants and those other conditions of service which are *not* allotted to the Treasury. . . . As things stand . . . the Treasury and the Prime Minister cannot lawfully delegate those functions to the departments and agencies; they cannot be delegated to another Minister – the relevant Secretary of State, for example – let alone to agencies which are responsible for the day-to-day management of the staff that they employ. Whether it is sensible or not – I do not think that it can be – decisions affecting the working conditions of all 560,000 or so civil servants must conform to rules laid down by the two central departments, and those rules, like the laws of the Medes and Persians, must then be obeyed. (213 HC Deb. 6s. c. 458)

These arrangements were now 'wholly inappropriate', Waldegrave argued, constituting as they did 'an immensely complicated system of hurdles set up when the Treasury was, in effect, the personnel department of a small Civil Service'. The Conservative Government wanted 'to introduce . . . more variegated styles of employment in our great Public Service', the Minister added (*ibid.*, c. 463), and the 1992 legislation was designed to facilitate the delegation of Civil Service personnel management functions previously exercised from the centre down to departments and agencies (*ibid.*, c. 406–1). Such functions were to be 'progressively devolved' (*ibid.*, c. 464).

By April 1994, all agencies employing 2,000 or more staff were required to be ready to implement their own pay and grading structures, and, well in advance of this deadline, the Civil Service unions recognised one implication of this. John Ellis wrote:

The Inland Revenue has always had its own grading structure, but pay rates were negotiated with the Treasury. Now it negotiates its own pay structures and as from 1 April 1993 has been considered independent from the Treasury. At a recent meeting with Treasury officials to discuss London weighting, when an attempt was made by the General Secretary [of the Inland Revenue Staff Federation] to deal with a particular problem in the Inland Revenue, it evoked the response: 'we do not negotiate on Inland Revenue issues any more' and 'we will not be drawn on matters concerning [the] Inland Revenue'. The message could not be clearer: once delegation has taken place there will be little redress available from the Treasury for unions at national level. (*CCSU Bulletin*, May 1993, p. 227)

Besides the Board of Inland Revenue, the Board of Customs and Excise, and the Health and Safety Executive, twenty-one agencies were destined to become fully delegated areas for pay determination purposes, leading Ellis to observe:

Together these organizations account for around 307,000 employees, i.e. about 88 per cent of staff employed in agencies and well over half of all staff employed in the Civil Service. This means that these staff are now outside the national pay determination agreements with the national Civil Service unions.

'Slowly but surely these policies will cause chaos to develop throughout the Civil Service because of the multiplicity of grading structures and different rates of pay that are bound to emerge', Ellis predicted (*CCSU Bulletin*, March 1994, p. 42); and when, with effect from October 1994, a Recruitment and Retention Allowance replaced, among other things, Local Pay Additions and London weighting as part of Civil Service pay, naturally enough this only applied to that part of the Civil Service still subject to the Treasury (*CCSU Bulletin*, May/June 1994, p. 65). The Civil Service Management Code, issued in January 1994, did contain requirements that departments, in drawing up their staff handbooks, should observe the central departments' rules and principles (*CCSU Bulletin*, January 1994, p. 4), but the uniformities of the kind that had characterised the Civil Service Pay and Conditions of Service Code that it had replaced could not be replicated in the same way. The Civil Service (Management Functions) legislation of 1992 was not just 'a technical Bill of restricted scope' as it was presented as being to the House of Commons (213 HC Deb. 6s. c. 451). The Fultonite, John Garrett, recognised its potential at the time, observing:

The big change embodied in the Bill is the end of the national Civil Service. That is the point of the Bill: agency employees – at present, civil servants – will be subject to terms and conditions, employment regulations, recruitment and training policies and rights peculiar to the agency concerned. Instead of having a national Civil Service, we shall have a conglomerate of agencies, all with different terms and conditions. (*ibid.*, c. 463)

Within the Civil Service, meanwhile, the Mueller Report, a radical initiative in its own right, was being implemented. 'The standard pattern of working' was being increasingly displaced by a much wider 'range and diversity of working arrangements', the Earl of Caithness, the then Paymaster General, wrote in the foreword to a Treasury publication in 1990, adding: 'Part time working, for example, has grown tremendously over the last few years' (Treasury, 1990, p. 1). The Treasury later reported:

> Between 1984 and 1992 the number of non-industrial part timers has increased from 16,029 to 43,590. Nearly 16 per cent (41,213) of all women non-industrial staff now work part time. Whilst the proportion of men working part time is still low – 0.9 per cent – the number working part time has risen from 954 in 1984 to 2,377 in 1992. (*Civil Service Statistics 1992*, p. 14)

As at April 1992, of the 368,045 staff in all departments (excluding agencies) 7 per cent were part-timers and 2 per cent were casuals, and in the agencies the figures were 11 per cent and 5 per cent respectively (Treasury and OPSS, 1993, Annex X). It remained the case, of course, that 'most of us continue to work on permanent 41/42 hour contracts' as the central departments observed of civil servants in a contemporary internal document (*ibid*., section 6), and it was an unsurprising finding of this study that 'full time permanent employment was easier to manage' (*ibid*., section 8).

The various structural changes within central government since 1988 and the possible fragmentation of the Higher Civil Service that might result led Sir Robin Butler, the Head of the Home Civil Service, and Sir Peter Levene, the Prime Minister's Adviser on Efficiency and Effectiveness, to commission a special study in July 1992 to study future personnel arrangements at that level. The result was the Oughton Report, published in November 1993, John Oughton being the head of the Efficiency Unit. The supporting team included not only higher civil servants but also personnel drawn from the private sector. The report was commissioned 'to consider the policies and practices for ensuring the adequate supply of suitably qualified people to fill senior posts in departmental headquarters, agencies and executives, whether from internal sources or after open competition'. The study examined 'current arrangements in departments for identifying and developing those with potential, for appointing to top posts, and the tenure under which staff are currently employed' (Efficiency Unit, 1993a, p. 1). The report recommended that 'the key principles of recruitment through fair and open competition, promotion through merit, the emphasis on integrity, objectivity and impartiality, and non-politicization as the foundation for a permanent Civil Service continue to remain valid and should be preserved' (*ibid*., p. 7). Quite how anybody could reasonably dissent would be a mystery had not the Report noted an observation by a Permanent Secretary that 'we often need to create order out of chaos – indeed that is often what effective public adminstration is' (*ibid*., p. 15). After all, it had been the style of the Higher Civil Service that had offended the Thatcher Government, and when one Grade 2 official told the study team that 'the drive should be to find people who can show added value, not ask clever questions' (*ibid*., p. 22) he or she hit the nail on the head. A similar official insisted that 'even for high policy, you need to know the trade' (*ibid.*, p. 27), and a group of Grade 3 staff observed that 'Grade 1s and 2s need to be persuaded to leave their rooms. They see themselves as top policy advisers to Ministers, not managers' (*ibid.*, p. 24). The study team concluded that 'there should be more explicit criteria for the selection appraisal, development and promotion of staff at Grades 3 and above, and the Cabinet Office should ensure that these are built effectively into the relevant processes over the next year' (*ibid.*, p. 29). A private sector director told the team that 'the biggest weakness of the Civil Service was in the fact that people tend to stay in a particular job for only a relatively short period of time before being moved to another post' (*ibid.*, p. 49), a view confirmed by a Permanent Secretary who observed that 'the current caricature of a successful career is to get yourself whizzed around as many posts as possible, rubbing shoulders with very senior people. In reality, people need at least a couple of specialisms' (*ibid.*, p. 50). An agency Chief Executive thought that 'high flyers should be identified on the basis of their achievements (as they come through the organization), not a specially watered flower bed' (*ibid.*, p. 31). Much the same was being said at and around the time of the Fulton Report. The study team drew up an action list to remedy matters, notably that 'the Treasury and the First Civil Service Commissioner should jointly arrange for a further review of the recruitment arrangements for the fast stream entry, to report with recommendations in 1994.' Further, 'each department should establish a process for identifying within the next two years a specific scheme to provide opportunities for staff with high potential on fast stream and management development programmes to gain extended first hand experience of front line service delivery' (*ibid.*, p. 66). Additionally, 'departments should introduce career anchors under which staff by Grade 5 level at the latest would nominate one or two functions or areas of work to which they would expect to return in the course of their careers' (*ibid.*, p. 67). As for the terms of employent, a private sector personnel director told the study team that in the organisation concerned 'there are no short term contracts but everyone is on four weeks' notice, including the Chairman' (*ibid.*, p. 69). An agency Chief Executive observed that 'a three year contract makes me feel less secure and more wary; discourages me from putting all my cards on the table . . . and encourages staff to believe that they can sit tight and resist change until my contract is over' (*ibid.*, p. 76). A Grade 2 official declared that 'you don't need short term contracts to get rid of the unsatisfactory performer, you just need the will' (*ibid.*, p. 77). Maybe, but the Oughton team needed to make specific recommendations and the most important of them was that:

> The Treasury should work up proposals for alternative contract terms of employment for the Senior Open Structure, so that the costs and benefits can be assessed, which would safeguard against politicization, but which would strike an appropriate balance between risks and rewards. . . . We recommend a contract of indefinite terms but with a clear, specific period of notice' (*ibid.*, p. 81)

The Oughton team clearly considered that the vast majority of the highest posts in the Civil Service should be filled by insiders, and took as a model one private sector organisation:

> in which 80 per cent of their vacancies were filled from within and the remaining 20 per cent through open advertisement, from which they might expect to fill some vacancies from outside their organization and some from insiders who matched the best outsiders. This does not compare too starkly with recent Civil Service experience. Over the last three years, 14 per cent of the vacancies in the Senior Open Structure have been openly advertised and that has led to 10 per cent of the vacancies being filled by people who were not career civil servants. (*ibid.*, p. 55)

This was as far as the Oughton team wished to go in changing the character of the Higher Civil Service, but it remained to be seen if the Conservative Government had similar views.

6 From reform to revolution in the British Civil Service?

When, in 1978, the Callaghan Labour Government responded to the modest reforming proposals of the English Committee on the Civil Service, it did so in the spirit that nothing much needed to be done. After all, there had been 'a number of radical changes in the organization and management of the Civil Service' since the Fulton Report of 1968 (Cmnd 7117, 1978, p. 3). The Fulton programme now seems tame by comparison with the policies towards the Civil Service that have been pursued by Conservative Governments in the Thatcher era and beyond; and the publication of the White Paper entitled *The Civil Service. Continuity and Change* in July 1994 provides a point of reference from which to examine the changes made in the decade and a half since 1979 and to assess whether or not a revolution in the Civil Service has taken place or is in prospect.

I THE CIVIL SERVICE WHITE PAPER OF 1994

'Here are some proposals which you will not find in William Waldegrave's White Paper on the Civil Service published on July 13th [1994]', *The Economist* (16 July 1994, p. 23) observed:

> Most top civil servants will not be put on fixed term contracts. Most of their jobs will not be given to people from the private sector. Their pay will not increase enormously nor will their numbers be cut hugely. The fast stream which separates the most promising recruits for special advancement will not be abolished. The French *cabinet* system which provides more political advice to Ministers will not be imported; nor will the American system of political appointments to the Civil Service; nor the German system of public law, which defines civil servants' duties to the public. Despite the damning evidence of subterfuge and dissembling un-covered by the Scott inquiry into arms related exports to Iraq, there is no pro-posal to reduce Civil Service secrecy or increase governmental accountability.

That 'radical reformers of all political stripes have urged such changes in recent years' need not be a recommendation in their favour, and the assessment of the White Paper made by Sir Peter Kemp, who had played a leading role in pushing through the Conservative Government's policies before his resignation from the Civil Service in 1992, was a markedly different one, for, he wrote:

> Just because one thinks that the mandarins got away with it in the recent Civil Service White Paper, this does not mean that there is not a lot of important stuff

there. It is not in fact really a policy document at all because what it enshrines is existing policy; for the great bulk of the Civil Service the changes now in hand will continue, while for mandarins the *status quo* will not change. That is presumably why the document is called *Continuity and Change*. But it is still important. (Kemp, 1994a, p. 49)

As Sir Peter Kemp's radical credentials could not be doubted, there seems good cause to examine what was actually in the White Paper, as opposed to what was not, taking into account related material published at the same time.

A major proposal in the White Paper was that a Senior Civil Service should be established by April 1996 covering staff at Grade 5 level and above, including all agency Chief Executives, and its members would be subject to new pay and contractual arrangements. It was observed that:

> The new Senior Civil Service that would emerge from this process would be broader than the existing Senior Open Structure, which is confined to the current Grades 1–3. The Government believes there is merit in such a development. It would strengthen the cohesion not only of the senior management of departments, but also of the wider Senior Civil Service. Entry to the Senior Civil Service from within a department or agency would be marked for the individual concerned by leaving negotiated group pay arrangements and moving to individually determined pay, and by acceptance of a written contract of service. It would be a signal to the individual and to his or her senior managers of the need to think more broadly, both in respect of the job to be done and, potentially, in career management terms, looking across the Civil Service and at opportunities for experience outside. The [Oughton] Report noted a step change in responsibility between the current Grades 7 and 5 – requiring the ability to manage through others and a greater role in representing the organization externally that accords with the Government's perception – and reinforces the case for extending the scope of the Senior Civil Service to encompass that level of responsibility. (Cm. 2627, 1994, para. 4.18)

Numbers in the highest three grades of the Civil Service had been reduced by 20 per cent since 1979, the White Paper noted. Increasingly, departments had been eliminating unnecessary layers of management (*ibid.*, para. 4.19); and senior management reviews conducted by departments would be the means of ensuring that the structure at that level matched the needs of the organisation and was not driven by a formal Service-wide grading system, as well as informing the process of moving senior staff on to new pay and contractual arrangements (*ibid.*, para. 4.20).

These senior management reviews were thought likely to continue a trend which had seen more than 50 per cent of the individuals who had left the Senior Open Structure in the previous seven years doing so before the normal retirement age, 30 per cent of them having departed as the result of voluntary or compulsory early retirement brought about by management. The Government, therefore, proposed to introduce explicit written contracts for members of the new Senior Civil Service, which would clarify the terms and conditions of employment for members of that Service, and which would normally be contracts in which employment would be for an indefinite term but with specified periods of notice. The Government did not favour fixed-term or rolling contracts, but it recognised that there could not be a single comprehensive contract for everyone, not least because of the delegation of many personnel responsibilities to departments and agencies (*ibid.*, paras. 4.31–4.35). As there might well be in future fewer distinctions in job security between employment in the senior levels of the Civil Service and that at comparable levels elsewhere in the public sector or in the private sector, the Government appreciated that there would be less justification for the existing discount in Civil Service salaries, especially as there would be open competition for some posts. The Government wanted to see a 'smaller but better paid Senior Civil Service' established. In future, there was to be a single pay range for all Permanent Secretaries up to and including the Head of the Home Civil Service, with the level and extent of the range being determined on the basis of the advice of the Review Body on Senior Salaries (the successor to the Review Body on Top Salaries). A remuneration committee was to determine the position of individual Permanent Secretaries within this range. Below Permanent Secretary level, the Government proposed 'to replace the present central grading structure' by 'a number of overlapping pay ranges broadly linked to levels of responsibility'. Individual Permanent Secretaries would control the pay progression of their staff taking account of performance, level of responsibility and marketability of their skills and experience. The operation of this system by Permanent Secretaries was to be monitored and adjusted as necessary centrally to try to ensure adequate coherence between departments (*ibid.*, paras 4.36–4.39). Subject to satisfying the Civil Service Commissioners where outside recruitment was involved, it was to be for departments to make appointments to and within the new Senior Civil Service, including appointments made following an internal competition, which did not fall within the category of posts where central approval was required, meaning posts at Grades 1, 1A and 2. Where such approval was needed, the Head of the Home Civil Service was to continue making recommendations to the Prime Minister, after a meeting of the Senior Appointments Selection Committee or following an open recruitment exercise conducted under the auspices of the Civil Service Commissioners (*ibid.*, para. 4.27).

'There is no successful country in the world which does not try to recruit early and develop some of its ablest men and women with the task of supporting elected Ministers in doing their jobs', the White Paper declared. So, it was no surprise that it also recorded that 'the Government believes that the Civil Service must continue to recruit its share of the most talented graduates' (*ibid.*, para. 4.23). This was effectively to endorse the fndings of a *Review of Fast Stream Recruitment*, which the Oughton Report had proposed, and which was published at the same time as the White Paper by the Office of Public Service and Science. The argument behind the Recruitment Studies Team's recommendation in favour of retaining a generalist Fast Stream was much the same as that advanced by the Atkinson Report in 1983, namely that, whatever the state of the graduate labour market generally, the market for the "best" graduates remains strongly competitive.' Of the fast-stream scheme, the Team stated:

> It is needed for hard, business reasons: without it, departments cannot be confident that policy support for Ministers would be adequately staffed and managed. Whatever the fluctuations in demand from year to year, it makes no sense for the Civil Service to withdraw from the top end of the graduate market. And as the participating departments are happy to share the same basic specification, and are convinced that a common approach to marketing and assessment gets better results than they could achieve on their own, there is no case for abandoning a common scheme. (Office of Public Service and Science, 1994a, paras 4.15–4.16)

Those who object to such a scheme most commonly do so from a position which either objects to elites in principle, or which believes that if such an elite must exist it should be a microcosm of British society or at least of its higher-education system. So, the debate tends to degenerate into 'a dialogue of the deaf' as the Recruitment Studies Team recognised (*ibid.*, para. 5.5). Yet, the Team still felt the need to suggest that the term fast stream should be abandoned because of its 'elitist connotations' (*ibid.*, para. 6.12). As the stated object of the scheme, whatever its name, was to select the ablest people available, then its aim was elitist, and, given the severe competition for talent at the level concerned, nothing was to be gained by disguise.

'Sir Robin [Butler] must feel that he has seen off the most far reaching political threat to the mandarins in modern times', *The Economist* (16 July 1994, p. 23) suggested, but, if so, the Civil Service at large did not seem to have been so fortunate. 'The size of the Civil Service continues to fall and now stands at 533,350', the White Paper stated (Cm. 2627, 1994, para. 3.32), announcing that 'the Government would expect Civil Service manpower to fall significantly below 500,000 over the next four years.' The means of doing this would be to continue the control of running costs (*ibid.*, para. 3.33), and there was to be special central provision for the short-term funding of any resulting early retirements (*ibid.*, para. 3.34). The White Paper emphasised that the Government was to persist with the 'prior options' process, under which activities were reviewed to see whether they should be abolished, privatised, contracted out or market-tested, or organised in an agency, although there would be in future a five-year period, instead of three years, between reviews after an agency was created (*ibid.*, para. 3.22). Whereas, though, previously, there had been a central impetus behind, and detailed oversight of, the *Competing for Quality* and privatisation initiatives, the Government thought that the time had come to give departments and agencies 'greater freedom and flexibility to develop programmes for improving efficiency which best meets their own needs' (*ibid.*, para. 3.20). Such programmes had a role to play in the efficiency plans that departments and agencies were to be required to draw up each spring to show how they were to stay within their running costs limits over the next three years (*ibid.*, para. 3.21). Proposals for the further delegation to departments and agencies of responsibilities for direct-entry recruitment were published separately (Office of Public Service and Science 1994b), and in the White Paper itself the Government made clear its intention to continue with its policy of disaggregating the Civil Service's pay and grading systems. From April 1996, below senior levels, existing national pay arrangements would be replaced and responsibilities would be delegated to all departments, and, in addition, the Government indicated its preference for each agency within a department having responsibility for its own pay and grading (Cm. 2627, 1994, para. 3.26). The presumption was that departments would want to develop 'flatter management structures' (*ibid.*, para. 3.29). The Government also envisaged the introduction of improved management information systems within departments (*ibid.*, para. 3.15), and it published separately proposals that departments should introduce resource accounting systems based on commercial principles (Cm. 2626, 1994). One view of this latter development was that it would 'bring about a long overdue revolution in government accounting', not least because for the first time the 'government's accounts will identify the true cost of its various activities' (Evans, 1994, pp. 31–2). Sir Peter Kemp may well have been nearer the mark when observing that 'when resource accounting comes up against cash control requirements, there are no prizes for guessing which is going to win' (Kemp, 1994b, p. 526).

'In the Whitehall battle over Civil Service reform, the evolutionaries have routed the revolutionaries', *The Economist* (16 July 1994, p. 23) wrote of the White Paper of 1994. Even if this Radical Right assessment was correct, which need not necessarily be conceded, there was more to the Civil Service than Whitehall. Sir Peter Kemp took a broader perspective:

> What the White Paper finally recognizes is that there are two (or perhaps many more) Civil Services. Essentially, on the one hand, there are top people we all think we know about, now about 3,500, to be entitled the Senior Civil Service, plus their supporters; on the other hand about 500,000 invisible people, who do the work. The White Paper at last addresses the existence of an enormously diversified set of services, delivering what needs to be done in the best way it can be done, whether publicly or privately. It finally buries the idea of the old monolithic Civil Service, which has hampered thinking for so long, leaving those described as civil servants simply bound together by familiar concepts of independence, impartiality etc., and by accountability through Ministers to Parliament and the iron hand of the public expenditure system. (Kemp, 1994a, p. 49)

'Where the White Paper lets us down', Sir Peter Kemp believed, was 'when we come to the . . . newly named Senior Civil Service' where 'practically nothing has changed', which meant that 'the Luddites seem to have won part of the battle' (*ibid.*, p. 50). Opposition to change need be neither unprincipled nor sinister, but based on a perception of the needs of the British system of government, which has its own character, to which that of the career Civil Service has been related. Whether one subscribes to that position or not, it seems evident that, since 1988 at least, proponents of change, while not winning all along the line, have had the best of 'the battle'. Indeed, the order of change in the Civil Service over the decade and a half down to the White Paper of 1994 has been such that the question of whether or not it has been revolutionary in scale seems an obvious matter to consider.

II INCREMENTALIST AND REVOLUTIONARY MODELS OF ADMINISTRATIVE CHANGE

If a revolution in the British Civil Service has taken place then it would be remarkable since, as one would expect and as their leading historian, Geoffrey Elton, once wrote, 'true administrative revolutions are rare.' They took place 'only when the State itself is being refashioned fundamentally'. Otherwise, public administration 'usually develops by slow degrees' (Elton, 1953, p. 424). After 1979, Conservative Governments did attempt to reshape the role of the state within Britain, and, while what was done would not match a New Right fundamentalist agenda, some economic liberal goals were realised, even if closer involvement with the European bureaucracy was pulling in another direction. From the Next Steps Report onwards at least, major changes were made in the machinery of British central government and in the Civil Service too. How important these changes were, as well as those which immediately preceded them, and their nature seems best assessed in terms of the historical development of the Civil Service, and Elton has provided an historical model of a kind, and, from the extensive literature about the public policy process, there is also the incrementalist model to consider.

Those who have found discussion of rationalist and incrementalist models of public policy making to be artificial (e.g. Smith and May, 1980, pp. 147–61) have failed to appreciate the political sub-text that runs through it. In the original Dahl–Lindblom formulation:

> Incrementalism is a method of social action that takes existing reality as one alternative and compares the probable gains and losses of closely related alternatives by making relatively small adjustments in existing reality, or making larger adjustments about whose consequences approximately as much is known as about the consequences of existing reality, or both. Where small increments will clearly not achieve desired goals, the consequences of large increments are not fully known, and existing reality is clearly unacceptable, incrementalism may have to give way to a calculated risk. Thus, scientific methods, incrementalism, and calculated risks are on a continuum of policy methods. (Dahl and Lindblom, 1953, p. 82)

When Charles Lindblom developed the incrementalist model not only as an explanation of developments in public policy but also as being the best means of proceeding (Lindblom, 1958, pp. 298–312; 1959, pp. 79–88; 1964, pp. 157–8; 1965; 1968; 1977; 1979, pp. 517–26; 1980; 1990; Braybrooke and

Lindblom, 1963; Lindblom and Cohen, 1979; Lindblom and Woodhouse, 1993) naturally enough this attracted the criticism of those who preferred 'scientific methods', meaning planning (Dror, 1964, pp. 153–7; 1968; 1971; 1986), and it also encouraged an alternative 'mixed scanning' thesis (Etzioni, 1967, pp. 385–92; 1968; 1986, pp. 8–14). From this last source came the telling criticism of the model which was that while incremental decisions were bound to outnumber fundamental or 'large' decisions, the latter's significance for societal decision making was not commensurate with their number. It was thus a mistake to relegate non-incremental decisions to the category of exceptions, especially in the case of war, which would be an obvious instance of fundamental decisions setting the context for the numerous incremental ones (Etzioni, 1967, p. 387). Lindblom's refinement of the model to embrace disjointed incrementalism did not dispose of this criticism, as he seemed to believe (Lindblom, 1979, p. 519). There was also the matter of what actually constituted an increment (Dempster and Wildavsky, 1979, pp. 371–89). Nevertheless, of the range of public policy models (e.g. Lane, 1993, pp. 69–89), that of Lindblom was addressed to British experience, from which the approved 'muddling through' approach to decision making was derived (Lindblom, 1958, p. 311). The political dimension in the model was the embracing of British Fabian socialism (Dahl and Lindblom, 1953, pp. 515–16), there being little difference between 'inevitable gradualness' and incrementalism. Fabianism has rarely travelled so well, but there is no doubting its importance as a tradition in the reform of the British Civil Service, and, entwined with it, the Lindblom model provides one prospective measure of the recent changes.

A famous interpretation of British administrative history provides another possible measure: 'There have been . . . only three administrative revolutions, though many changes and reforms, in English history', the distinguished constitutional historian, Geoffrey Elton, declared, adding that 'as might be expected, they were the work of dynamic Governments and of ages when the State was being made anew' (Elton, 1953, p. 425). The Anglo-Norman creation of a centralised feudal state governed by the Monarch in his or her household was said to be 'one such revolution' (*ibid.*, p. 424). The claims made on behalf of Ranulf Flambard as an administrative reformer (Southern, 1933, pp. 95–128; 1970, pp. 183–205; Harvey, 1975, pp. 175–93) can be noted in passing, as can the view that the Treasury had been established as the first government department by that time (Richardson and Sayles, 1963, pp. 225, 242) which seems rather early for such a development. The second administrative revolution was said by Elton to have taken place in the 1530s when medieval government was replaced by early modern government, when 'an administration relying on the household was replaced by one based exclusively on bureaucratic departments and officers of state' but one which was still 'responsible to the Crown' (Elton, 1953, pp. 424–5). This time Thomas Cromwell was treated as being the great administrative reformer. To put the matter mildly, other historians have not always shared that view, and, indeed, there have been those who did not believe that there had been a Tudor administrative revolution at all (Cooper, 1963, pp. 110–12; Harriss, 1963, pp. 8–39; Williams, 1963a, pp. 3–8; 1963b, pp. 39–58; Harriss and Williams, 1965, pp. 87–96; Beckingsale, 1978, pp. 152–3; Coleman and Starkey, 1986). Elton continued to defend the notion of the Tudor revolution (Elton, 1964, pp. 26–49; 1965, pp. 103–9) and it had been part of his original argument that:

> The principle then adopted was not in turn discarded until the much greater administrative revolution of the nineteenth century, which not only destroyed survivals of the medieval system allowed to continue a meaningless existence for some three hundred years, but also created an administration based on departments responsible to Parliament – an administration in which the Crown for the first time ceased to hold the ultimate control. (Elton, 1953, pp. 424–5)

In this case, the notion of an administrative revolution having taken place attracted only mild scepticism from historians (e.g. Cromwell, 1965–6, pp. 245–55), and debate largely concentrated on whether or not the revolution was primarily brought about by dynamic administrators or by Benthamism (MacDonagh, 1958, pp. 52–67; Parris, 1960, pp. 17–37; Hart, 1965, pp. 39–61), leaving unchallenged the unlikely assumption that the changes wrought in the middle quarters of the nineteenth century were revolutionary both in kind and in scale in a way that those which had fashioned the paraphernalia of twentieth-century collectivism were not. Elton at least thought that there was an 'essential unity' between the three administrative revolutions he had detected which was clearly 'reflected in what must be the basis of any administrative structure, the Civil Service itself. Thus,

> The medieval household system was served by men recruited from church and household; the middle period used clients of Ministers, trained in their service and promoted by and through them; this second method of supply lasted until it was replaced by the modern Civil Service with its examinations. (Elton, 1953, p. 425)

The development of that modern Civil Service, though, was by no means straightforward, and the complexities of the form that it took matters for the analysis of the most recent changes.

III CIVIL SERVICE TRADITIONS AND THE NEW PUBLIC MANAGEMENT

Three main reforming traditions have characterised the modern development of the British Civil Service. Two of them have been primarily external to the Civil Service: namely, economic liberalism and Fabian socialism. The other important tradition has been self-generated reform from within the Civil Service itself. It was the case, of course, that the economic liberal W.E. Gladstone put Sir Charles Trevelyan, of the Treasury, and Sir Stafford Northcote, then of the Board of Trade, to work on their famous Civil Service reform programme, and that the Liberal Prime Minister was instrumental in bringing forward the Order in Council of 1870 relating to competitive examinations. So, as one would anticipate, there never has been a neat divide between the various traditions. The role of civil servants and their supporting organisations in Civil Service reform was a more prominent one than tended to be commonly conceded. The importance of the Fabian contribution was never likely to be understated. Most of the outside literature about the Civil Service was written by Fabians. Their reforming proposals came to be as familiar to the Civil Service as if they were friends. Indeed, they were well intentioned, in the sense that the Fabians too believed in mass bureaucracy. The aggressive tone of the opening chapter of the Fulton Report disguised for some the modest nature of that essentially Fabian document's main proposals. The resulting establishment of the Civil Service Department actually emphasised the Service's separateness and standing. Indeed, from the Service's perspective, the only jarring note in the Fulton Report was that the Committee's Management Consultancy Group had introduced 'business methods' on to the Fabian agenda. Previously, advocacy of this approach had been left to economic liberals. Managerialism in some form now had the seal of approval from both external reforming traditions. Whether the Civil Service took managerialism very seriously even then seems doubtful. Lord Bancroft recalled:

> Certainly in the years after the Fulton Report a great deal of work was done on accountable management, and on playing at shops, with one unit charging another for services in monopoly money as if they were in a trading situation with profits and losses and so on. It was just a charade. (interview, 1988)

When economic liberalism came to be persisted with in the Thatcher era and beyond, the 'charade' was over, and the Conservative Governments' policies towards the Civil Service were characterised by a determination to reshape that Service as far as possible in line with private sector mores. Market-testing and contracting-out policies were the logical outcome of this approach, and the Next Steps programme and the Mueller proposals were plainly antipathetic to the continuance of a career Civil Service of the existing type and scale.

The significance of the Conservative Governments' policies seems best evaluated against an historical background, and one can note at once the existence of a dominant interpretation of the history of the Civil Service. The former Labour Minister and Civil Service staff association leader, Lord Houghton, who had joined the Board of Inland Revenue as long before as 1915, expounded a version of this interpretation when opposing the Civil Service (Management Functions) legislation of 1992 in the House of Lords. 'When I look back over my lifetime with, in, and for the Civil Service, I realize that the whole trend from the Administration has been towards uniformity', Lord Houghton declared. He added:

> From the very beginning, the miscellaneous assortment of public servants in different departments, doing different jobs and whose pay in many cases was not

fixed centrally, called for some better and more orderly arrangements to govern their service, pay and conditions under which they were to do their work. Every big organization of the Civil Service has tended towards a greater concentration on grading, recruitment, scales of pay and opportunities, all of which have been related to the standard of qualification on entry of our public servants. . . . The entry examinations and the standards that were set for entry have all related to the educational system. That is why the structure of the British Civil Service has gone the way that it has. (538 HL Deb. 5s. c. 19–20)

'Centralization, uniformity, standardized recruitment' were all now being cast aside, Lord Houghton complained. For 'the Government are proposing reforms which are equal in significance and importance to those made over one hundred years ago in an entirely opposite direction' (538 HL Deb. 5s. c. 1066).

So, on this view, the Conservatives since 1979 have been turning the clock back, away from the 'rationality' of the development of the career Civil Service since the Northcote–Trevelyan Report of the 1850s. That document rightly remains *the* reference point in the history of the British Civil Service, but what happened subsequently was not as straightforward as it has been often portrayed in the Whig manner with Progress eventually triumphing over the Forces of Darkness. Gladstone saw the Civil Service reforms in terms of Parliamentary reform (Fry, 1969, p. 33), whereas by the time that they were implemented party politics and constitutional conventions had changed so as to frustrate this ambition (Greenaway, 1985, pp. 157–69). Gladstone had wanted to use the 'intellectual' part of the reformed Civil Service not only to conduct the business of government departments more efficiently but also as a source of recruitment to the House of Commons to improve its quality. The First Division or Administrative Class, of course, did become a form of political class, but one placed in a subordinate role behind the previously nascent constitutional convention of ministerial responsibility. Hence, the Northcote–Trevelyan Report only partially fulfilled its political author's intentions and, inevitably, the translation of the Report's four main principles into practice was imperfect too. The structure of the Civil Service never did match Northcote and Trevelyan's division of labour between 'intellectual' and 'mechanical' work. It was never simply a matter of there being a First Division and a Second Division. Similarly, the Northcote and Trevelyan principle of promotion by merit only was well worth stating, to register opposition to promotion solely by seniority, but in any organisation of much size the latter principle was bound to have a place, as it came to do, for instance, in the limits set on promotion fields. Further, it was the exceptional period when the Civil Service was unified, and that civil servants only and always were recruited by open competition was not the case. This was not just a matter of ex-armed forces recruitment after both world wars or of the importing of irregulars during those wars. The MacDonnell Majority Report detected no fewer than seven methods of appointment to the Civil Service in 1914, while recognising that, since the Order in Council of 1870, open competition had established itself as 'the normal method' of direct-entry recruitment to the Service, 'deviation from which requires justification on some specific ground of public policy' (Cd. 7338, 1914, p. 24), notably the appointment of 'Professional, Technical and Scientific Officers' (*ibid.*, p. 27).

Where the Houghton view was right was that for more than a hundred years from the establishment of the Civil Service Commission in 1855 onwards, it was clear what the normal order of things was intended to be in relation to direct-entry requirement to the main part of the Civil Service. What the view ignored was that between 1963 and 1969 the Commission had ceased to conduct its own open competitive examinations to the Classes concerned. Executive Class recruitment on the basis of GCE qualifications plus interview had begun in 1956, at which date similar Clerical Class recruitment, first begun experimentally in London in 1953, became nationwide. In 1964, the Commission began the process of delegating clerical recruitment to departments, and by 1966 this had become the chief method of entry (Reader, 1981, p. 55). Bringing the Civil Service Commission within the Civil Service Department in 1968 was a mark of its diminished role and status, which was emphasised in 1972, when the relationship first made in 1859 between Civil Service superannuation and the necessity for a certificate of qualification from the Commissioners was severed (Civil Service Commissioners, 106th Report, 1973, pp. 13–14). Some ground seemed to be recaptured when, by means of an Order in Council in 1978, the Commissioners' certificate of qualification was made a requirement whether the appointment to the Civil Service was permanent or not (112th Report, 1979, pp. 6–7, 21–9). By means of an Order in Council of 1981, though, responsibility for recruitment to grades below Executive Officer and its equivalent was transferred entirely to departments and, while such recruitment had to be by merit and by fair and open competition, there was no call for a certificate of qualification from the Commissioners (116th Report, 1983, pp. 7–8, 19–30). An Order in Council in 1991 transferred to departments and agencies the responsibility for recruitment to all grades below Grade 7 level, thus extending their area of responsibility from 85 per cent of recruits a year since 1983 to over 95 per cent. The certificate of qualification vanished altogether, being replaced, where necessary, by the Commissioners' written approval before appointment. The Civil Service Commission vanished too. As part of the Next Steps programme, it was replaced by two discrete organisations, the Office of the Civil Service Commissioners, and the Recruitment and Assessment Services Agency (124th Report, 1991, pp. 1–4, 30–6). The OPSS study, *Responsibilities for Recruitment to the Civil Service*, published in 1994, envisaged the Civil Service Commissioners being 'the custodians of the principles of openness, fairness and merit for all Civil Service recruitment' (Office of Public Service and Science, 1994b, para. 4.10) with the executive responsibilty for recruitment in line with those principles being assigned to Permanent Secretaries in departments and to agency Chief Executives (*ibid.*, para.

4.13). Yet another Order in Council was anticipated, setting out the still further restricted role of the Commissioners (*ibid.*, para. 6.23).

With the common bond of centralised recruitment having come to be undermined in the manner described, what else was left of the 'uniformity' that Lord Houghton, like others, had seen as characterising the structure of the Civil Service? It needs to be recognised that, in the strict sense, it was only exceptionally that there had been anything formally resembling a unified Civil Service. It was only between 1919 and the implementation of the Eden–Bevin reforms that what at various times was called the Foreign Service or the Diplomatic Service was treated as not being a separate entity. 'There was no such single thing as the Civil Service', Sir Henry Primrose of the MacDonnell Commission had correctly remarked about the disparate pre-1914 arrangements (Chapman and Greenaway, 1980, p. 17). The Tomlin Commission observed in 1931:

> Examined historically it will be found that the Civil Service in the past existed as a group of independent departments, and that it is only by a gradual process that a measure of common regulation and common staffing has been developed. It is perhaps significant of this development that the phrase 'the Civil Service' has only gradually come to be used in the instruments regulating the Civil Service in place of phrases such as 'civil officers of His Majesty's Service' or 'officers in His Majesty's civil establishments'. (Cmd. 3909, 1931, para. 13)

What the Tomlin Commission called 'the tendency to unification of the Service' had been 'brought about by several different causes' (*ibid.*, para. 14). One was provision for superannuation (*ibid.*, para. 15). A second was common recruitment and, much more slowly, regulations about conditions of employment such as minimum hours of work for all permanent civil servants (*ibid.*, para. 16). Another was the development of classes common to the Service, about which the Commission noted:

> The Playfair Commission (1874–5) and the Ridley Commission (1886–90), in order to promote efficient organization, recommended that various departments should be staffed by clerks recruited from common examinations and paid on the same scales. The adoption of their recommendations led to the creation of a number of classes common to the Service. . . . Thus practice was still further extended as a result of the recommendations of the Reorganization Committee of 1920. (*ibid.*, para. 17)

That Committee had been set up as part of the Whitley system of joint consultation, first established in 1919 and identified by the Commission as another unifying factor, together with Civil Service arbitration arrangements (*ibid.*, para. 22). The most important factor had to be the development of Treasury control from 1919 onwards, whereby the consent of that department was required in relation to the numbers, grading, remuneration and conditions of service of all civil servants (*ibid.*, para. 18), and the role accorded to the Head of the Civil Service (*ibid.*, para. 20).

The structure of the Civil Service always was more complicated than the familiar picture of it largely comprising what originally were called the Treasury or Reorganisation Classes – the Administrative, Executive and Clerical Classes – and this was not just a matter of, for instance, the Service employing members of thirty-three different professions at the time of the Tomlin Commission (*ibid.*, para. 10). The Treasury memoranda submitted to that Commission showed that, in 1929, the numbers in what it called 'Other Executive Classes', meaning departmental classes, were more than twice as great as those in the Executive Class itself, even if the numbers in the Clerical Class exceeded those in the Departmental Clerical Classes (Tomlin, Treasury Introductory Memoranda, 1930, paras. 33, 35, 42–3, 44). By the time of the Priestley Commission of 1953–5, the most important changes recorded by the Treasury in its memorandum were those which had led to the development of various classes of specialists, most notably those in the Scientific Civil Service and in the Works Group of Professional Classes. When one looked closely at what was still treated as the main part of the Service, it turned out that about 44 per cent of the members of the Executive Class were in Departmental Executive Classes. Members of Departmental Clerical Classes constituted about 31 per cent of the Clerical Class (Priestley, Treasury Factual Memorandum, 1954, paras. 267, 360). The Treasury Factual Memorandum submitted to the Fulton Committee of 1966–8 was much less clear about the relative proportions, but the material submitted about Departmental Classes indicated that they were much the same as at the time of Priestley, and the Executive Class was shown as being linked for pay purposes to no less than 277 Departmental Classes (Fulton, evidence, vol. 4, pp. 409-41).

'Look at the job first' was 'the guiding principle' on which the Fulton Committee believed the future organisation of the Civil Service should be based (Cmnd 3638, 1968, para. 24) and it recognised that there would be advantage in each department recruiting its own staff independently and devising its own grading system to match the needs of its work and staff. 'But the Civil Service cannot be run in this way', the Fulton Committee declared; 'The Service must be a flexible, integrated whole; it must continue to be a unified Service. Its structure should be designed accordingly as a structure that is common throughout' (*ibid.*, para. 196). The Committee recommended that 'Classes as such should be abolished' and that 'all civil servants should be organized in a single grading structure' (*ibid.*, para. 192). In proposing a unified grading structure of this kind which was 'essentially a pay structure' and which was 'not designed to determine the organization of the work' (*ibid.*, para. 221), the Committee believed itself to have recommended 'a fundamental change' (*ibid.*, para. 192). If implemented, it would have been a remarkable one, given that the Commiteee recorded the size of the Civil Service as being 471,600 in 1968 (*ibid.*, para. 294): but it would also have been a change in an integrationist direction, and thus along the lines that Sir Warren Fisher had pioneered, indeed taking it to its logical conclusion. The needs of the work and the interests of the career Civil Service did not necessarily cohere, to put the matter mildly, and the Fulton Committee stated that the former should be paramount while not relating that to the Service's structure. Even on integrationism, the Committee was inconsistent. Of the Swedish Civil Service, the Committee wrote that 'its attractions' were 'great and clear' while recognising, as it had to do, that 'the Swedes do not rely on a single monolithic organization' (*ibid.*, p. 138). Then again, if the Civil Service adopted 'accountable management', as the Committee recommended (*ibid.*, paras 150–4), for this to mean anything substantive at all, it had to be promotive of diversity.

The links between the heavily circumscribed managerialism to be found in the Fulton Report and the New Public Management developed in the period after 1979 were weak ones. Such managerialism as the Fulton Committee embraced was largely designed to operate alongside the career Civil Service, only modifying its practices. As the FMI illustrated, the New Public Management was intended to be more intrusive, in many ways undermining of Civil Service behaviour. The New Public Management, of course, was by no means simply a British phenomenon. Indeed, links with the writings of the American engineer, F.W. Taylor, called *Scientific Management*, first published in 1911, were intelligently made in one study (Pollitt, 1990, pp. 13–17, 61, 69, 174, 176, 177). The New Public Management tended to attract an interpretative literature of a quality that flattered the subject (e.g. Perry and Kraemer, 1983; Kooiman and Eliassen, 1987; Hood, 1990a, 1990b; 1991; Rainey, 1991; Massey, 1993; Metcalfe, 1993) and which tended to be deflective in discussion of developments in the British Civil Service. Thus, the authors of one able study wrote of the Thatcher Government's efficiency strategy that 'at best, its implementation would drag British government kicking and screaming back into the 1950s' (Metcalfe and Richards, 1990, p. 17). Raynerism and the FMI bore no relation at all to the Civil Service of the 1950s, which had been largely left to its own devices in terms of organising itself, and which had been unconditionally granted the Priestley pay formula.

The focus of discussion about the New Public Management needs to be the position of individual civil servants and the impact that it has made upon them. What as early as 1914 had come to be the special status of civil servants was glimpsed by Arthur Boutwood of the MacDonnell Commission in a note of reservation:

> The relative independence conferred upon the established civil servant by what may fairly be called an assured position and assured prospects creates a status which is superior to that of the employee who is completely dependent upon his employer. Probably this higher status is an unintended result of the steps taken to remove from the Civil Service the evils consequent upon a widespread abuse of patronage. Now that it exists, however, it has a value other than the value given to it by its historical connections. It makes possible, and brings within measurable distance, a higher kind of business organization. The incidental creation of this new status was an upward step, important although unobserved, in social

development, and the possibilities it brings within view extend far beyond the Civil Service, extend over the whole field of industry. (Cd. 7338, 1914, p. 117)

The idea that the career Civil Service model could be applied across the board in a market economy on any long-term basis was nonsense, but Boutwood did anticipate some elements of the manner in which not only public corporations were to develop but also private business corporations. Of the career Civil Service, Boutwood wrote that 'in an organization of this higher type, the comparative independence of the subordinate agencies deprives the controlling agency of certain coercive powers, or (at least) imposes limitations upon the exercise of those powers' (*ibid.*). Indeed it did, and Whitleyism was eventually to add to the limitations. The introduction of the Whiteley system of joint consultation in 1919 was a 'Big Bang' that 'brought in a revolution overnight' in the Civil Service, Lord Houghton observed (*CCSU Bulletin*, July 1994, p. 86). In reality, as Houghton had written elsewhere, while Whitleyism was important in that it conferred rights, progress in the inter-war period was slow and 'the ever open door' only came with the Second World War (*Whitley Bulletin*, June 1969, pp. 84–9). Whitleyism then proceeded to condition the existence of line managers in the Civil Service, in the opinion that the Fulton Committee's Management Consultancy Group, with national agreements precluding changes in grading structures and related duties (Report, 1968, para. 337). The Group commented:

> The unique constraints upon the line manager in the Civil Service are fundamental to any consideration of its managerial style . . . he cannot hire or dismiss, he cannot reward merit by any form of payment, he cannot promote, he cannot reprimand formally, he cannot even stop the annual increment of an unsatisfactory subordinate . . .. The only action that a manager in the Service can take to ensure that the system recognizes the strengths and weaknesses of a subordinate is in marking subordinate's annual confidential report form and . . . there are powerful conventions which discourage exceptionally good or bad markings. (*ibid.*, para. 335)

The Group wrote that 'the emphasis upon equity and fair chances for all deprives the line manager of what in industry is his main motivational tool' (*ibid.*, para. 336), and added that centralised control of expenditure by the Treasury imposed on the Civil Service line managers affected far less scope for financial initiative than was common in the private sector (*ibid.*, para. 338).

Those who believed that the Thatcher Government was trying to impose 'an impoverished concept of management' upon the Civil Service (Metcalfe and Richards, 1990, p. 16) seemed not to recognise that within the Civil Service management had been impoverished anyway, if not quite the same way. The nature of the career Civil Service as it had developed made this so. That the flirtation with Taylorism which the future Royal Institute of Public Administration initially engaged in (Pollitt, 1990, p. 15) failed to impress the Treasury was as unsurprising as that department's dismissive attitude towards management thinking in the Bridges era (Chapman, 1988, pp. 248–58). The Plowden Report in 1961, though, had made it clear that this outlook had to change. The Civil Service needed to develop a New Public Management of its own. What was required was obvious professionalisation and, while the Treasury made efforts particularly with management training in the 1960s, there was nothing resembling a New Public Management in place by 1979, and the Thatcher Government gradually introduced its own version. The Civil Service was bound to be in a difficult position anyway in dealing with politically imposed managerialism, but to have to face this threat unarmed hardly helped. The confidence of the past had gone. In 1985, a distinguished civil servant, Anne Mueller referred to the cult management book of the time by Peters and Waterman, *In Search of Excellence,* as if it had lessons for the British Civil Service (Mueller, 1985b, pp. 1, 17), whereas several of the American companies that the writers had chosen as models of efficiency were soon in severe difficulties.

Worse was to come. In 1993, the Conservative Minister, William Waldegrave referred to the American book by Osborne and Gaebler, *Reinventing Government,* as if it had relevance for the British Civil Service (Waldegrave, 1993a, p. 12; 1993b, p. 4) and the Head of the Home Civil Service later did the same (Butler, 1994, pp. 263–70), whereas the only value that the volume could have was to serve a short-term purpose in the American political debate. Osborne and Gaebler stated that they had chosen 'an audacious title' for their book (Osborne and Gaebler, 1992, p. xv). It was also a misleading title on two counts: firstly, government, which was never defined, was equated with bureau activity, as it it had no connection with politics; secondly, the authors treated the American Constitution as if it was sacrosanct, whereas the constitutional arrangements were one source of the veto powers which Lindblom detected many years ago as bedeviling the effective working of the American political system (Lindblom, 1965, pp. 238–9, 266–7, 298–9, 325–6) and, hence, of its public bureaucracy. Even a self-styled polemical defender of American public administration against Osborne and Gaebler and other detractors acknowledged the disadvantages that flowed from the 'gridlock' between the various branches of government, and recognised too that a succession of 'outrageous federal deficits' meant that Americans as citizens were unwilling to give as much to the Republic as they took out of it (Goodsell, 1994, p. xi). It was this problem that Osborne and Gaebler attempted to address:

> Most of our leaders still tell us that there are only two ways out of our repeated public crises: we can raise taxes, or we can cut spending. For almost two decades, we have asked for a third choice. We do not want less education, fewer roads, less health care. Nor do we want higher taxes. We want better education, better roads, and better health care, for the same tax dollar. (Osborne and Gaebler, 1992, p. 22)

The political leaders cited were right. To rely on the supposed 'third choice' to bridge the gap between public revenues and expenditure was both irresponsible and unconvincing, since there was no hard evidence to show that the difference in efficiency between public administration and the various forms of alternative provision was of the order required. Osborne and Gaebler did not produce such evidence. They stated that 'we believe deeply in government' while being against 'the system' which was restricted to meaning 'one-size-fits-all' forms of public bureaucracy (*ibid.*, pp. xviii–xix). The unwillingness of the electorate to fund government activities was assumed to be resentment about techniques, and a list of alternatives was produced (*ibid.*, pp. 31, 290–8, 332–47). Government was to be assigned the role of 'steering' not 'rowing' (*ibid.*, pp. 25–48) and 'empowering' rather than 'serving' (*ibid.*, pp. 49–75) as if the distinctions could easily hold in practice and as if 'steering' in some circumstances was not 'serving' and 'rowing' was not an example of power in action, meaning 'empowering'. Supposedly morally uplifting stories of the kind that Osborne and Gaebler used in their book did not prove anything, and one example demonstrating that their ideas worked in the least likely environment would be better than all their other examples added together. *Reinventing Government* did not address traditional issues of government and administration at all. There was nothing about such matters as spans of control, or accountability, or conventions versus laws. Osborne and Gaebler wrote in the Progressive idiom that runs from the 1880s in the United States. It never had much relation to British concerns, and while information about different ways of doing things has interest, whether these ways are better merits a level of analysis not presented (O.A. Hartley, personal communication, 1993).

If examples of efficiency were believed to be needed by the Civil Service then seeking them abroad was understandable, if unrewarding, given that British private sector management, apart from the retail chain Marks and Spencer and a handful of other companies, had its own past reputation for amateurism to live down (Erickson, 1959; PEP, 1965; Keeble, 1992). The efficiency of banks and insurance companies compared unfavourably with that of social security local offices, according to the Fultonite, John Garrett in evidence to the Treasury and Civil Service Committee in 1994. He added:

> The Civil Service is remarkably efficient at running large transaction processing operations and has a long record of innovation in office automation. It is often forgotten that the Scientific and Technical Civil Service has an outstanding record of discovery and innovation in, for example, aviation, environmental protection and agriculture, from which private industry has benefited immeasurably. The idea that the Government simply consumes wealth and is a burden on the public and on industry is also a fallacy. Very many public services add value: training, support for industry, the regions and exports, research, construction.

Garrett believed that there was 'no objective evidence, to sustain 'the commonly held idea that government services are inherently inefficient because in general they are not motivated by profit and are dominated by unionized producer interests', and he lauded 'the ideal of public service' (HC 27-II, 1993–4, p. 100). This was not 'objective evidence' either, and even the Fulton Committee, primed by its Management Consultancy Group including Garrett, had found Whitleyism to be inhibitive of effective management (Cmnd 3638, 1968, para. 271), and this was before the homely, traditional form of Whitleyism had given way to the aggressive Civil Service unionism of the 1970s and early 1980s (Fry, 1985, pp. 122–45). The majority of civil servants may well have upheld 'the ideal of public service' all along, but disinterestedness, one of that ideal's hallmarks, contrasted starkly with the assertion of self-interest by unions, who did not lack a measure of rank-and-file support.

With the defeat of the unions in the 1981 strike, the Civil Service was poorly placed to defend itself against Conservative Governments seeking radical change. Thereafter, the blows rained upon the career Civil Service, and, far from relenting, the pace eventually came to quicken until the scale of change moved so far beyond the recognised boundaries of Civil Service reformism for it to be a matter of serious debate whether or not a revolution in the Civil Service was taking place or in prospect.

IV TOWARDS A REVOLUTION IN THE CIVIL SERVICE?

What lay behind the Conservative Governments' drive for change in the Civil Service and the rest of the public sector from 1979 onwards, according to William Waldegrave in 1993, was the belief that 'the unprecedented expansion of the State during and after the [Second World] War had not really been taken into account in the structures for managing it.' Waldegrave added:

> The transformation had left government directing a substantial proportion of the national wealth – somewhere between 40 and 50 per cent . . . a vigorous debate about the optimum share of the wealth that the State should control began in the 1960s and 1970s. Contributions ranged from the most unreconstructed corporatists who wanted to scale the commanding heights of the economy, to the advocates of a pre-modern minimalist administration, who resented government even pottering about on the economic equivalent of the South Downs. Both these extremes were quite impractical (although from my point of view the hearts of the minimalists were at least in the right place). However, this debate overlooked an essential point. In the post-war world of unpredecentedly rising expectations . . . the question of how the State *managed* its expenditure was every bit as important as the *extent* of its economic activity. (Waldegrave, 1993b, pp. 1–2)

This could hardly be the case, since in relation to public sector activities Governments tended to have responsibilities for financing and political accountability which they would not have otherwise, and freeing themselves from these commitments was one of the attractions of, for example, privatising public enterprises, where the introduction of private sector management disciplines was presumed to lead to greater efficiency. There was no mystery about the reality that public sector management had been previously relatively neglected, because the reasons were much the same as why there was in fact no 'vigorous debate' about the role of the state in Britain for many years. Keynesianism ruled from the early 1940s to the mid-1970s, and since high public expenditure was deemed to be the guarantor of a form of full employment that was defined in practice in terms of everybody having a job but not necessarily being fully employed doing it, then there were few political or any other incentives to economise on either public spending or staffing, and there was plenty of union power as well as electoral sentiment to help to sustain the existing order. The economic liberal revival within the Conservative Party in Opposition in the 1960s promoted a largely internal debate and plans were made in relation to the role and machinery of central government which were not substantially added to in the 1970s, but the Heath Government in between had eventually practised the politics of full employment. The IMF crisis of 1976 brought the Keynesian era to an end, but if the Managed Economy could no longer be managed in the same way, the Welfare State part of the dispensation persisted, and this was the prime reason why Conservative Governments after 1979 could neither alter the pattern of public expenditure dramatically nor introduce more than cuts in the rate of growth of such spending in all but the most exceptional areas. So, the little economies of the 'good housekeeping' kind had to be sought and the emphasis was on bringing about a management revolution in the Civil Service and elsewhere in the public sector, a daunting enough task but not when compared with promoting anything resembling a British economic miracle.

'The history of reform in the Civil Service, going back over many years, has been a history . . . of changing the labels, not changing the substance', Peter Kemp told the Treasury and Civil Service Committee in 1989 (HC 348-I, 1988–9, evidence, q. 3), and of the Next Steps programme he was clear that 'it is not my intention as Project Manager . . . to go in for "badge engineering" or cosmetic change. We must ensure that the changes bring about real and lasting improvements in efficiency and delivery of services' (*ibid.*, p. 3). The 'bones of previous Civil Service reforms litter the wayside and so for that matter do the bones of people who attempted to do them', Kemp observed in 1990 (HC 481, 1989–90, evidence, q. 14), adding:

> One of the fears I have about Next Steps reform . . . is the idea that the car can swerve back to the middle of the road. In this case we actually want to change the direction on a lasting basis. So I think it probably will always be necessary to have a force to make things and keep things changing. (*ibid.*, q. 47)

Only Prime Ministerial support could provide the necessary force and Margaret Thatcher and John Major did so. Kemp spelt out that the future relationship between departments and agencies to use the 'Rothschild jargon' would be a customer/contractor one, which meant that there was no need for departments to continue to engage in a 'hands-on' form of 'double guessing' (HC 420, 1988–9, evidence, q. 4016). The existence of no more than 'strategic control' meant that the centre of departments would have changed roles with implications for their culture and size (HC 481, 1989–90, evidence, q. 39). There were obvious implications for the Treasury and for the Civil Service too. 'We have come a long way . . . already' from the days when 'Civil Service pay systems were totally rigid . . . and determined centrally', Kemp remarked in 1990, seeing advantages himself in a 'sum of money' approach with its distribution largely left to individual managerial discretion (*ibid.*, q. 35). There was no commitment to 'standardized Civil Service grades', and Kemp himself saw virtues in 'the classic management dictum that there must be no more than four grades from shop floor to boss' (*ibid.*, q. 34). This was the expression of a personal preference, but when Kemp observed that 'agencies are neither a short step to privatization nor a protection against it' (HC 420, 1988–9, evidence, q. 4067) his remarks reflected Government policy, and the direction of this was plainly the promotion of further incursions into the Civil Service.

So, had Conservative Governments since 1979 brought about a revolution in the Civil Service? *The Economist* (21 December 1991, p. 28) was dismissive: 'The Government describes Next Steps, its programme of reform in the Civil Service, as a "quiet revolution". Quiet it is. A revolution it isn't.' Yet, when the White Paper of 1994 appeared, *The Economist* (16 July 1994, p. 23) wrote that it represented 'a retreat from the Civil Service revolution of the past few years'. This was because 'the centrally imposed programme of privatization and market testing, whereby departments are obliged to seek private tenders for much of their work, is to be dropped.' Sir Peter Kemp did not think that the political prominence given to market testing had been a benefit in terms of its delivery, and saw no disadvantage in delegating responsibility nearer the work to be done (Kemp, 1994a, p. 50), and pressures on running costs were an incentive for departments and agencies to seek economies. Kemp, though, was also sceptical about there having been a Civil Service revolution, writing in 1993 that 'at the centre, in Whitehall, old attitudes and the old guard prevail', adding, presumably with his own resignation from the Civil Service in mind, that 'the only heads that have rolled have been among the revolutionaries themselves.' Of the Civil Service changes, Sir Peter wrote that 'these are welcome breakthroughs but they do not add up to a revolution' (Kemp, 1993, p. 8), believing that what had been done 'lacks the qualities of a real revolution, save perhaps by the modest standards of what has gone before' (*ibid.*, p. 45). When the *Fundamental Review of H.M. Treasury's Running Costs* (Treasury, 1994) was published, Graham Mather, from the Radical Right, saluted the 'October Revolution at the Treasury' which, because it would be used as the model for change elsewhere in Whitehall, marked 'the beginning of the end of an under-performing Service running on Victorian lines' (*The Times*, 20 October 1994). That a knife had been directed at the heart of the Civil Service, the Treasury, was remarkable in itself, but it remained to be seen if the cuts were made both there and in other departments. What was clear was that any hopes which the Civil Service had that Mrs Thatcher's departure would bring to an end the 'permanent revolution' were mistaken, another commentator observed. Far from stilling the revolution, John Major spurred it on, and, on this view, 'one of his most significant bequests to his successor is likely to be a Civil Service vastly different from that created by the Northcote–Trevelyan reforms 140 years ago and largely unchanged until recent years' (Willman, 1994, p. 64).

Since there is no universally agreed definition of what constitutes a revolution, whether or not the order of change brought about in the Civil Service during the Thatcher era and beyond has been revolutionary has to be a matter that cannot be settled beyond dispute. The same can be said of the Eltonian model. The utility of Lindblom's incrementalist model has to be limited because developments tend to be defined as incremental unless they are not. All that said, though, the Civil Service of 1979 was not the creature of the Northcote–Trevelyan Report, even if it had a remarkable number of characteristics that derived from that document, and a largely self-governing Service was the main author of the many subsequent changes that were made in terms of structure and recruitment and, critically, during the Warren Fisher era, of administrative culture. The radical peacetime Governments of twentieth-century Britain, those of Campbell-Bannerman, Asquith and Attlee, did not engage in Civil Service reform. The most that the Wilson Governments could do was to engage in what Peter Kemp called 'the business of shiny shop windows or just changing names' (HC, 420, 1988–9, evidence, q. 4016). The Heath Government ended up doing much the same. There were links between the Thatcher era and that of Heath in terms of Conservative ideas, of course, and when the White Paper of 1970 was not listed as one of the predecessors of the Ibbs Report, it was understandable that David Howell wrote to Sir Robin Ibbs to say, 'I feel like Trotsky, written out of history.' Howell's Black Book of 1970 had a list of candidates for agency treatment that was much the same as the Next Steps programme (interview, 1989). The important difference was the relative lack of interest that the Heathites took in practice in changing the Civil Service itself. This can be illustrated by the eventual fate of the Property Services Agency, which was set up by the Heath Government in 1972 on the basis of conventional Civil Service staffing. 'The Property Services Agency is to be dismantled', one of the Civil Service unions lamented in 1989, and 'departments will be able to replace government services with private contractors' (*NUCPS Journal*, October 1989, p. 3). 'The Property Services Agency Projects Division has been given away with an £84 million handshake to Tarmac', the same union protested in 1992. 'The deal includes the Government picking up the tab for 900 redundancies – half the workforce' (*NUCPS Journal*, October 1992, p. 1). The Thatcher and Major Governments were engaged in a different order of change.

If there has been a revolution in the British Civil Service it would have to be dated from the Next Steps Report of 1988. Mrs Thatcher was said by an economic adviser, Alan Walters, to have adopted a 'stepping stones' approach in several major policy areas (Walters, 1986, pp. 4–5). The Next Steps initiative was a logical development of the FMI (Andren, 1992, p. 5), which was later described by John Major as 'part of a coherent strategy for management reform' (*ibid.*, p. 7). The FMI was dramatic stuff by past standards, and, by the same criterion, the scale of related activity was remarkable too, but, essentially, the mass career Civil Service had survived. Of the Thatcher Governments' policies towards the Civil Service down to the beginning of 1988, Roy Campbell's famous lines seemed appropriate (Campbell, 1985, p. 176):

> They use the snaffle and the curb all right,
> But where's the bloody horse?

It came mainly in the form of the Next Steps programme which was implemented at a relentless pace. The Oughton Report in 1993 recorded that 'the Next Steps initiative . . . has created 92 agencies encompassing some 350,000 staff working on Next Steps lines with a further 54 candidates announced.' The Report added that 'a reasonable assumption might be that about 75 per cent of the Civil Service might work on such lines by the mid-1990s' (Efficiency Unit, 1993a, p. 16). The Fultonite prescription would have been for agencies to have remained within departments abiding by central Civil Service pay and employment rules (HC 27-II, 1993–4, evidence, p. 101). The 'underlying agenda' of the Fulton Report had been 'to prize the executive operations of government out of the hands of the mandarins and give them to professionally qualified people' (*ibid.*, q. 1626). Inevitably, 'market testing, or contractorization, or piecemeal privatization by tender' was scorned (*ibid.*, p.101), much like the mandarins whom it was possible to despise as easily as it was to admire the broad mass of civil servants such as counter clerks (*ibid.*, q. 1612). The Thatcher Governments and their successors combined an unsentimental view of both the Higher Civil Service and the mass of the Civil Service, with the latter being the main target. The 'independent' position of established civil servants always gave offence, and the consistent aim behind Conservative policies towards the Civil Service was the extension of managerial prerogatives, not least to damage the unions, who were eventually to face a multiplicity of bargaining units and individualised contracts of employment. The security of tenure of established civil servants was to be undermined, and recruitment, pay, and grading were to be decentralised. When the Civil Service Commission was abolished, and the administration of the Civil Service pension scheme was even considered for market testing (Treasury, 1992e; *The Times*, 19 October 1994; *FDA News*, November 1994, p. 1–2), this really was radicalism.

Reformism had given way to a revolution in the Civil Service at large. What the Conservative Government was engaged in was a Long March through Whitehall, according to a Minister, Stephen Dorrell, in 1992: 'The conventional question was "what can we sell?" That question must now be turned on its head. Now we ask ourselves "what must we keep?" What is the inescapable core of government?' (*The Times*, 23 November 1992). That Chinese Communist parallels were sought at all by a British Conservative Minister was strange enough, but, as they were, as one Civil Service union pointed out, the Cultural Revolution directed against the bureaucracy would be the more apposite (*NUCPS Journal*, December 1992, p. 2). Attacking the Civil Service had become a shibboleth of contemporary Conservatism, an inevitably unconvincing surrogate for the inability of Conservative Governments after 1979 to bring about a transformation of the performance of the British economy. This was the 'permanent revolution' that mattered above all, and, while few would expect this to be achieved in a decade and a half, it was no compensation to learn that 'New Zealand has adopted some of our Civil Service reforms' (Waldegrave, 1993a, p. 12). Developments in public administration in New Zealand had their interest (Boston *et al.*, 1991; Wistrich, 1992, pp. 119–35; Boston, 1993, pp. 14–29; HC 27-IX, 1993–4, evidence, pp. 262–70, q. 2294–2355), but much less than those in countries which economic liberals cited as successful economies. The idea that Japan was simply an economic liberal miracle could not survive knowledge of its tradition of technocratic bureaucracy (Koh, 1989). The Civil Service has played an important and technocratic role in the economic development of Singapore (Meow, 1985; Regnier, 1987; Sandhu and Wheatley, 1989), and a survey of the East Asian economic miracle conducted by the World Bank, an organization given to favouring market philosophy, emphasised the role of reputable Civil Services in promoting economic advance (World Bank, 1993, pp. 174–80).

The British adminstrative style was never technocratic. Sir Warren Fisher led it down a different road. Fisher's heirs within the Senior Civil Service were threatened by the management revolution, which encouraged different forms of accountability and structure and, through the Next Steps arrangements, the recasting of the role of the Treasury and of the policy elites in other departments and the reduction of numbers. As for what Sir Peter Kemp chose to call 'the real Civil Service; the half million men and women who are actually out there doing the management and executive jobs' (Kemp, 1994b, p. 525), many had cause to feel that the revolution had already taken place.

Bibliography and references

I ARCHIVE MATERIAL

Lord Boyle of Handsworth. Brotherton Library, University of Leeds.
Conservative Party Archive. Bodleian Library, University of Oxford.
Fulton Committee on the Home Civil Service 1966–8. Committee on the Civil Service (Fulton Committee). PRO: BA 1/1–97. Public Record Office.

II OFFICIAL PUBLICATIONS

All Command Papers and House of Commons Papers are published by HMSO, London. This is not necessarily the case with the publications of government departments and other official bodies.

A Command Papers

C 1713. 1984. (Northcote–Trevelyan) *Report on the Organization of the Permanent Civil Service.*
Cd 7338. 1914. *Fourth Report of the* (MacDonnell) *Royal Commission on the Civil Service.*
Cd 9230. 1918. *Report of the* (Haldane) *Machinery of Government Committee.*
Cmd 1581. 1922 *First Interim Report on National Expenditure.*
Cmd 1582. 1922. *Second Interim Report of the* (Geddes) *Committee on National Expenditure.*
Cmd 1589. 1922. *Third Report of the* (Geddes) *Committee on National Expenditure.*
Cmd 3909. 1931. *Report of the* (Tomlin) *Royal Commission on the Civil Service.* Treasury Factual Memorandum and Minutes of Evidence published separately.
Cmd 3920. 1931. *Report of the* (May) *Committee on National Expenditure.*
Cmd 9613. 1955. *Report of the* (Priestley) *Royal Commission on the Civil Service.* Treasury Factual Memorandum and Minutes of Evidence published separately.
Cmnd 1432. 1961. *Control of Public Expenditure* (Plowden Report).
Cmnd 3638. 1968. *The Civil Service.* Vol. 1, *Report of the* (Fulton) *Committee 1966–8.* Vol. 2, *Report of a Management Consultancy Group.* Vol. 3 (1), *Surveys and Investigations, Social Survey of the Civil Service.* Vol. 3(2), *Surveys and Investigations.* Vol. 4, *Factual, Statistical and Explanatory Papers.* Vol. 5(1), *Proposals and Opinions.* Parts 1 and 2, *Government Departments and Staff Associations.* Vol. 5(2), *Proposals and Opinions.* Parts 3 and 4, *Organizations and Individuals.*
Cmnd 4156. 1969. *Report of the* (Davies) *Committee of Inquiry. The Method II System of Selection for the Administrative Class of the Home of Civil Service.*

Cmnd 4506. 1970. *The Reorganization of Central Government* (Heath White Paper).

Cmnd 4814. 1971. *A Framework for Government Research and Development* (Roths-child Report).

Cmnd 5332. 1973. *The Dispersal of Government Work from London* (Hardman Report).

Cmnd 7057. 1978. *Report of the* (Armitage) *Committee on Political Activities of Civil Servants.*

Cmnd 7117, 1978. *The Civil Service: Government observations on the eleventh Report from the Expenditure Committee, session 1976–77, H.C. 535.*

Cmnd 8170. 1981. *The Future of the Civil Service Department: Observations on the first Report from the Treasury and Civil Service Committee, session 1980–81, H.C. 54.*

Cmnd 8293. 1981. *Efficiency in the Civil Service.*

Cmnd 8504. 1982. *Administrative Forms in Government.*

Cmnd 8590. 1982. *Report of the* (Megaw) *Inquiry into Civil Service Pay.*

Cmnd 8616. 1982. *Efficiency and Effectiveness in the Civil Service: Government obser-vations on the third report from the Treasury and Civil Service Committee, session 1981–82 H.C. 236.*

Cmnd 9058. 1983. *Financial Management in Government Departments.*

Cmnd 9297. 1984. *Progress in Financial Management in Government Departments.*

Cmnd 9465. 1985. *Acceptance of Outside Appointments by Crown Servants: Govern-ment observations on the eighth Report from the Treasury and Civil Service Commit-tee, session 1983–84, H.C. 302.*

Cmnd 9525. 1985. *Review Body on Top Salaries. Report no. 22: Eighth report on top salaries.*

Cmnd 9702-I. 1986. *The Government's Expenditure Plans 1986–87 to 1988–89.*

Cmnd 9841. 1986. *Civil Servants and Ministers: Duties and responsibilities. Govern-ment response to the seventh Report from the Treasury and Civil Service Committee, Session 1985–86, H.C. 92.*

Cmnd 9916. 1986. *Westland plc: The defence implications of the future of Westland plc. The Government's decision-making: Government response to the third and fourth Reports from the Defence Committee, Session 1985–86, H.C. 518 and 519.*

Cm. 78. 1987. *Accountability of Ministers and Civil Servants: Government response to the first Report from the Treasury and Civil Service Committee, session 1986–87, H.C. 62, and to the first Report from the Liaison Committee, session 1986–87, H.C. 100.*

Cm. 524. 1988. *Civil Service Management Reform: The next steps. The Government reply to the eighth Report from the Treasury and Civil Service Committee, session 1987–88, H.C. 494.*

Cm. 585. 1989. *Ministry of Defence Business Appointments: Government response to the second and ninth reports from the Defence Committee, session 1987–88, H.C. 392 and H.C. 622.*

Cm. 841. 1989. *Developments in the Next Steps Programme: The Government reply to the fifth Report from the Treasury and Civil Service Committee, session 1988–89, H.C. 348.*

Cm. 914. 1989. *The Financing and Accountability of Next Steps Agencies.*

Cm. 1261. 1990. *Improving Management in Government: The Next Steps agencies. Review 1990.*

Cm. 1263. 1990. *Progress in the Next Steps Initiative: The Government reply to the eighth Report from the Treasury and Civil Service Committee, session 1989–90, H.C. 481.*

Cm. 1599. 1991. *The Citizen's Charter. Raising the Standard.*

Cm. 1730. 1991. *Competing for Quality: Buying better public services.*

Cm. 1760. 1991. *Improving Management in Government: The Next Steps agencies. Review 1991.*

Cm. 1761. 1991. *The Next Steps Initiative: The Government's reply to the seventh Report from the Treasury and Civil Service Committee, session 1990–91, H.C. 496.*

Cm. 2101. 1992. *The Citizen's Charter: First Report.*

Cm. 2111. 1992. *The Next Steps Agencies: Review 1992.*

Cm. 2290. 1993. *Open Government.*

Cm. 2430. 1993. *Next Steps Agencies in Government: Review 1993.*

Cm. 2540. 1994. *The Citizen's Charter: Second Report, 1994.*

Cm. 2626. 1994. *Better Accounting for the Taxpayer's Money: Resource accounting and budgeting in Government.*

Cm. 2627. 1994. *The Civil Service: Continuity and change.*

B House of Commons Select Committee Reports

HC 308. 1964–5. *Sixth Report from the Estimates Committee: Recruitment to the Civil Service.*

HC 535. 1976–7. *Eleventh Report from the Expenditure Committee: The Civil Service.* Vol. I, *Report.* Vol. II, *Minutes of Evidence.* Vol. III. *Appendices.*

HC 54. 1980–1. *First Report from the Treasury and Civil Service Committee: The future of the Civil Service Department.*

HC 216. 1980–1. *Fourth Report from the Treasury and Civil Service Committee: Acceptance of outside appointments by civil servants.*

HC 171. 1981–2. *Sixth Report from the Committee of Public Accounts: Control of Civil Service manpower.*

HC 236. 1981–2. *Third Report from the Treasury and Civil Service Committee: Efficiency and effectiveness in the Civil Service.* Vol. I, *Report.* Vol. II, *Minutes of Evidence.* Vol. III, *Appendices.*

HC 150, 1983–4. *Fourteenth Report from the Committee of Public Accounts: Manpower control – reviewing the need for work.*

HC 302. 1983–4. *Eighth Report from the Treasury and Civil Service Committee: Acceptance of outside appointments by Crown servants.*

HC 92. 1985–6. *Seventh Report from the Treasury and Civil Service Committee: Civil servants and Ministers, duties and responsibilities.* Vol. I, *Report.* Vol. II, *Annexes, Minutes of Evidence, and Appendices.*

HC 518. 1985–6. *Third Report from the Defence Committee: Defence implications of the future of Westland plc.*

HC 519. 1985–6. *Fourth Report from the Defence Committee: Westland plc: The Government's decision-making.*

HC 61, 1986–7. *Thirteenth Report from the Committee of Public Accounts: The Financial Management Initiative.*

HC 62. 1986–7. *First Report from the Treasury and Civil Service Committee: Ministers and civil servants.*

HC 100. 1986–7. *First Report from the Liaison Committee: Accountability of Ministers and civil servants to select committees of the House of Commons.*

HC 358-I. 1986–7. *Treasury and Civil Service Committee Sub-Committee: Civil Service recruitment, training and career management, and public sector manpower. Minutes of evidence and appendices.*

HC 392. 1987–8. *Second Report from the Defence Committee: Business appointments. The acceptance of appointments in commerce and industry by members of the armed forces and officials of the Ministry of Defence.*

HC 494. 1987–8. *Eighth Report from the Treasury and Civil Service Committee: Civil Service management reform: The next steps. Vol. I, Report. Vol. II, Annexe, Minutes of Evidence and Appendices.*

HC 622. 1987–8. *Ninth Report from the Defence Committee: Business appointments. Observations on the Government's reply to the second Report, session 1987–88.*

HC 217. 1988–9. *Sixth Report from the Treasury and Civil Service Committee: Presentation of information on public expenditure.*

HC 348, 1988–9. *Fifth Report from the Treasury and Civil Service Committee: Developments in the Next Steps programme.*

HC 383. 1988–9. *Fourth Report from the Defence Committee: Statement on the defence estimates 1989.*

HC 420. 1988–9. *Thirty Eighth Report from the Committee of Public Accounts: The Next Steps initiative.*

HC 14. 1989–90. *First Report from the Defence Committee: The appointment of the Head of Defence Export Services.*

HC 260. 1989–90. *Fifth Report from the Treasury and Civil Service Committee: The Civil Service Pay and Conditions Code.*

HC 481. 1989–90. *Eighth Report from the Treasury and Civil Service Committee: Progress in the Next Steps initiative.*

HC 177. 1990–1. *Third Report from the Home Affairs Committee: Next Steps agencies.*

HC 178. 1990–1. *Third Report from the Select Committee on Procedure: Parliamentary questions.*

HC 269. 1990–1. *Fourth Report from the Treasury and Civil Service Committee: The acceptance of outside appointments by Crown servants.*

HC 496. 1990–1. *Seventh Report from the Treasury and Civil Service Committee: The Next Steps initiative.*

HC 617. 1990–1. *Fifth Special Report from the Treasury and Civil Service Committee: The Civil Service pay and Conditions Code. The Government's observations on the fifth Report from the Committee, session 1989–90, H.C. 260.*

HC 48. 1991–2. *First Special Report from the Treasury and Civil Service Committee: The acceptance of outside appointments by Crown servants. The Government's observations on the fourth Report from the Committee, session 1990–91, H.C. 269.*

HC 390. 1992–3. *Sixth Report from the Treasury and Civil Service Committtee: The role of the Civil Service; interim report. Vol. I, Report. Vol. II, Minutes of Evidence and Appendices.*

HC. 27. 1993–4. *Fifth Report from the Treasury and Civil Service Committee: The role of the Civil Service. Vol. I, Report. Vol. II, Minutes of Evidence. Vol. III, Appendices to the Minutes of Evidence.*

HC. 154. 1993–4. *Eighth Report from the Committee of Public Accounts: The proper conduct of public business.*

C Government Departments and Other Official Bodies

Allen Report. 1979. *Report of the Committee on the Selection Procedure for the Recruitment of Administration Trainees.* London: Civil Service Commission.

Anderson Report. 1923. *Report of the Committee on Pay etc. of State Servants.* London: HM Treasury.

Andren, P. 1992. *Developing the Strategic Management Approach: A historical perspective.* London: HM Treasury.

Atkinson Report. 1983. *Selection of Fast Stream Graduate Entrants to the Home Civil Service, the Diplomatic Service, and the Tax Inspectorate; and of Camdidates from Within the Service.* London: Civil Service Commission.

Cabinet Office. 1986. *Reforms at Work in the Civil Service.* London: Cabinet Office.

Cassells, J.S. 1983a. *Review of Running Costs: Report to the Prime Minister.* London: HMSO.

Cassells, J.S. 1983b. *Review of Personnel Work in the Civil Service: Report to the Prime Minister.* London: HMSO.

Civil Service College. Annual Reports.

Civil Service Commissioners. Annual Reports.

Civil Service Department. *Civil Service Statistics* (since 1981, Treasury).

Clements-Bedford Report. 1992. *Fast Stream Cohort Research: Ten to twenty year follow up. Analysis of the relationship between CSSB procedures and subsequent job performance.* London: Recruitment and Assessment Services.

Coster Report. 1984. *Training for Senior Management Study: Outline proposals for a senior management development programme.* London: Management and Personnel Office.

Durham, P. (ed.) 1987. *Output and Performance Measurement in Central Government: Some practical achievements.* Treasury Working Paper No. 45.

Efficiency Unit. 1984. *Consultancy Inspection and Review Services in Government Departments: Report to the Prime Minister.* London: Cabinet Office.

Efficiency Unit. 1985. *Making Things Happen: A report on the implementation of government efficiency scrutinies.* London: Cabinet Office.

Efficiency Unit. 1988. *Improving Management in Government: The next steps. Report to the Prime Minister* (Ibbs Report/Next Steps Report). London: HMSO.

Efficiency Unit. 1991. *Making the Most of Next Steps: The management of Ministers' departments and their executive agencies. Report to the Prime Minister* (Fraser Report). London: HMSO.

Efficiency Unit. 1993a. *Career Management and Succession Planning Study* (Oughton Report). London: HMSO.

Efficiency Unit. 1993b. *The Government's Guide to Market Testing.* London: HMSO.

Efficiency Unit. 1994a. *Multi-Disciplinary Scrutiny of Public Sector Research Establishments.* London: HMSO.

Efficiency Unit. 1994b. *The Government's Use of External Consultants.* London: HMSO.

Eland Report. 1985. *Scrutiny of the Means of Identifying and Developing Internal Talent. Central Report and Action Plan.* London: Management and Personnel Office.

Goldman, Sir S. 1973. *The Developing System of Public Expenditure Management and Control,* Civil Service Studies 2. London: Civil Service Department.

Goldsworthy, D. 1991. *Setting up Next Steps.* London: HMSO.

Heaton–Williams Report. 1974. *Civil Service Training: Report by R.N. Heaton and Sir L. Williams.* London: Civil Service Department.

Lewis, S. (ed.) 1986. *Output and Performance Measurement in Central Government. Progress in Departments.* Treasury Working Paper no. 38. London: HM Treasury.

Management and Personnel Office. 1983. *Civil Service Management Development in the 1980s.* London: MPO.

Management and Personnel Office. 1984. *Government Purchasing: A multi-department review of Government contract and procurement procedures.* London: MPO.

Management and Personnel Office. 1985. *Office Accommodation: A multi-department review of the management of Government office accommodation.* London: MPO.

Management and Personnel Office. 1987. *The Challenge of Change in the Civil Service.* London: MPO.

Mueller Report. 1987. *Working Patterns: A study document by the Cabinet Office (Management and Personnel Office).* London: HM Treasury.

National Audit Office. 1986a. *The Rayner Scrutiny Programmes 1979–1983.* HC 322 (1985–6). London: HMSO.

National Audit Office: 1986b. *The Financial Management Initiative.* HC 588. (1985–6). London: HMSO.

National Audit Office. 1987. *The Ministry of Defence and Property Services Agency: Control and management of the defence estate.* HC 131 (1986–7). London: HMSO.

National Audit Office. 1989a. *Ministry of Defence: Control and use of manpower.* HC 342 (1988–9). London: HMSO.

National Audit Office. 1989b. *Manpower Planning in the Civil Service.* HC 398 (1988–9). London: HMSO.

National Audit Office. 1989c. *The Next Step Initiative.* HC 410 (1988–9). London: HMSO.

National Audit Office. 1992. *Local Pay Additions.* HC 259 (1991–2). London: HMSO.

Office of Public Service and Science. 1994a. *Review of Fast Stream Recruitment.* London: OPSS.

Office of Public Service and Science. 1994b. *Responsibilities for Recruitment to the Civil Service.* London: OPSS.

Reader, K.M. 1981. *The Civil Service Commission 1855–1975.* Civil Service Studies 5. London: Civil Service Department.

Treasury. 1984a. *Budgetary Control Systems: Implementation Report by the Cabinet Office (MPO)/Treasury Financial Management Unit.* London: HM Treasury.

Treasury. 1984b. *Top Management Systems: Report by the Cabinet Office (MPO)/Treasury Financial Management Unit.* London: HM Treasury.

Treasury. 1985a. *Policy Work and the F.M.I. Report by the Cabinet Office (MPO)/Treasury Financial Management Unit.* London: HM Treasury.

Treasury. 1985b. *Top Management Systems: Second report by the Cabinet Office (MPO)/Treasury Financial Management Unit.* London: HM Treasury.

Treasury. 1985c. *Resource Allocation in Departments: Role of the Principal Finance Officer, Report by the Cabinet Office (MPO)/Treasury Financial Management Unit.* London: HM Treasury.

Treasury. 1986a. *Multi-Departmental Review of Budgeting: Executive summary and final central report.* London: HM Treasury.

Treasury. 1986b. *Using Private Enterprise in Government: Report of a multi-departmental review of competitive tendering and contracting for services in Government departments.* London: HM Treasury.

Treasury. 1987a. *Flexible Pay: A new pay regime in the Civil Service.* London: HM Treasury.

Treasury. 1987b. *Agreement on the Pay, Pay System, Organization and Personnel Management Agreements for Grades and Groups Represented by the Institution of Professional Civil Servants.* May 1987. London: HM Treasury.

Treasury. 1987c. *New Pay Arrangements in the Inland Revenue: Text of the provisional agreement between H.M. Treasury and the Board of Inland Revenue (on behalf of the official side) and the Inland Revenue Staff Federation.* November 1987. London: HM Treasury.

Treasury. 1988. *New Pay Arrangements for Grades 5, 6 and 7: Text of the agreement between H.M. Treasury (on behalf of the official side), and the Association of First Division Civil Servants, the Institution of Professional Civil Servants and the National Union of Civil and Public Servants.* July 1988. London: HM Treasury.

Treasury. 1989a. *New Pay Arrangements for Executive, Office Support and Related Grades: Text of the agreement between H.M. Treasury (on behalf of the official side) and the National Union of Civil and Public Servants.* April 1989. London: HM Treasury.

Treasury. 1989b. *New Pay Arrangements for Clerical and Secretarial Grades: Text of the agreement between H.M. Treasury (on behalf of the official side) and the Civil and Public Services Association.* April 1989. London: HM Treasury.

Treasury. 1990. *Made to Measure: Patterns of work in the Civil Service.* London: HM Treasury.

Treasury. 1991. Civil Service Pay. *Treasury Bulletin* 2 (Autumn), 45–9. London: HM Treasury.

Treasury. 1992a. *New Pay Arrangements for Grades 5, 6 and 7: Text of the agreement between H.M. Treasury (on behalf of the official side), and the Association of First Division Civil Servants, the Institution of Professionals, Managers and Specialists, and the National Union of Civil and Public Servants.* September 1992. London: HM Treasury.

Treasury. 1992b. *Agreement on the Pay, Pay System, Organization and Personnel Management Arrangements for Grades and Groups Represented by the Institution of Professionals, Managers and Specialists.* November 1992. London: HM Treasury.

Treasury. 1992c. *New Pay Arrangements for Executive, Office Support and Related Grades: Text of the agreement between H.M. Treasury (on behalf of the official side) and the National Union of Civil and Public Servants.* October 1992. London: HM Treasury.

Treasury, 1992d. *New Pay Arrangements for Clerical and Secretarial Grades: Text of the agreement between H.M. Treasury (on behalf of the official side) and the Civil and Public Services Association.* November 1992. London: HM Treasury.

Treasury. 1992e. *Efficiency Scrutiny of the Administration of the Principal Civil Service Pension Scheme.* December 1992. London: HM Treasury.

Treasury. 1994. *Fundamental Review of H.M. Treasury's Running Costs.* London: HM Treasury.

Treasury and OPSS 1993. *A Picture of Flexible Working in Government Departments and Agencies.* London: HM Treasury.

Trosa Report. 1994. *Next Steps: Moving on.* London: Office of Public Service and Science.

Wardale Report. 1981. *Chain of Command Review: The open structure.* London: Civil Service Department.

Wilding, R.W. 1979. *The Professional Ethic of the Administrator*. Civil Service College Working Paper no. 10.

III FURTHER SOURCES

Abromeit, H. 1986. *British Steel: An industry between the state and the private sector*. Heidelberg: Berg.

Allen, F.H. 1981. 'The basis and organization of recruitment', *Management Services in Government*, 36, 21–8.

Amery, L.S. 1947. *Thoughts on the Constitution*. Oxford: Oxford University Press.

Amery, L.S. 1953. *My Political Life*, Vol. II. London: Hutchinson.

Anderson, B. 1986. 'Thatcherites who would prefer to be without Thatcher', *The Spectator* 26 July.

Baker, K. 1993. *The Turbulent Years*. London: Faber and Faber.

Baldwin, S. 1935. *This Torch of Freedom: Speeches and addresses*. London: Hodder and Stoughton.

Balfour, Lord. 1927. *Opinions and Argument 1910–1927*. London: Hodder and Stoughton.

Balfour, Lord. 1928. 'Introduction', in W. Bagehot, *The English Constitution*. London: Oxford University Press.

Beckingsale, B.W. 1978. *Thomas Cromwell: Tudor minister*. London: Macmillan.

Benn, T. 1981. *Arguments for Democracy*. London: Cape.

Birkenhead, Lord. 1961. *The Prof in Two Worlds: The official life of Professor F.A. Lindemann, Viscount Cherwell*. London: Collins.

Birkenhead, Lord. 1965. *Halifax: The life of Lord Halifax*. London: Hamish Hamilton.

Birkenhead, Lord. 1969. *Walter Monckton: The life of Viscount Monckton of Brenchley*. London: Weidenfeld and Nicolson.

Blackstone, T. and Plowden, W. 1988. *Inside the Think Tank: Advising the Cabinet 1971–1983*. London: Heinemann.

Blake, R. 1955. *The Unknown Prime Minister: The life and times of Andrew Bonar Law 1858–1923*. London: Eyre and Spottiswoode.

Blake, Lord, and Cecil, H. 1987. *Salisbury: The man and his policies*. London: Macmillan.

Boston, J. 1993. 'Financial management reform: principles and practice in New Zealand', *Public Policy and Administration* 8, 14–29.

Boston, J., Martin, J., Pallott, J. and Walsh, P. (eds) 1991. *Reshaping the State: New Zealand's bureaucratic revolution*. Auckland: Oxford University Press.

Bray, A.J.M. 1987. *The Clandestine Reformer: A study of the Rayner scrutinies*. (Strathclyde Papers on Government and Politics no. 55). Glasgow: University of Strathclyde.

Braybrooke, D., and Lindblom, C.E. 1963. *A Strategy of Decision*. London: Collier-Macmillan.

Breton, A. 1974. *The Economic Theory of Representative Government*. Chicago: Adline-Atherton.

Bridges, Sir E.E. 1950. *Portrait of a Profession: The Civil Service tradition*. Cambridge: Cambridge University Press.

Bridges, Sir E.E. 1954. 'The reforms of 1854 in retrospect', *Political Quarterly* 25, 316–23.

Buchanan, J.M. 1960. *Fiscal Theory and Political Economy*. Chapel Hill: University of North Carolina Press.

Buchanan, J.M. 1975. *The Limits of Liberty: Between anarchy and Leviathan*. Chicago: University of Chicago Press.

Buchanan, J.M., and Tullock, G. 1962. *The Calculus of Consent*. Ann Arbor: University of Michigan Press.

Buchanan, J.M., and Wagner, R.E. 1977. *Democracy in Deficit: The political legacy of Lord Keynes*. New York: Academic Press.

Buchanan, J.M. *et al*. 1978. *The Economic of Politics*. London: Institute of Economic Affairs.

Butler, E., Pirie, M., and Young, P. 1985. *The Omega File*. London: Adam Smith Institute.

Butler, Sir R. 1993. 'The evolution of the Civil Service: a progress report', *Public Administration* 71, 395–406.

Butler, Sir R. 1994. 'Reinventing British government', *Public Administration* 72, 263–70.

Butler, R.A. 1948. 'Reform of the Civil Service', *Public Administration*, 26, 169–72.

Butler, R.A. 1949. 'Conservative policy', *Political Quarterly*, 20, 317–25.

Butler, Lord. 1971. *The Art of the Possible*. London: Hamish Hamilton.

Campbell, J. 1993. *Edward Heath*. London: Cape.

Campbell, J. *et al*. 1990a. 'Conservative Party policy making 1965–70, Part I', *Contemporary Record* 3, no. 3 (February), 36–8.

Campbell, J. *et al*. 1990b. 'Conservative Party policy making 1965–70, Part II', *Contemporary Record* 3, no. 4 (April) 34–6.

Campbell, R. 1985. *Collected Works*, Vol. I: *Poetry*. Craighill: Donker.

Carlton, D. 1981. *Anthony Eden: A biography*. London: Allen Lane.

Cecil, Lady G. 1932. *Life of Robert Marquis of Salisbury*, vol. IV: *1887–1892*. London: Hodder and Stoughton.

Chamberlain, Sir A. 1930. 'Civil Service traditions and the League of Nations', *Public Adminstration*, 8, 3–9.

Chamberlain, Sir A. 1935. *Down The Years*. London: Cassell.

Chandos, Lord. 1962. *Memoirs*. London: Bodley Head.

Chapman, L. 1978. *Your Disobedient Servant*. London: Chatto and Windus.

Chapman, L. 1980. 'Action not words', *The Spectator*, 17 May.

Chapman, L. 1982. *Waste Away*. London: Chatto and Windus.

Chapman, R.A. 1984. *Leadership in the British Civil Service: A study of Sir Percival Waterfield and the creation of the Civil Service Selection Board*. London: Croom Helm.

Chapman, R.A. 1988. *Ethics in the British Civil Service*. London: Routledge.

Chapman, R.A., and Greenaway, J. 1980. *The Dynamics of Administrative Reform*. London: Croom Helm.

Churchill, W.S. 1906. *Lord Randolph Churchill*, Vol. I. London: Macmillan.

Civil and Public Services Association and National Union of Civil and Public Servants. 1988. *Changing Working Patterns. In whose interest?* London: CPSA and NUCPS.

Clarke, Sir R.W. 1978. *Public Expenditure Management and Control: The development of the Public Expenditure Survey Committee*. London: Macmillan.

Cole, M. (ed.) 1956. *Beatrice Webb's Diaries 1924–1932*. London: Longmans, Green.

Coleman, C. and Starkey, D. (eds) 1986. *Revolution Reassessed: Revisions in the history of Tudor government and administration*. Oxford: Clarendon Press.

Colville, J. 1985. *The Fringes of Power: Downing Street diaries 1939–1955*. London: Hodder and Stoughton.

Cooper, Sir F. 1981. 'Management and money', *Management Services in Government* 36, 5–20.

Cooper, J.P. 1963. 'A revolution in Tudor history', *Past and Present* 26, 110–12.

Coster, P.R. 1987. 'The Civil Service senior management programme', *Employment Gazette* June, 291–300.

Council of Civil Service Unions. 1992. *Competing for Quality: Jobs for sale*. London: CCSU.

Council of Civil Service Unions. 1993. *CCSU Comments on the Government's Guide to Market Testing*. London: CCSU.

Craig, F.W.S. (ed.) 1975. *British Central Election Manifestos 1900–1974*. London: Macmillan.

Croham, Lord. 1985. *Would Greater Openness Improve or Weaken Government?* The Chancellor's Lecture 1984. University of Salford.

Cromwell, V. 1965–6. 'Interpretations of nineteenth century administration: an analysis', *Victorian Studies* 9, 245–55.

Crossman, R.H.S. 1972. *Inside View*. London: Cape.

Dahl, R.A., and Lindblom, C.E. 1953. *Politics, Economics and Welfare*. New York: Harper and Row.

Dale, H.E. 1941. *The Higher Civil Service of Great Britain*. London: Oxford University Press.

Dempster, M.A.H., and Wildavsky, A. 1979. 'On change; or there is no magic size for an increment', *Political Studies* 27, 371–89.

Dilks, D. 1984. *Neville Chamberlain*, Vol. I: *Pioneering and Reform 1869–1929*. Cambridge: Cambridge University Press.

Dror, Y. 1964. 'Muddling through: "science" or inertia?', *Public Administration Review* 24, 153–7.

Dror, Y. 1968. *Public Policy Making Re-examined*. Scranton, Penn.: Chandler.

Dror, Y. 1971. *Design for Policy Sciences*. New York: American Elsevier.

Dror, Y. 1986. *Policy Making Under Adversity*. New Brunswick: Transaction.

Dunnill, F. 1956. *The Civil Service: Some human aspects*. London: Allen and Unwin.

Dutton, D. 1985. *Austen Chamberlain: Gentleman in politics*. Bolton: Ross Anderson.

Eden, Sir A. 1960. *Full Circle*. London: Cassell.

Egremont, Lord. 1968. *Wyndham and Children First*. London: Macmillan.

Elder, N.C.M. 1970. *Government in Sweden*. Oxford: Pergamon.

Elliot, W. 1948. 'Where will Civil Service expansion end?', *Public Administration* 26, 250–2.

Elton, G.R. 1953. *The Tudor Revolution in Government: Administrative changes in the reign of Henry VIII*. London: Cambridge University Press.

Elton, G.R. 1964. 'The Tudor revolution: a reply', *Past and Present* 29, 26–49.

Elton, G.R. 1965. 'A revolution in Tudor history?', *Past and Present* 32, 103–9.

Erickson, C.J. 1959. *British Industrialists Steel and Hoisery 1850–1950*. Cambridge: Cambridge University Press.

Etzioni, A. 1967. 'Mixed scanning: a "third" approach to decision making', *Public Administration Review* 27, 385–92.

Etzioni, A. 1968. *The Active Society*. London: Collier-Macmillan.

Etzioni, A. 1986. 'Mixed scanning revisited', *Public Administration Review* 46, 8–14.

Evans, H. 1981. *Downing Street Diary: The Macmillan years 1957–1963*. London: Hodder and Stoughton.

Evans, M. 1994. 'The true cost of government', *Parliamentary Brief* 3, no. 1, 31–2.

Feiling, K. 1946. *The Life of Neville Chamberlain*. London: Macmillan.

Fowler, N. 1991. *Ministers Decide*. London: Chapmans.

Fry, G.K. 1969. *Statesmen in Disguise: The changing role of the administrative class of the British Home Civil Service 1853–1966*. London: Macmillan.

Fry, G.K. 1974. 'Civil Service salaries in the post-Priestley era 1956–1972', *Public Administration* 52, 319–33.

Fry, G.K. 1979. *The Growth of Government: The development of ideas about the role of the state and the machinery and functions of government in Britain since 1780*. London: Cass.

Fry, G.K. 1981. *The Administrative 'Revolution' in Whitehall: A study of the politics of administrative change in British central government since the 1950s*. London: Croom Helm.

Fry, G.K. 1983. 'Compromise with the market: the Megaw Report on Civil Service pay 1982', *Public Administration* 61, 90–6.

Fry, G.K. 1985. *The Changing Civil Service*. London: Allen and Unwin.

Fry, G.K. 1991. 'A reconsideration of the British general election of 1935 and the electoral revoluton of 1945', *History* 76, 43–53.

Fry, G.K. 1993. *Reforming the Civil Service: The Fulton Committee on the British Home Civil Service 1966–1968*. Edinburgh: Edinburgh University Press.

Gibbon, Sir G. 1943. 'The civil servant: his place and training', *Public Administration* 21, 85–90.

Gilbert, M.J. 1966. *The Roots of Appeasement*. London: Weidenfeld and Nicolson.

Gilbert, M.J. 1976. *Winston S. Churchill*, Vol. V: *1922–1939*. London: Heinemann.

Gilbert, M.J. 1979. *Winston S. Churchill*, Vol. V: *Companion*, Part I: *Documents 1922–1939*. London: Heinemann.

Gilbert, M.J. 1988. *Winston S. Churchill*, Vol. VIII: *1945–1965*. London: Heinemann.

Gilbert, M.J., and Gott, R. 1963. *The Appeasers*. London: Weidenfeld and Nicolson.

Goodsell, C.T. 1994. *The Case for Bureaucracy*. Chatham NJ: Chatham House.

Gosling, R. and Nutley, S. 1990. *Bridging the Gap: Secondments between government and business*. London: Royal Institute of Public Administration.

Greenaway, J.R. 1985. 'Parliamentary reform and Civil Service reform: a nineteenth century debate reassessed', *Parliamentary History* 4, 157–69.

Greenaway, J.R. 1992. 'British Conservatism and bureaucracy', *History of Political Thought* 13, 129–60.

Greenleaf, W.H. 1983. *The British Political Tradition*, Vol. II: *The Ideological Inheritance*. London: Routledge.

Hardcastle, A. *et al.* 1983. *Management Information and Control in Whitehall*. London: RIPA.

Harriss, G.L. 1963. 'A revolution in Tudor history? Medieval government and statecraft', *Past and Present* 25, 8–39.

Harriss, G.L., and Williams, P. 1965. 'A revolution in Tudor history?', *Past and Present* 31, 87–96.

Hart, J. 1965. 'Nineteenth century social reform: a Tory interpretation of history', *Past and Present* 31, 39–61.

Hartley, K. 1986. 'Economic models of Civil Service reform', in A. Shenfield *et al.*, (ed.) *Managing the Bureaucracy*. London: Adam Smith Institute.

Harvey, S.P.J. 1975. 'Domesday Book and Anglo-Norman governance', *Transactions of the Royal Historical Society*, 5s., 25, 175–93.

Headlam, Sir C. *et al.* 1946. *Some Proposals for Constitutional Reform.* London: Eyre and Spottiswoode.

Healey, D.W. 1989. *The Time of My Life.* London: Michael Joseph.

Heath, A.F. 1981. *Social Mobility.* Glasgow: Fontana.

Heath, E., and Barker, A. 1978. 'Heath on Whitehall reform', *Parliamentary Affairs* 31, 363–90.

Heclo, H. 1977. *A Government of Strangers: Executive politics in Washington.* Washington, D.C.: Brookings Institution.

Heclo, H., and Salamon, L.M. (eds.) 1981. *The Illusion of Presidential Government.* Boulder, Col.: Westview Press.

Heclo, H. and Wildavsky, A. 1974. *The Private Government of Public Money.* London: Macmillan.

Hennessy, P. 1989a. 'The Civil Service', in D. Kavanagh and A. Seldon (eds) *The Thatcher Effect.* Oxford: Clarendon Press.

Hennessy, P. 1989b. *Whitehall.* London: Secker and Warburg.

Hennessy, P., Morrison, S. and Townsend, R. 1985. *Routine Punctuated by Orgies: The Central Policy Review Staff 1970–1983.* Strathclyde Papers on Government and Politics no. 31. Glasgow: University of Strathclyde.

Heseltine, M. 1980. 'Ministers and management in Whitehall', *Management Services in Government* 35, 61–8.

Heseltine, M. 1987. *Where There's a Will.* London: Hutchinson.

Hewart, Lord. 1929. *The New Despotism.* London: Benn.

Home, Lord. 1976. *The Way the Wind Blows.* London: Collins.

Hood, C. 1990a. *Beyond the Public Bureaucracy State? Public administration in the 1990s.* London: London School of Economics.

Hood, C. 1990b. 'Public administration: lost an empire, not yet found a role?', in A. Leftwich (ed.) *New Developments in Political Science.* Aldershot: Elgar.

Hood, C. 1991. 'A public management for all seasons?', *Public Administration,* 69, 3–19.

Hoskyns, Sir J. 1983. 'Whitehall and Westminster: an outsider's view', *Parliamentary Affairs* 36, 137–47.

Hoskyns, Sir J. 1984. 'Conservatism is not enough', *Political Quarterly* 55, 3–16.

Hoskyns, Sir J. *et al.* 1986. *Re-skilling Government: Proposals for the experimental introduction of ministerial cabinets.* London: Institute of Directors.

Howard, A. 1987. *Rab: The life of R.A. Butler.* London: Cape.

Howell, D. 1968. *Whose Government Works?* London: Conservative Political Centre.

Howell, D. 1970. *A New Style of Government.* London: Conservative Political Centre.

Howell, D. 1971. *A New Style Emerges.* London: Conservative Political Centre.

Hurd, D. 1979. *An End to Promises: Sketch of a government 1970–74.* London: Collins.

Institute of Directors. 1986a. *Re-skilling Government Seminar.* London: Institute of Directors.

Institute of Directors. 1986b. *Re-skilling Government: The boundaries of the reform process.* London: Institute of Directors.

James, R.R. 1972. *Ambitions and Realities: British politics 1964–70.* London: Weidenfeld and Nicolson.

James, R.R. (ed.) 1974. *Winston S. Churchill: His complete speeches 1897–1963,* Vol. III: *1914–1922.* London: Chelsea House.

James, R.R. 1986. *Anthony Eden*. London: Weidenfeld and Nicolson.

Jenkins, S., and Sloman, A. 1985. *With Respect Ambassador: An inquiry into the Foreign Office*. London: BBC.

Koh, B.C. 1989. *Japan's Administrative Elite*. Berkeley: University of California Press.

Jessel, D. 1980. 'Mandarins and ministers', *The Listener*, 11 December.

Jones, G.W. 1976. 'The Prime Minister's secretaries: politicians or administrators?', in J.A.G. Griffith (ed.) *From Policy to Administration: Essays in honour of William A. Robson*. London: Allen and Unwin.

Jones, R.W. 1964. 'The model as a decision maker's dilemma', *Public Administration Review* 24, 158–60.

Kahn, H.R. 1962. *Salaries in the Public Services in England and Wales*. London: Allen and Unwin.

Katzman, R.A. 1980. *Regulatory Bureaucracy: The Federal Trade Commission and antitrust policy*. Cambridge, Mass.: MIT Press.

Keeble, S.P. 1992. *The Ability to Manage: A study of British management 1890–1990*. Manchester: Manchester University Press.

Keeling, D. 1971. 'The development of central training in the Civil Service 1963–1970, *Public Administration*, 49, 51–71.

Kellner, P., and Crowther-Hunt, Lord. 1980. *The Civil Servants: An inquiry into Britain's ruling class*. London: Macdonald.

Kemp, Sir P. 1993. *Beyond Next Steps: A Civil Service for the twenty-first century*. London: Social Market Foundation.

Kemp, Sir P. 1994a. 'The mandarins emerge unscathed', *Parliamentary Brief* 2, no. 10, 49–50.

Kemp, Sir P. 1994b. 'The Civil Service White Paper: a job half finished', *Public Administration* 72, 525–32.

King, A. (ed.) 1976. *Why is Britain Becoming Harder to Govern?* London: BBC.

Kooiman, J., and Eliassen, K. (eds) 1987. *Managing Public Organizations: Lessons from contemporary European experience*. London: Sage.

Lane, J.E. 1993. *The Public Sector: Concepts, models and approaches*. London: Sage.

Laski, H.J. 1938. *Parliamentary Government in England*. London: Allen and Unwin.

Laski, H.J. 1942. 'Introduction', in J.P.W. Mallalieu (ed.) *Passed to you Please*. London: Gollancz.

Laski, H.J. 1943. 'The education of the civil servant', *Public Administration* 21, 13–23.

Laski, H.J. 1951. *Reflections on the Constitution*. Manchester: Manchester University Press.

Lawson, N. 1992. *The View from No. 11: Memoirs of a Tory radical*. London: Bantam Press.

Legge-Bourke, H. 1950. *Master of the Offices: An essay and correspondence on the central control of His Majesty's Civil Service*. London: Falcon Press.

Lerner, A.P. 1944. *The Economics of Control: Principles of welfare economics*. New York: Macmillan.

Letwin, S.R. 1992. *The Anatomy of Thatcherism*. London: Fontana.

Levitt, M. 1985. *Productivity in Central Government*. London: Public Finance Foundation.

Lewis, R., and Maude, A. 1949. *The English Middle Classes*. London: Phoenix House.

Likierman, A. 1982. 'Management information for ministers: the MINIS system in the Department of the Environment', *Public Administration* 60, 127–42.

Lindblom, C.E. 1958. 'Policy analysis', *American Economic Review* 48, 298–312.

Lindblom, C.E. 1959. 'The science of "muddling through" ', *Public Administration Review* 19, 79–88.

Lindblom, C.E. 1964. 'Contexts for change & strategy: a reply', *Public Administration Review* 24, 157–8.

Lindblom, C.E. 1965. *The Intelligence of Democracy.* New York: Free Press.

Lindblom, C.E. 1968. *The Policy Making Process.* Englewood Cliffs, N.J.: Prentice Hall.

Lindblom, C.E. 1977. *Politics and Markets.* New York: Basic Books.

Lindblom, C.E. 1979. 'Still muddling, not yet through', *Public Administration Review* 39, 517–26.

Lindblom, C.E. 1980. *The Policy Making Process*, 2nd edn. Englewood Cliffs, NJ: Prentice Hall.

Lindblom, C.E. 1990. *Inquiry and Change.* London: Yale University Press.

Lindblom, C.E., and Cohen, D.K. 1979. *Usable Knowledge.* New Haven, Conn.: Yale University Press.

Lindblom, C.E. and Woodhouse, E.J. 1993. *The Policy Making Process*, 3rd edn. Englewood Cliffs, NJ: Prentice Hall.

MacDonagh, O. 1958. 'The nineteenth century revolution in government: a reappraisal', *Historical Journal* 1, 52–67.

Macdonald, G. 1937. 'Sir Henry Craik', in J.R.H. Weaver (ed.) *The Dictionary of National Biography 1922–1930.* London: Oxford University Press.

Mackenzie, G.C. 1981. *The Politics of Presidential Appointments.* New York: Free Press.

Macmillan, H. 1969. *Tides of Fortune 1945–1955.* London: Macmillan.

Macmillan, H. 1972. *Pointing the Way 1959–1961.* London: Macmillan.

Macmillan, H. 1973. *At the End of the Day 1961–1963.* London: Macmillan.

Major, J. 1989. 'Public service management: revolution in progress', speech to the Audit Commission, 21 June.

Marshall, G. 1984. *Constitutional Conventions: The rules and forms of political accountability.* Oxford: Clarendon Press.

Massey, A. 1993. *Managing the Public Sector: A comparative analysis of the United Kingdom and the United States.* Aldershot: Elgar.

Mather, G. 1991. *Government by Contract.* London: Institute of Economic Affairs.

Meow, S.C. 1985. 'The Civil Service', in J.S.T. Quah, C.H. Chee and S.C. Meow (eds) *The Government and Politics of Singapore.* Singapore: Oxford University Press.

Metcalfe, L. 1993. 'Public management: from initiation to innovation', in J. Kooiman (ed.) *Modern Governance: New government–society interactions.* London: Sage.

Metcalfe, L., and Richards, S. 1990. *Improving Public Management*, 2nd edn. London: Sage.

Moore, N.E.A. 1984. 'The Civil Service College: what it is and what it is not', *Management Services in Government* 39, 96–103.

Moran, Lord. 1966. *Winston Churchill: The struggle for survival 1940–1965.* London: Constable.

Mothio, H. 1989. *Top Management Information Systems in Whitehall.* London: London PA Consulting Group.

Mueller, A. 1985a. *The Civil Service in the Year 200.* CIPFA Centenary Conference. 19 June.

Mueller, A. 1985b. *Better Results through People in the Civil Service*. RIPA, Belfast, 11 October.

Murray, K.A.G. 1990. *Reflections on Public Service Selection*. Privately published.

Namier, Sir L.B. 1955. *Personalities and Powers*. London: Hamish Hamilton.

Nelson, M. 1982. 'A short, ironic history of American national bureaucracy', *Journal of Politics*, 44, 747–78.

Niskanen, W.A. 1971. *Bureaucracy and Representative Government*. Chicago: Aldine.

Niskanen, W.A. *et al.* 1973. *Bureaucracy: Servant or master?* London: Institute of Economic Affairs.

Nottage, R., and Stack, F. 1972. 'The Royal Institute of Public Administration 1922–1939', *Public Administration*, 50, 281–304.

O'Halpin, E. 1989. *Head of the Civil Service: A Study of Sir Warren Fisher*. London: Routledge.

Osborne, D., and Gaebler, T. 1992. *Reinventing Government*. New York: Addison-Wesley.

Parris, H. 1960. 'The nineteenth century revolution in government: a reappraisal reappraised', *Historical Journal* 3, 17–37.

Peden, G.C. 1979. *British Rearmament and the Treasury 1932–1939*. Edinburgh: Scottish Academic Press.

Percy, Lord E. 1933. 'The Civil Service under modern conditions of legislation and administration', *Public Administration*, 11, 3–14.

Perry, J., and Kraemer, K.L. (eds) 1983. *Public Management: Public and private perspectives*. Calif.: Mayfield.

Peters, C., and Nelson, M. (eds) 1979. *The Culture of Bureaucracy*. New York: Holt, Rinehart and Winston.

Peters, T.J., and Waterman, R.H. 1982. *In Search of Excellence: Lessons from America's best run companies*. New York: Harper and Row.

Petrie, Sir C. 1940. *The Life and Letters of Sir Austen Chamberlain*, Vol. II. London: Cassell.

Petrie, Sir C. 1958. *The Powers behind the Prime Minister*. London: MacGibbon and Kee.

Pirie, M. 1988. *Privatization in Theory and Practice*. London: Adam Smith Institute.

Pliatzky, Sir L. 1982. *Getting and Spending: Public expenditure, employment and inflation*. Oxford: Blackwell.

Pliatzky, Sir L. 1986. 'Can government be efficient?', *Lloyds Bank Review*, 159, 22–32.

Political and Economic Planning. 1965. *Thrusters and Sleepers. A Study of Attitudes in Industrial Management*. London: Allen and Unwin.

Pollitt, C. 1984. *Manipulating the Machine: Changing the pattern of ministerial departments 1960–1983*. London: Allen and Unwin.

Pollitt, C. 1990. *Managerialism and the Public Services: The Anglo-American experience*. Oxford: Blackwell.

Ponting, C. 1985. *The Right to Know: The inside story of the Belgrano Affair*. London: Sphere.

Ponting, C. 1986. *Whitehall: Tragedy and farce*, London: Hamish Hamilton.

Posner, R.A. 1974. 'Theories of economic regulation', *Bell Journal of Economics and Management* 5, 335–58.

Powell, E. 1953. 'Conservatives and social services', *Political Quarterly* 24, 156–66.

Prior, J. 1986. *A Balance of Power*. London: Hamish Hamilton.

Pyper, R. 1985. 'Sarah Tisdall, Ian Willmore and the civil servants' "right to leak" ', *Political Quarterly* 56, 72–81.

Rainey, H.G. 1991. *Understanding and Managing Public Organizations*. San Francisco: Jossey-Bass.

Ramsden, J. 1980. *The Making of Conservative Party Policy: The Conservative research department since 1929*. London: Longman.

Rayner, Lord. 1984. *The Unfinished Agenda*. London: University of London.

Regnier, P. 1987. *Singapore: City state in South East Asia*. London: Hurst.

Richards, D. 1993. *Appointments in the Higher Civil Service*. Strathclyde Papers in Government and Politics no. 93. Glasgow: University of Strathclyde.

Richardson, H.G., and Sayles, G.O. 1963. *The Governance of Medieval England from the Conquest to Magna Carta*. Edinburgh: Edinburgh University Press.

Ridley, N. 1973. *Industry and the Civil Service*. London: Aims of Industry.

RIPA Working Group. 1987. *Top Jobs in Whitehall: Appointments and promotions in the senior Civil Service*. London: RIPA.

Roberts, A. 1991. *'The Holy Fox': A biography of Lord Halifax*. London: Weidenfeld and Nicolson.

Robertson, K.G. 1982. *Public Secrets: A study in the development of government secrecy*. London: Macmillan.

Robson, W.A. (ed.) 1956. *The Civil Service in Britain and France*. London: Allen and Unwin.

Robson, W.A. 1971. 'The reorganization of central government', *Political Quarterly* 42, 87–90.

Robson Brown, Sir W. *et al.* 1963. *Change or Decay*. London: Conservative Political Centre.

Rose, K. 1969. *Superior Person: A portrait of Curzon and his circle in late Victorian England*. London: Weidenfeld and Nicolson.

Rubinstein, W.D. 1986. 'Education and the social origins of British elites 1880–1970', *Past and Present*, 112, 163–207.

Rubinstein, W.D. 1993. *Capitalism, Culture and Decline in Britain 1750–1990*. London: Routledge.

Saltman, L.M., and Lund, M.S. (eds) 1981. *The Reagan Presidency and the Governing of America*: Washington D.C.: Urban Institute Press.

Sandhu, K.S., and Wheatley, P. (eds) 1989. *Management of Success: The moulding of modern Singapore*. Singapore: Institute of South East Asian Studies.

Seldon, A. 1981. *Churchill's Indian Summer: The Conservative Government 1951–1955*. London: Hodder and Stoughton.

Selznick, P. 1966. *TVA and the Grassroots: A study in the sociology of formal institutions*. New York: Harper and Row.

Semple, M. 1979. 'Employment in the public and private sectors 1961–1978', *Economic Trends*, 313, 90–108.

Shuckburgh, Sir E. 1986. *Descent to Suez: Diaries 1951–1956*. London: Weidenfeld and Nicolson.

Sisson, C.H. 1966. *The Spirit of Administration*. 2nd edn. London: Faber and Faber.

Sisson, C.H. 1971. 'The great management hoax', *The Spectator*, 27 February.

Smith, G., and May, D. 1980. 'The artificial debate between rationalist and incrementalist models of decision making', *Policy and Politics* 8, 147–61.

Smith, P. (ed.) 1972. *Lord Salisbury on Politics: A selection from his articles in the Quarterly Review 1860–1883*. Cambridge: Cambridge University Press.

Southern, R.W. 1933. 'Ranulf Flambard and early Anglo-Norman administration', *Transactions of the Royal Historical Society* 45, no. 16, 95–128.

Southern, R.W. 1970. *Medieval Humanism and Other Studies*. Oxford: Blackwell.

Stigler, G. 1971. 'The theory of economic regulation', *Bell Journal of Economics and Management* 2, 3–21.

Stigler, G. 1972. 'The process of economic regulation', *The Antitrust Bulletin* 17, 207–35.

Taylor, F.W. 1947. *Scientific Management*. New York: Harper.

Taylor, R. 1975. *Lord Salisbury*. London: Allen Lane.

Thatcher, M. 1993. *The Downing Street Years*. London: Harper Collins.

Theakston, K., and Fry, G.K. 1989. 'Britain's administrative elite: permanent secretaries 1900–1986', *Public Administration* 67, 129–47.

Thompson, J.W. 1984. 'Fast stream training at the Civil Service College', *Management Services in Government*, 39, 48–54.

Thompson, R.W. 1976. *Churchill and Morton*. London: Hodder and Stoughton.

Tullock, G. 1965. *The Politics of Bureaucracy*. Washington D.C.: Public Affairs Press.

Tullock, G. 1976. *The Vote Motive. An Essay in the Economics of Politics With Applications to the British Economy*. London: Institute of Economic Affairs.

Wade, E.C.S., and Phillips, G.G. 1977. *Constitutional and Administrative Law*, 9th edn. London: Longman.

Waldegrave, W. 1978. *The Binding of Leviathan: Conservatism and the future*. London: Hamish Hamilton.

Waldegrave, W. 1993a. *Public Service and the Future: Reforming Britain's bureaucracies*. London: Conservative Political Centre.

Waldegrave, W. 1993b. *The Reality of Reform and Accountability in Today's Public Service*. London: Public Finance Foundation.

Walker, N. 1961. *Morale in the Civil Service*. Edinburgh: Edinburgh University Press.

Walker, P. 1991. *Staying Power*. London: Bloomsbury.

Wallace, W. 1977. *The Foreign Policy Process in Britain*. London: Royal Institute of International Affairs.

Walters, A. 1986. *Britain's Economic Renaissance: Margaret Thatcher's reforms 1979–1984*. Oxford: Oxford University Press.

Warner, N. 1984. 'Raynerism in practice: anatomy of a Rayner scrutiny', *Public Administration* 62, 7–22.

Wass, Sir D. 1984. *Government and the Governed*. London: Routledge and Kegan Paul.

Wheare, K.C. 1954. *The Civil Service in the Constitution*. London: Athlone Press.

Wheeler-Bennett, Sir J. (ed.) 1968. *Action this Day: Working with Churchill*. London: Macmillan.

Williams, G. 1956. 'The myth of "fair" wages', *Economic Journal* 66, 621–34.

Williams, M. 1972. *Inside Number Ten*. London: Weidenfeld and Nicolson.

Williams, P. 1963a. 'A revolution in Tudor history? Dr Elton's interpretation of the age', *Past and Present*, 25, 3–8.

Williams, P. 1963b. 'A revolution in Tudor history' The Tudor state', *Past and Present*, 25, 39–58.

Willman, J. 1994. 'The Civil Service', in D. Kavanagh and A. Seldon (eds) *The Major effect*. London: Macmillan.

Wilson, H. 1976. *The Governance of Britain*. London: Weidenfeld and Nicolson.

Wistrich, E. 1992. 'Restructuring government New Zealand style', *Public Administration* 70, 119–35.

Woolton, Lord. 1959. *Memoirs*. London: Cassell.

Wootton, B. 1955. *The Social Foundations of Wage Policy*. London: Allen and Unwin.

World Bank. 1993. *The East Asian Miracle: Economic growth and public policy*. Oxford: Oxford University Press.

Young, H. 1993. *One of us: A biography of Margaret Thatcher*. London: Pan.

Young, H., and Sloman, A. 1986. *The Thatcher Phenomenon*. London: BBC.

Young, J.W. (ed.) 1988. *The Foreign Policy of Churchill's Peacetime Administration 1951–1955*. Leicester: Leicester University Press.

Index